GETTING AT THE AUTHOR

Getting at the Author

Reimagining Books
and Reading
in the Age of
American Realism

BARBARA HOCHMAN

University of Massachusetts Press
AMHERST

Copyright © 2001 by University of Massachusetts Press
All rights reserved
Printed in the United States of America
LC 00-048883
ISBN 1-55849-287-9
Designed by Jack Harrison
Set in Adobe Caslon by Graphic Composition, Inc.
Printed and bound by Sheridan Books, Inc.

Library of Congress Cataloging-in-Publication Data

Hochman, Barbara.
Getting at the author : reimagining books and reading in the age of American realism /
Barbara Hochman.
p. cm. — (Studies in print culture and the history of the book)
Includes bibliographical references and index.
ISBN 1-55849-287-9 (cloth : alk. paper)
1. American fiction—19th century—History and criticism.
2. Realism in literature.   3. Fiction—Appreciation—United States—History—19th century.
4. Authors and readers—United States—History—19th century.
5. Books and reading—United States—History—19th century.
6. Criticism—United States—History—19th century.
7. Reader-response criticism.   I. Title.   II. Series.

PS374.R37 H64 2001
813'.40912—dc21
00-048883

British Library Cataloguing in Publication data are available.

This book is published with the support and cooperation of the University of Massachusetts Boston.

To the memory of my father

GUNTHER J. SPEYER

1913–2000

CONTENTS

CONTENTS

PREFACE

This book has been in the making for ten years. It has taken many turns and benefited from the help of many people and institutions. A brief account of its genesis will serve here as both preface and acknowledgments.

The project began as an effort to interpret the recurrent figure of the woman onstage in the fiction of Theodore Dreiser, Edith Wharton, and Henry James. In this phase of its conception the study was enriched by my participation in an NEH Summer Seminar directed by Emory Elliott at Princeton (1988). Two articles came out of my work there. In an essay on Edith Wharton's *House of Mirth*, I took Lily's appearance onstage in the much-debated "tableaux vivants" episode as a scene of reading, and Lily herself as a figure for the writer. Shortly thereafter, in a discussion of Dreiser's *Sister Carrie*, I suggested that Carrie's experience as an amateur actress in *Under the Gaslight* reflects Dreiser's own experience in the writing and editing of his novel.

I remained convinced that there was more to say about the recurrent image of the writer as public performer. Why did so many American novelists at the close of the nineteenth century imagine themselves as actress, singer, or public speaker—visibly displayed to an audience, often exhilarated, but also vulnerable and exposed? My ongoing interest in the implications of this figure led me to reflect on the realist strategy of authorial self-effacement. The objective or "invisible" narration of realist texts began to look like the other side of the coin.

Examining numerous reviews and essays of the period, I encountered a heated debate about the withdrawal of the authorial narrator. This debate, often carried on in the same journals that serialized the work of James and Wharton, reflected changing assumptions about the relation of the author to both narrator and reader. Keeping this debate in mind, I explored how Henry James identified the rewards and dangers of being a novelist with the pleasures and pitfalls of being a woman onstage.

The reading process now came into sharper focus. The question became, How was the act of reading itself imagined, not only by "canonical" novelists but also by other fiction writers of the period, including those who had not survived in the literary canon? How did educators, reviewers, and nonprofessional readers conceptualize the reading experience at the end of the nineteenth century? This stage of the project took me to the American Antiquarian Society, where I participated in a Summer Seminar, "Reading Culture, Reading Books," directed by Robert Gross and Mary Kelley. Access to nineteenth-century sources and the seminar's lively discussion of reading habits combined to convince me that in the course of the nineteenth century, the interplay of reading conventions and narrative strategies had reshaped certain pleasures of the text for both authors and readers. I particularly want to thank Robert Gross and Mary Kelley for their insights and encouragement. I am grateful as well to John Hench, Caroline Sloat, Joanne Chaison, and the entire staff of the American Antiquarian Society.

In the winter of 1997 I had the opportunity to present my ideas in an NEH Institute, "Books and the Imaginary," at Dartmouth College. My warm thanks to Walter Stephens, director of the institute, and to the other participants for their responses and challenges.

Additional thanks are in order.

Emory Elliott and Donald Pizer have been unstinting with their encouragement and support for many years.

Other colleagues and friends read parts of the manuscript, listening, questioning, prodding, and arguing: Joan Acocella, Jonathan Auerbach, Elizabeth Freund, Robert Griffin, Zvi Jagendorf, Irene Kacandes, Marcus Klein, Lee Clark Mitchell, Hana Wirth-Nesher, Zephyra Porat, Karen Schiff, Mark Seltzer, and David Stewart.

I extend particular thanks to Walter Benn Michaels for useful comments at a critical juncture, to John Landau for skepticism at a great many junctures, to Naomi Landau for invaluable library help, and to Hamutal Yellin for her work on the index. The anonymous readers for the University of Massachusetts Press offered many cogent suggestions. Thanks to Carol Betsch, managing editor, for her patience and efficiency throughout the production process. And thanks to Paul Wright for believing in this project for a long time.

I am also grateful for financial support provided by the American Antiquarian Society, the National Endowment for the Humanities, the Cohen-Porter Fund, the Swiss Association for North American Studies, Tel Aviv University, and Ben-Gurion University of the Negev. This support made it possible for me to present my ideas at the Summer Seminars and Institute I have mentioned and at conferences of the American Studies Association; the Modern Language Association; the Society for the History of Authorship, Reading and Publishing; and the Swiss Association for North American Studies.

Finally, for ongoing intellectual, emotional, and moral support, special thanks to Baruch Hochman.

Portions of chapter 4 have appeared in my articles "The Rewards of Representation: Edith Wharton, Lily Bart, and the Writer/Reader Interchange," *Novel: A Forum on Fiction* 24.2 (Winter 1991), Copyright NOVEL Corp. © 1991; "Disappearing Authors and Resentful Readers in Late Nineteenth-Century American Fiction: The Case of Henry James," *English Literary History* 63.1 (Spring 1996), © Johns Hopkins University Press 1996. A portion of chapter 5 has appeared in my "Self-Disclosure in the Fiction of Frank Norris," *Norris Studies* 9 (Spring 1989). I am grateful to these journals for permission to reprint.

BARBARA HOCHMAN

Jerusalem, Israel

GETTING AT THE AUTHOR

INTRODUCTION

Reimagining Books and Reading in the Age of American Realism

author, n. writer of book
The Concise Oxford Dictionary of Current English

"Every book should have I-places in it . . . places where one's soul can come up to the surface and look out through the ice and say things."[1] In 1902 the author of these words was fighting a losing battle. At the turn of the century the impersonal voice was fast becoming the sign of authority and value in American literature and criticism (as in history, ethnography, medicine, and other fields). Although many writers resisted this development, others heartily endorsed it. By 1900 the aesthetic of authorial self-effacement—what Frank Norris called "suppression of the author's personality" in fiction—had become a basic tenet of literary realism.[2]

This book provides a cultural perspective on the realist commitment to objective narration. It also is a study of interpretive conventions—of assumptions that turn-of-century readers brought to a book before opening it. I stress a reciprocal dynamic: reading habits are influenced by narrative strategies and vice versa in an ongoing cycle. The rhetoric of fiction, especially when it changes direction, is always implicated in the shifting expectations and desires of contemporary readers.[3] This process is one of continual readjustment among writers, readers, editors, publishers, reviewers, and others. At the same time, such tugs and pulls play themselves out within a larger field of cultural forces: the shift in reading habits and narrative conventions around the turn of the century implied changing ideas about many areas of public and private experience. My prime concern, however, is how these larger changes reshaped long-standing assumptions about the pleasures of a text. Such assumptions are culturally specific and can be reconstructed.

Throughout the nineteenth century a narrating voice was associated with the idea of an author speaking through it.[4] The author was generally presumed to be a human being whose "individuality" emerged from his or her text in the

I

course of the reading experience. As a repository of authorial character, a book was a reader's "friend," and reading was "a kind of conversation" with the writer. This way of reading was reinforced by rhetorical strategies, particularly the use of a narrator whom the reader, often addressed as "you," was encouraged to associate with the author of the work—a real, sometimes biographically concrete person, and always a writer and storyteller.

The widespread practice of "reading for the author" was partly the product of a culture that privileged the idea of individual autonomy and the concept of character but that also affirmed family and community. The imagined network of relations among writers, texts, and readers reflected governing assumptions about social relations more generally. In the first half of the nineteenth century, when most Americans lived in self-contained communities and many spent their lives in the place where they had been born, prevailing notions about an author's relation to text and reader were grounded in a relatively stable sense of the relations between oneself and others. An author's character, presumed to be implicit in his or her book, could give reading the feel of a reciprocal exchange—a virtual relationship of sorts.

By the 1880s and 1890s, however, many questions had arisen about the integrity of the self and its place in the world. Uncertainty about the relation of the self to its own modes of expression and self-representation contributed to an imagined rupture between author and text.[5] Like the sense of disjunction that emerged in many areas of American life, the idea of an author as separate and distant from his or her book crystallized during this period. In the course of the nineteenth century, America was changing from a relatively coherent culture in which most people lived within a familiar community network to a heterogeneous society in which families were increasingly dispersed and daily life involved a growing number of transactions with strangers.[6] This development alone had serious consequences for the way people experienced themselves in relation to others. "One's self—for other people—is one's expression of one's self," Mme. Merle tells Isabel Archer in *Portrait of a Lady* (1880), challenging Isabel's assumptions about the seamless unity of the inner and outer woman.[7] By the 1890s the sense of fragmentation that had begun to inform both the idea of community and that of the self had infiltrated the imagined integrity of author and text. As the concept of projected "personality" challenged the notion of integral "character,"[8] a feeling of uncertainty subverted the assumption that the reading process was a human transaction or exchange in which, as Noah Porter had expressed it, a reader could "confer with [an author] through his book."[9]

Toward the end of the century Henry James, Frank Norris, Edith Wharton, and others began stressing authorial "removal" from the text as a goal of narration. But the self-consciously impersonal realist or naturalist narrator was a controversial phenomenon when it first appeared. Most of the late nineteenth-century fiction that would later constitute the academic canon thwarted the expectations of contemporary fiction readers by eliminating the chatty authorial storyteller, with his or her emotional appeals and meta-fictional asides.[10] The new narrators rarely addressed (or even referred to) the reader directly, and almost never said "I" while telling their tale. By renouncing this well-worn narrative convention, the realists alienated numerous readers for whom the sense of writer-reader interchange was a primary pleasure of fiction reading.[11]

Many popular novels around the turn of the century continued to employ precisely the kind of narrating persona that had been rejected by writers of realism. Owen Wister, Francis Marion Crawford, Winston Churchill, and others used a rhetoric of direct address to reinforce an image of the reader as an active collaborator in a shared enterprise. Their narrators were often sharply delineated authorial figures who spoke about themselves as they told their stories, offering the reader a reassuring sense of human exchange and community such as realist works neither enacted nor depicted. The divide between "popular" and "serious" fiction deepened partly along these lines. During most of the twentieth century, the novelists who went on conceptualizing the reader as peer and confidant were forgotten or dismissed, at least in the classroom; those who scorned the rhetoric of direct address, affirming the absent author and "transparent" text, became the mainstay of the literary canon.

Discussions of American realism often begin by recalling that realist fiction was under attack on several fronts from the moment it appeared. In the century since realism became a literary force, its "low" subject matter, loose structure, and relation to reality have been repeatedly castigated, defended, and reinterpreted.[12] Although the battle over realism is often reexamined, certain charges against it are rarely recalled. The realist ideal of the story that "tells itself" was fiercely attacked in its time; yet this part of the argument is generally overlooked today because "suppression of the author's personality," so offensive to late nineteenth-century readers and reviewers, is the one element of realist poetics that was embraced by the academy. The explicit goal of depersonalized, objective narration accounts for much of the resistance to literary realism in its own time. But the anger that greeted the disappearance of the authorial persona is forgotten today because the realists prevailed. It is precisely the blessing of institutionalized literary study that has rendered this feature of realism invisible in its original form, as a contested site.

In 1920 T. S. Eliot made a powerfully influential claim: poetry, he suggested, is "not the expression of personality, but an escape from personality."[13] Well into the twentieth century, however, American reviewers continued to celebrate "the flavor of [an author's] personality" in fiction.[14] Although such reviewers were out of touch both with a gestating modernism and with incipient narrative theory, they were not out of touch with popular taste. Novels such as Owen Wister's *The Virginian*, George Du Maurier's *Trilby*, and Kate Wiggin's

Rebecca of Sunnybrook Farm were more popular in their own time than the work of writers who would outlive them in the canon, if not always in the bookstores. I suggest that the popularity of these novels derived in part from the use of a narrating voice that could be readily identified with the author's own "person." The "friendly" authorial narrators of popular fiction invited their readers to participate imaginatively in the life experience, the moral vision, and the aesthetic process through which they shaped the represented world of the text.

By contrast, realist writers took history, anthropology, and journalism as their model for narration; they argued for self-effacement, objectivity, and truth. One effect of such impartial, "nonintrusive" storytelling was the implication that the reader too was an outsider—a distant, silent, even passive observer, a kind of "dazed spectator."[15] Many turn-of-century readers refused to embrace this position, reluctant to exchange the role of active indigenous participant for that of foreign correspondent.

As Walter Ong has suggested, every author defines some kind of "reader role" for the consumer of the text.[16] In Wolfgang Iser's terms, every text offers a reader "a particular role to play" even when the reader might appear to be excluded or ignored. Yet as Iser himself points out, the act of reading always generates a certain tension between the "role offered by the text and the real reader's own disposition."[17] Culturally conventional assumptions can be as powerful as a reader's "own disposition" in creating a gap between the role offered by a text and the role accepted by a reader. Writers can never count on a perfect fit between the reader role inscribed in a work and the readiness of readers to comply with their instructions.[18] Many late nineteenth-century readers and reviewers resisted the role of silent onlooker that was implicit in the realist idea of the text as a transparent window or a reflecting mirror.[19] They reacted strongly and negatively to the unfamiliar reader role prescribed by texts which had eliminated a compelling, individualized narrating persona and the very idea of writer-reader relations.

"The trouble with most realism," Sarah Orne Jewett wrote in 1890, "is that it isn't seen from any point of view at all and so its shadows fall in every direction."[20] The lack of an authoritative point of view—the very thing that was increasingly valorized by literary studies in the course of the twentieth century—was anathema to many readers (and writers) of the period for whom the "objectivity" of realism was simply a withholding of authorial presence. As one of the prime pleasures of reading seemed about to disappear, many readers resisted.

In "First Steps toward a History of Reading," Robert Darnton makes a number of suggestions about how we might infer the reading habits, the underlying assumptions, of readers who have long been dead. Toward the end of the essay he invokes Walter Ong's idea of a "reader role" to suggest that one could compare the "implicit readers of [particular] texts with the actual readers of the past, and, by building on such comparisons, to develop a history as well as a theory of reader response."[21] Using dozens of unpublished letters written by an eighteenth-century French bourgeois, he anchors the notion of "romantic sensitivity" in a particular subject who has never before been credited with a role in the shaping of literary taste.[22]

Darnton proposes a double-pronged approach, one that takes account of a literary text on the one hand, and of reading practices that have engaged it on the other. But it is still the case today, as Roger Chartier wrote in 1989, that the two perspectives—on texts and on real readers—often remain "disjoined."[23] In the present study I have tried to combine them by contextualizing late nineteenth-century American fiction within reading practices of the period. I have read many texts with the purpose of extrapolating reader roles, scenes of reading, and figures for the reader and the author. I have asked what these images and scenarios can tell us about contemporary reading practices and vice versa.

Both Darnton and Chartier suggest that we consider the implied readers of literary works in relation to "real" reading habits. But the reading habits of real readers constitute a major problem of conceptualization in and of themselves. It is not only that written comments by nineteenth-century readers (especially nonprofessional readers) are few and far between.[24] It is also that, as James Machor has emphasized, the comments left in diaries or letters present their own challenges to interpretation.[25]

How then are we to reconstruct the experience of actual readers who have been dead for over a hundred years? I have not created an in-depth portrait of one particular historical subject, like Darnton's bourgeois (or Carlo Ginzburg's miller, or the nineteenth-century women readers whose letters and diaries Barbara Sicherman and Mary Kelley have examined).[26] Instead, my "readers" are often generalized extrapolations—triangulations—based on disparate sources. I have drawn on the work of many scholars who have examined the letters, diaries, and commonplace books of nineteenth-century readers; but I have also looked at published essays and reviews of the period, and at the personal letters and published comments of well-known writers. Precisely because the sources are so disparate, they deserve particular attention where they point to shared practices.

I have approached each of my sources with the same questions in mind: How was the reading public and the act of reading itself conceptualized by readers, writers, reviewers, and educators in the second half of the nineteenth century? What was the place of the author in the reading experience? Considering my texts in the light of one another, I have reconstructed widely shared but also changing assumptions about the way authors were imagined in relation to their books. I have related these changing assumptions to certain aspects of American social reality on the one hand, and to the protocol for reading inscribed in both popular and canonical fiction on the other.

In *Revolution and the Word*, Cathy Davidson points to a problem of method in any attempt to infer reading habits from "published assessments" of particular works. Since most readers, as Davidson notes, "do not write about what they read," it can be misleading to generalize about reading practices on the basis of published essays and reviews.[27] But numerous published comments (by both familiar writers and forgotten ones) have been entirely ignored—either because they contradict an author's better-known ideas or because they have long been seen as dated and irrelevant to academic discourse. Outmoded or "insignificant" comments are not reprinted. But, like contemporary discussions of "minor" works or of reading habits themselves, they provide valuable insight into interpretive norms of the period.

Although "most readers do not write about what they read," most writers tend to be voracious readers. The reading habits of well-known authors should not be disqualified as evidence of more general trends just because academics have sequestered them in a "high" cultural preserve. Throughout most of the twentieth century, literary scholars have extrapolated practices and values that canonical writers shared with one another, and have focused attention on these writers and their codified criteria as if they inhabited a distinct realm, entirely apart from popular taste. The work of Lawrence Levine, Richard Brodhead, Joan Shelley Rubin, and others has created new perspective on how "high," "low," and "middlebrow" cultures developed in America. But our heightened critical awareness of this hierarchical stratification should not prevent us from noting the predilections and practices that canonical authors shared with people who did not read or write for a living. I suggest that the reading habits of James, Howells, Wharton, and others often dovetailed with the interpretive conventions of the "common" reader.

Much valuable work on the theory and practice of reading has emphasized the difference between the interpretive conventions of readers inside and outside the literary professions. Janice Radway, for one, has highlighted the fallacy of assuming that "ordinary readers read as trained readers do."[28] But sometimes "trained readers" do in fact read like "ordinary" ones. If we are to avoid throwing out the baby with the bathwater, we should not ignore the forgotten ways in which well-known canonical writers read for pleasure. To do so is to overestimate—and reinforce—the rigid division between levels of culture that emerged in the course of the nineteenth century.[29]

A related point worth emphasizing here is that the reading practices of any one individual are likely to vary. Even canonical authors can be erratic in their tastes and interpretive practices. Novelists are not necessarily more consistent in their modes of reading than the rest of us. As authors make their way into the literary canon, they come to occupy a fixed place in the tradition and often acquire a rigid profile. Our sense of individual authors as highly integrated, consistent figures is a legacy of the New Criticism, with its emphasis on the unity of literary texts. But the critical uniformity attributed to authors such as James, Norris, and Cather is, like the canon itself, a construction of professionals. As Henry James came to be seen as "the master" of an increasingly rarefied literary technique, his appreciation of Owen Wister and his "incurable liking" for H. G. Wells disappeared from view.[30] Insofar as Frank Norris became known as "the boy Zola" and Willa Cather as a feminist, their enthusiasm as readers of George Du Maurier's *Trilby* was overlooked or elided. Jack London was not famous for his delight in *Rebecca of Sunnybrook Farm.*[31]

My juxtaposition of sources reveals forgotten assumptions about reading—about what was seen to be legitimate, important, and pleasurable in a turn-of-century text. The idea of a book as the reader's "friend" and reading as "a kind of conversation" with an author—these and other turn-of-century assumptions are no longer readily apparent, at least to academics, partly because they have been declassed. Throughout most of the nineteenth century, the digressive, self-reflexive narrator was associated with the writer of the text and often seen as the repository of moral, social, and intellectual values. In the course of the twentieth century, this friendly narrator (now seen as the intrusive narrator) became a sign of inferior writing for people who, in Henry James's phrase, "[took] their fiction seriously."[32] Yet reading habits were not transformed in one fell swoop. Even the most eloquent and consistent advocates of authorial invisibility (like James) found it stubbornly difficult to imagine a text without an author or to dissociate the idea of a book from that of a reciprocal human transaction. Insofar as writers of realism were also avid readers, they themselves often relished playing the very kind of reader role that they refused to inscribe in their own texts. In addition, many writers who affirmed the value of making the reader forget the author were deeply ambivalent about being invisible themselves.

The desire for an author, like the illusion if not the conviction of interchange, remained an important motive for reading at the turn of the century. Indeed, one could argue that the desire for an author has never entirely disappeared (see figure 1).[33] Still, the convention of reading for the author was a ground of considerable conflict in the 1880s and 1890s. This conflict became a watershed in the development of both the novel and literary studies; it also reflected some pressing tensions in turn-of-century American life.

Chapter 1 defines and exemplifies the interpretive convention that I call "reading for the author." In antebellum America, discussions of books and reading tended to assume a certain congruence between the words of a book and what Frank Norris later called "the man behind the pen." An author's "personality" or "individuality" (terms often used interchangeably) was generally perceived as an asset to both spoken and written discourse. For most writers, reviewers, and educators of the period, the self-evident condition for making sense of a

FIGURE 1. Encouraged by publishers, the practice of "reading for the author" continues today. From *The New York Times*, July 22, 1994, A5. *Courtesy of Barnes & Noble, Inc.*

text was a concrete image of "one's author" and a sympathetic writer-reader "relationship." Chapter 1 concludes by isolating some of the cultural factors that combined to challenge friendly reading practices toward the end of the century.

In chapter 2 I suggest that the struggle over impersonal, "objective" narration was deeply colored by social and demographic change. Daniel Borus and Amy Kaplan have shown that as an increasingly heterogeneous reading public was courted and in part created by new modes of marketing and advertising in the 1880s and 1890s, many authors grew increasingly anxious about whom they were addressing in their work. I suggest that such anxiety informs and even accounts for the rise of the depersonalized and disembodied realist narrator. The rhetorical ideal of authorial self-effacement, partly generated in the attempt to foster increased imaginative distance between the author and the invisible mass of disparate readers, not only influenced the shape of the literary canon but also left indelible traces on the imagery and structure of realist texts.

Chapter 3 demonstrates how "friendly reading," a well-established convention at midcentury, was later associated primarily with popular fiction that never received the academic stamp of approval. Novels such as *Rebecca of Sunnybrook Farm, The Virginian, Richard Carvel,* and *Trilby* defied the realist agenda in narration as in setting and thematics. As the "Great Immigration" from eastern and southern Europe made cultural diversity increasingly threatening to many readers across the country, the authorial narrators of popular fiction endorsed reassuring images of cultural cohesion. Yet a closer look at some of these best-sellers reveals that they themselves could no longer take friendly reading habits for granted, even as they capitalized on a widespread desire to do so.

In chapters 4 and 5 I turn to the more avid proponents of authorial remoteness or removal from the work. I argue that the realist stance with regard to narration created problems even for those writers who were most committed to it. Having defined the novelist's rhetorical posture as impersonal and distant from both text and reader, many authors discovered the drawbacks of trying to situate themselves above their work "like the God of Creation," invisible and indifferent.[34] Writers who no longer said "I" even in their "own book," as one commentator put it, were led to reimagine their place in the text and their relation to readers through a series of surrogate figures.[35]

Chapter 4 takes the image of a woman onstage as one such representative of authorial presence in the text. At once seductive and vulnerable, the recurrent figure of the actress reflects authorial ambivalence about self-representation in realist works of the period. In chapter 5 I explore a more oblique set of figures for the writer (and the reader). Once writer-reader relations were no longer envisioned as intercourse or interchange, they were often imagined as a more treacherous give-and-take. Amid growing uncertainty about how to conceptualize an author's relation to book and reader, many novelists imagined the act of reading itself as a hostile attempt to "get at" the withheld figure concealed behind the words on the page.

This book follows realism into the first two decades of the twentieth century. By then the idea of the author as a knowable, palpable human being communing with an actively participating reader had virtually disappeared from American fiction, at least from the novels that would later make up the literary canon. In the 1920s Edith Wharton, Percy Lubbock, and others (following James) made the story that "tell[s] itself" an essential criterion of "great" fiction.[36] Although many people continued to read "for the author," the narrative strategy of showing rather than telling became the mark of the truly "professional" novelist. Over much of the twentieth century, generations of students were taught to see the literary text as a self-enclosed structure, quite independent of the author who created it. The figure of the author became increasingly extraneous to the act of reading—dissolved into the language of the work and resurrected at best as a textual "function." In literature departments all over the world, the idea of authorial presence in fiction grew increasingly absurd, and its turn-of-century advocates were quite lost to view.

Today the personal "I" has regained legitimacy; writers of all kinds are now prepared to talk about themselves in their work. Not only have the first-person pronoun and autobiographical discourse recovered their respectability in literature and criticism,[37] but also the wish for intercourse (often called feedback) has returned to writer-text-reader relations with a vengeance. Interactive fiction, video games, "responsive" computerized toys (not to speak of the Internet)—a virtual reality of give-and-take abounds, eroding the objectifying and distancing realist model whose institutionalization this book traces. Reading habits continue to be renegotiated via changing texts and contexts.

We have become increasingly aware that every book is shaped not only by explicit intentions and rhetorical strategies but also by the writer's psychological and cultural history. That awareness is central to the present study, which tells the story of several discredited assumptions about authors, books, and reading that were commonly accepted a hundred years ago. Both my attempt to create a new perspective on familiar works of fiction and my effort to reconstruct lost reading habits have been constrained and colored by my own relation to books and reading. But it is my hope that the very constraints and even inconsistencies of my own reading practices have given me empathic access to interpretive conventions that have disappeared from view.

1

Reading for the Author: "Friendly Reading" in Nineteenth-Century America

I sit with Shakespeare and he winces not.

W. E. B. Du Bois, *The Souls of Black Folk* (1903)

At the start of Jack London's novel *The Sea-Wolf* (1904), Humphrey Van Weyden is rescued by a sealing ship after a ferry wreck. The ship saves him from drowning in the icy waters of the Pacific, but it effectively imprisons and enslaves him. Several months later, his fortunes take a dramatic turn for the better, with the appearance of Maude Brewster, another rescued castaway, who turns out to be a poet from Van Weyden's own familiar background. Although they have never met before, Humphrey and Maude soon recognize each other. Before long, Hump becomes aware that love has dawned: "Love had come, when I least expected it . . . it had come! Maude Brewster! My memory flashed back to that first thin little volume on my desk, and I saw before me, as though in the concrete, the row of thin little volumes on my library shelf. How I had welcomed each of them! . . . They had voiced a kindred intellect and spirit, and as such I had received them into a camaraderie of the mind; but now their place was in my heart."[1] Hump's reflections suggest that he has long loved Maud, identifying her "intellect and spirit" with the material beauty of the slim bound volumes of her work. It has only remained to link the image to the person. Like London himself, who made some lasting friends through his publications,[2] Hump here works within a model of reading as a reciprocal human transaction which had wide currency throughout the nineteenth century.

London himself, to be sure, did not fully endorse the assumptions that lead to romance between Hump and Maude. Like other realist and naturalist authors, London often mocked the goal of spiritual "communion" between writer and reader; he identified with an ethos of professionalism and affirmed a rhetorical strategy of authorial self-effacement. As we have noted, realist writers of the 1880s and 1890s conceptualized the text as a window or a mirror. They insisted that their readers were looking at a world, not engaging in "a kind of conversation" with the author of the book.[3] In Henry James's formulation, situations were to "speak for themselves."[4] The realist aesthetic thus posed a direct challenge to the idea of a book as a catalyst for proto-personal intercourse between writer and reader.

The discussion in this chapter will define and exemplify the interpretive convention that I call "reading for the author," which, I suggest, was a common practice in antebellum America. I want primarily to outline the norms of a reading convention that prevailed throughout much of the nineteenth century. But I also intend to emphasize that even the most clearly conceptualized reading conventions shape particular acts of reading only up to a point. Finally, I explore some of the tensions that threatened the primacy of this way of reading altogether. Toward the end of the nineteenth century, as those tensions came to the forefront, the realist aesthetic formalized the ideal of the invisible author and the story that "tells itself." As a result, "friendly reading" came to be seen as an inferior practice, unworthy of those who claimed a place in the emerging "high" literary culture of the period.[5]

Only Connect: Reading for the Author at Midcentury

For readers in the early and middle years of the nineteenth century, an image of the author seemed a natural concomitant of fiction reading. A sense of connection to "one's author" was considered an inevitable, legitimate, indeed desirable part of the reading experience. Affirmed in essays and reviews, the idea of continuity between literary discourse and authorial presence received additional support from the conception of rhetoric as it was taught in schools. Primers emphasized that emotional appeals could work only "if the orator felt the same emotions [he expressed]";[6] "sincerity" was promoted as an essential component of persuasive discourse.[7] As with writing, so with reading; readers were enjoined to extrapolate the human spirit implicit in printed words. Even after the Civil War, many educators, editors, and men of letters agreed that effective reading involved a meeting of minds, a kind of communion between author and reader. The value of forming a sympathetic relationship with an author by reading a text was routinely emphasized in manuals with titles such as *A Handbook for Readers, How to Read a Book,* and the still more authoritative and oft-reprinted *Books and Reading: What Books Shall I Read and How Shall I Read Them?* by Noah Porter, president of Yale (first published in 1871).[8] The practice of reading aloud—im*person*ation—was commonly recommended as an aid to understanding.[9] The habit of thinking about books as embodiments of authors—"gentlemen in parchment"[10]—was reflected in a widespread discourse representing books as people. "Books are only makeshifts for men," in the words of one commentator; or, as Bronson Alcott put it, "Good books . . .

[l]ike living friends . . . have their voice and physiognomies, and their . . . company is prized as old acquaintances."[11]

It is important to recognize that this way of reading was not yet an active search for the "man behind the pen,"[12] as it would be at the end of the century. Rather, it was an interpretive convention that involved taking for granted the imaginative unity of author and text. The habit of reading for the author had little to do with the revelation of biographical details. As Nina Baym has shown, the author was conceptualized in terms of tone, style, and represented moral attitudes, associated with the qualities of the text itself in a closed circle. "A poet's life is in his work," as one characteristic review of poetry put it in 1851.[13] Those aspects of a writer's life that were *not* in his or her work were considered out of bounds, at least for public discussion.[14] But since the words of a book were presumed to express the ideas and the character of a particular person, the sense of authorial presence was felt to be a natural and benign pleasure of reading.[15]

In 1850 the idea of books as friends and reading as a kind of conversation with the author was embraced not only by educators and reviewers, but also by readers who did not read (or write) for a living. Reading for the author was a long-standing interpretive convention; it cut across the lines of gender, region, race, and class.[16] In an article on women's reading in antebellum America, Mary Kelley cites numerous excerpts from letters, diaries, and commonplace books that refer to books as companions and the author as a person to love or to hate.[17] "I like him not," one Philadelphia woman wrote in her diary after reading Rousseau. "Or his ideas," she added.[18] Although Kelley's discussion is not directly concerned with the figure of the author as a factor in the reading experience, her citations repeatedly reflect this reading practice.[19] The work of Ronald and Mary Zboray provides additional evidence that for many nineteenth-century readers, some idea of intercourse with an author was a staple pleasure of reading. "The author has knowledge," Benjamin Waterhouse of Boston conceded to his wife after reading a travelogue, "but I detest the fellow."[20]

Antebellum authors were generally imagined as real people who could be known by their words like one's neighbors or other social acquaintances. Aspects of authorial character were presumed to emerge clearly in the course of the reading experience and were considered central to it. Nineteenth-century reviewers discussed works of fiction as expressions of an individual personality to whom the review itself was often addressed, directly or indirectly, as if reviewer, author, and reader were part of a homogeneous community, or as if the reviewer knew the author personally (which indeed he or she often did). The more fully a work encouraged and sustained a sense of common ground and personal contact through reading, the more positive the critical response to the work was likely to be.[21]

A discussion of Nathaniel Hawthorne's *Scarlet Letter* published in the *North American Review* in 1850 focuses first and foremost on the preface of the novel, praising the good fortune that has removed Hawthorne himself from the Custom House and brought him "back to our admiring, and, we modestly hope, congenial society."[22] The reviewer notes with satisfaction that Hawthorne's "'removal'... has saved those finer and more delicate traits in which genius peculiarly manifests itself, from being... obliterated... through the influence of the atmosphere" (136). Praising Hawthorne's "rare... individuality" (137), the reviewer admits outright "that we like the preface better than the tale" (139). This enthusiasm for Hawthorne's preface stems largely from the emerging image of a biographically concrete and humanly palpable Hawthorne. Moreover, the reviewer's preference for the Custom House section of the novel was far from unusual. Hawthorne himself speaks of the phenomenon as widespread, and Henry James refers to it in his 1879 book on Hawthorne, noting that Hawthorne "wrote to his publisher, when there was a question of his undertaking another novel, that what had given the history of Hester Prynne its 'vogue' was simply the introductory chapter."[23]

Even at midcentury, of course, commentators often raised questions about the extent to which a text could or should give its reader "intimate" knowledge of the author. "There is... a natural disposition with us to judge an author's personal character by the character of his works," Edwin Whipple wrote in 1850. "We find it difficult to understand the common antithesis of a good writer and a bad man.... The greater the writer, the more pertinaciously we sophisticate away the faults of the man."[24] This passage takes for granted that readers tend to equate "an author's personal character" with "the character of his works"; but it simultaneously acknowledges that such a practice does not really make sense. "The antithesis of a good writer and a bad man" is a "common" one, Whipple suggests. By noting that readers often resort to sophistry in order to ensure the desired harmony between discourse and "personal character," Whipple implies that the readerly desire for continuity is naively wishful; yet he includes himself when he writes that "*we* find it difficult" to abide the contradiction between a "bad man" and a "good writer." The readiness to infer the person from the work is represented here as a typical, even inevitable way of reading, a "natural disposition."[25]

It makes sense to recall in this context that writers often sought to establish a boundary between their authorial personas and their more private selves. In his preface to the *The Scarlet Letter,* Hawthorne noted that although he imagined his reader as a friend, and was impelled to indulge an autobiographical impulse, yet he would keep "the inmost me behind a veil." Writing to the editor Thomas Wentworth Higginson in 1862, Emily Dickinson made a point of underscoring the fact that the "I" of her poetry was not Emily Dickinson but "a supposed person."[26] Such attempts to sharpen the line between an author and his or her representation in public discourse implicitly acknowledged, but also defied, widely shared interpretive practices.

Antebellum reviewers tended to respect authorial attempts to direct and delimit reading conventions. Reviewers in such well-established journals as the *Atlantic Monthly* or the *North American Review* strongly encouraged the notion that an imagined relationship, created through reading, would not violate the boundaries of decorum and discretion that characterized middle-class social relations generally. Thus the previously cited discussion of Hawthorne's *Scarlet Letter* begins by devoting considerable attention to the autobiographical implications of Hawthorne's introductory section; but it ends with these remarks:

> We hope to be forgiven if in any instance our strictures have approached the limits of what may be considered personal. We would not willingly trench upon the right which an individual may claim, in common courtesy, not to have his private qualities or personal features discussed to his face, with everybody looking on. But Mr. Hawthorne's example in the preface, and the condescending familiarity of the attitude he assumes therein, are at once our occasion and our apology. (148)[27]

These lines rest on assumptions that have since become irrelevant to discussion of a literary work: antebellum reviewers generally assumed not only that reviews were part of a conversation between authors and readers but also that, like most men and women in polite society, readers who sought to "know" their author well would respect the conventions of "common courtesy," including what would soon come to be called the "right to privacy." Certain ways of reading, however, could violate conventional norms.[28] In 1850 the "limits of what might be considered personal" were fluid, uncertain, and the source of considerable concern to reviewers and authors alike. The Hawthorne reviewer's apology for an inadvertent overstepping of limits endorses a decorum of reading, but it also reflects an uncomfortable suspicion that a living author could be rudely intruded upon by interpretive practices.

Noting that the preface to *The Scarlet Letter* had triggered widespread concern for Hawthorne's welfare, the review praises certain "qualities of [Hawthorne's] heart, which, by an unconscious revelation through his style, like the involuntary betrayal of character in a man's face and manners, have won the affection of other than personal friends" (136). This formulation might seem to suggest that contemporary readers, as David Leverenz has put it, took "the still waters of [Hawthorne's] persona . . . to be as 'natural' as a limpid stream."[29] Equating Hawthorne's "written style" with his "face and manners," the review certainly reinforces the identification of author with text. But at the same time it reflects a reading practice that made many writers uncomfortable: if an "unconscious revelation of style" could expose endearing qualities, it might just as easily constitute an "involuntary betrayal" of less appealing characteristics.[30]

Another contemporary review of Hawthorne illustrates more clearly how the interpretive convention of reading for the author could not always be confined within the limits of social decorum, even at midcentury. Herman Melville's discussion of Hawthorne's *Mosses from an Old Manse,* published in 1850 under a pseudonym ("A Virginian Spending July in Vermont"), shows how thoroughly the idea of an author colored the experience of reading for one "eagle-eyed reader," as Melville refers to himself.[31] Melville's representation of reading Hawthorne suggests that, for Melville, to read a text was to proliferate questions about the writer's "personal character"—his heart, soul, mind, physiognomy. In this sense, although Melville was, to be sure, an especially articulate nineteenth-century reader, his reading practices were characteristic of many others'. Like the readers who wrote to Susan Warner after reading *The Wide Wide World,*[32] or those who descended on Louisa May Alcott's home in Concord after the publication of *Little Women,*[33] Melville sought personal contact with Hawthorne after reading his work. Soon after writing his review of Hawthorne's *Mosses,* Melville began to cultivate a friendship with Hawthorne. But Melville had already assumed that to read Hawthorne's text with responsive care was to find its author vividly, even intimately present to his imagination.[34]

Melville was explicit, indeed emphatic, about his ability to infer "Nathaniel Hawthorne" from the text. He goes so far as to ask those who know Hawthorne to corroborate his inferences: "I submit it, then, to those best acquainted with the man personally, whether the following is not Nathaniel Hawthorne" (1040). Sketching the author as he enters "a room in neglected attire, with the aspect of a thinker, but somewhat too rough-hewn and brawny for a scholar," Melville proceeds to elaborate the qualities of what nineteenth-century biographers often referred to as the "inner man": "His face was full of sturdy vigor, with some finer and keener attribute beneath; though harsh at first, it was tempered with the glow of a large, warm heart, which has force enough to heat his powerful intellect through and through" (1040).[35] Of course, Melville had good reason to believe that the image he claimed to have inferred through his reading would be accurate: he had already met Hawthorne before writing the review.[36] By pretending never to have done so ("I never saw the man" [1040]), Melville underscores his own acuity as a reader; he has read through Hawthorne's attempt to "hoodwink the world, with respect to himself" (1041), and approached a "thorough and acute appreciation of what [Hawthorne] is" (1041). But Melville's disingenuousness in putting his inferences to the test does not merely foreground Melville's own sensitivity as a reader; it also legitimizes the interpretive practice of such deduction.

Like many other reviews of the period, Melville's discussion supports the idea of reading as a communion of spirit, a meeting of minds or best selves. Noting that he has found in Hawthorne ideas that he himself has previously expressed, Melville asserts that "th[is] charm[ing] . . . coincidence shows . . .

a parity of ideas . . . between a man like Hawthorne and a man like me" (1042). For Melville, moreover, the sense of like-mindedness ("parity") extends beyond a relationship of two to a sense of community. What begins as a relation imagined as private—an intimacy between reader and book in a hayloft—ends by widening into an imagined community created through reading. Reading here is figured at once as a ground of communication or friendship, even love, and as a ground of cohesion or cultural authority. Suggesting that "genius" is not "individually developed in any one man" of a particular period, Melville insists that the "great fullness and overflowing" of a mind like Hawthorne's "may be . . . shared by a plurality of men of genius" (1042). This "plurality" would presumably include Melville as well.

Like the practice of reading for the author, the association of reading with an imagined community of the "like-minded" is characteristic of mid-nineteenth-century reading practices more generally. In antebellum America, as Ronald and Mary Zboray have shown, books often served to strengthen ties between friends and relations, who participated in reading as a shared activity. Books were regularly read aloud in the family, inscribed with comments, discussed in letters, and passed around from hand to hand. Circulating across the generations in the home but also over distances, books could recall and imaginatively reinstate absent family members, even deceased ones.[37]

For many nineteenth-century women in particular, as Barbara Sicherman notes, "reading remained . . . a social and collective as well as individual endeavor, one firmly rooted in relationships."[38] Engaged in as a "collective" practice, reading books enabled many women to consolidate not only a sense of connection to others but also a durable sense of self.[39] Sicherman and Kelley suggest that by sharing the ideas and fantasies stirred by reading with family members and with peers, many young women succeeded in imagining their way out of gender and class restrictions. In some cases, what began as imagined agency or wished-for social mobility ended by providing the conviction or security that led to a sense of cultural empowerment and real achievement.

For all of these nonprofessional readers—but also for Melville—the gratification of reading derived in part from the power of a text to facilitate imaginative participation in a network of relationships based on elective affinities. Like the relatively privileged women discussed by Sicherman and Kelley, and like the Zborays' antebellum middle-class readers (men and women from New England), Melville and other prominent nineteenth-century men of letters experienced reading as a "collective" endeavor "firmly rooted in relationships." Anticipating a deepening friendship, Melville often reflected on his reading in letters to Hawthorne. But, as I have already noted, Melville also experienced his private act of reading *itself* as a form of human intercourse. Communing with Hawthorne's text alone in his hayloft (real or imaginary), Melville generated a vividly imagined involvement with the writer of the book.

Reading for the Author: Incipient Dangers

Inferring Hawthorne's "best self" from the text, Melville appropriates the author as a worthy companion. Yet even as Melville's review shows how he makes reading the ground of an imagined relationship, it also exposes the difficulty of confining writer-reader relations to the model of a courteous social transaction. The very credence Melville gave to the practice of drawing inferences about authorial character created problems for his own relation to readers. It is as if the legitimacy he himself lent to reading for the author made him hesitate when he was the writer: if Melville could plumb the depths of Hawthorne's "heart" and "soul," what might his own readers infer from his text? I have noted Melville's disingenuousness about never having seen "this Hawthorne" (1034), but his false position vis-à-vis his own readers deserves further attention. In his Hawthorne review, Melville did not simply employ a pseudonym; he fleshed out his persona of the vacationing Virginian by inventing supporting details.[40] As Michael Gilmore has suggested, the strategy of disguise reflects Melville's anxiety about being identified as "Melville" in his spiritual affinities and his literary ambitions.[41] The point that deserves further emphasis here is that the deviousness of Melville's self-representation reflects not only his ambivalence about being discovered within his own text but also some of the issues at stake in reading for the author as an interpretive convention more generally.

Like other readers of the period, Melville believed that every piece of writing, whatever its subject, was also about its author. "If you rightly look for it," he claims, "you will almost always find that the author himself has somewhere furnished you with his own picture" (1040). Melville's insights into "Nathaniel Hawthorne" gain direct support from this widely shared conviction. Indeed, despite his own paraphernalia of camouflage, Melville assumed, as Gilmore notes, that "no effort at concealment [could] . . . wholly eliminat[e] a writer from his work" (61). But what exactly is the danger of appearing in one's text as oneself? Melville's own "eagle-eyed" inferences suggest that literary disguises can be penetrated; his caution about self-representation implies that an author may expose essential qualities of character will he nill he. If Melville imagined being read by others as he himself read Hawthorne, he might well have feared being not simply recognized but penetrated, overwhelmed, or consumed by his own readers—"relish[ed] . . . to his very bones," as he himself claims to have relished "this Hawthorne" (1040). Being relished may sound enviable, but the image also implies vulnerability, even danger, a sense of being too close to another for comfort.

Reading as eating was a familiar, indeed pervasive, trope in nineteenth-century discussions of books and reading. Melville invokes it repeatedly as he renders his delight in Hawthorne: "How aptly might the still fall of his ruddy thoughts into your soul be symbolized by the 'the thump of a great apple . . .

falling . . . from the mere necessity of perfect ripeness'!" (1034). Throughout the nineteenth century, educators, reviewers, and others used the imagery of food and drink not just to render the manifold pleasures of reading but to stress the difference between an active and a passive relation to books. Recent feminist critics in particular have focused attention on the negative emphasis of such metaphors, especially when used to describe women readers.[42] Both the selection and consumption of literary works were figured in terms of the contrast between a discriminating palate or a healthy diet on the one hand and the evils of addiction on the other.[43] But another range of implications is present in the recurrent invocation of this trope. When Cotton Mather attacked the pernicious effect of "impure" literature, he noted that it would be better for such works to be "thrown into the *fire,* than to be laid before the *eye,*" by which route they could "cast [hot] coals into your bosom."[44] The notion of such boundary-breaking violence is implicit in many images that figure reading as consumption of a text—and its author.

"To what infinite height of loving wonder and admiration I may yet be borne," Melville writes, "when by repeatedly banquetting on these Mosses, I shall have thoroughly incorporated their whole stuff into my being—that I can not tell" (1040–41). Melville's "banquetting" on Hawthorne's "Mosses," his "incorporat[ion]" of them into his "being," yields "loving wonder and admiration." But to "relish" and "incorporate" an author may also be to dismember, transform, or destroy. Insofar as a text is intimately associated with its writer, the image of reading as eating may come to suggest a kind of cannibal feast. What will be left of "this Hawthorne" after he has been "relish[ed] . . . to his very bones"?

In all its forms, the notion of reading as eating depends on the porousness of boundaries between reader and text, a porousness that many twentieth-century theorists of reading struggled to conceptualize and explain. The forging of an imagined relationship with an author through reading depends on such porousness as well. Georges Poulet has suggested that the act of reading often creates the illusion of access to "otherness," as if a reader virtually comes to inhabit a consciousness not his or her own.[45] In Michael Steig's formulation, "The text itself . . . is perceived as an 'other.'"[46] But the very porousness that can create the "feel" of interaction and foster an exhilarating sense of merger or intimacy between reader and writer may under certain conditions become a source of discomfort instead. There is more than one way for reading to facilitate an imagined violation of physical barriers and social conventions. The capacity of fiction in particular to encourage transgressive fantasies had long given the novel a bad name.

When the novel as a genre first appeared, moralists and educators attacked it for promoting identification with imaginary creatures.[47] Such identification was seen as a potential threat to a reader's sense of his or her "place" and even self. The idea of an author served a corrective function in this context. Unlike fictional characters who presented a danger precisely because they were not "real," the figure of the author, conceptualized as a person worth knowing, became a prime value of literature. The fact that authors were "real" people made them especially valuable as both models and potential "friends."[48]

"I aspire to be acquainted with wiser men than this our Concord soil has produced, whose names are hardly known here," Henry David Thoreau writes in *Walden*.[49] Like Melville imagining a community of the great when reading Hawthorne, Thoreau assumes not only that books are to be identified with their authors, but also that authors of the "oldest and the best" books are "a natural and irresistible aristocracy in every society."[50] "Shall I hear the name of Plato and never read his book? As if Plato were any townsman and I never saw him,—my next neighbor and I never heard him speak. . . . But how actually is it? His Dialogues . . . lie on the next shelf and yet I never read them. . . . We should be as good as the worthies of antiquity, but partly by first knowing how good they were" (97).

To read the "worthies of antiquity" is to "see" them, to hear them "speak," to know them, to emulate them. Yet Thoreau goes on provocatively, insisting that "the works of the great poets have never yet been read by mankind, for only great poets can read them. . . . [O]f reading as a noble intellectual exercise [most men] know little or nothing; yet this only is reading, in a high sense, not that which lulls us . . . and suffers the nobler faculties to sleep the while, but what we . . . devote our most alert and wakeful hours to" (94). Like other contemporary commentators, Thoreau here draws a line between reading "which lulls us" and reading that is active, that keeps us "alert and wakeful." Even today, "there are probably words addressed to our condition exactly, which, if we could really hear and understand, would . . . put a new aspect on the face of things for us" (97). It does not require much interpretive pressure to see these words as a kind of protocol for the reading of *Walden* itself. Yet Thoreau knew that his conception of "serious reading" (90), reading "in a high sense," was only an ideal. Well aware that few people devote their "most alert and wakeful hours" to reading, Thoreau announces in his epigraph that his own intention is "to wake my neighbors up."

When Thoreau conceptualizes reading as "a noble intellectual exercise," he imagines authors as wise but also individuated and potentially accessible people. Even the great classical authors of antiquity are figured as "any townsman," a "next neighbor." Readers can come to know them, if only they are receptive, attentive, and alert. The act of reading is represented as deliberate, respectful (and exclusive) social intercourse. Yet Thoreau, like Melville, understood that reading habits were increasingly difficult to constrain within this model. A well-known passage in Thoreau's section "On Reading" castigates "those who [read] like cormorants and ostriches," attacking readers who "can digest all sort of [stuff], even after the fullest dinner of meats and vegetables" (95). Thoreau's vision of such readers as all-devouring animals or reading "machines" (imagery that becomes increasingly familiar as the century goes on) replaces the human element with a brutish impulse that omnivorously consumes and destroys. Thoreau associates this way of reading with inferior reading matter. Yet he could not be sure that destructive reading practices would necessarily be confined to "inferior" books. As we have noted, Thoreau explicitly articulates his fear that even "the great poets have never yet been read" in the "noble" way that they require. What then is to ensure that they (or he) cannot be consumed indiscriminately or torn to pieces like "gingerbread" (96)?

At the beginning of *Walden,* Thoreau explains (and thereby foregrounds) his decision to use the first-person pronoun, identifying his discourse with his own history, with himself. As Gilmore notes, the "conception of literature as synonymous with life and the person recurs throughout [*Walden*]" (46). "In most books, the *I*, or first person, is omitted," Thoreau writes. "In this it will be retained; that, in respect to egotism, is the main difference." Indeed, like Melville, Thoreau assumes that every book is really about its author: "We commonly do not remember that it is, after all, always the first person that is speaking. I should not talk so much about myself if there were any body else whom I knew as well. Unfortunately, I am confined to this theme by the narrowness of my experience. Moreover, I, on my side, require of every writer, first or last, a simple and sincere account of his own life" (3).

Nineteenth-century children were well schooled in the art of rhetoric and knew a great deal about adapting a literary persona to the occasion at hand. But this should not blind us to the fact that nineteenth-century readers (and writers) still linked the words of a text to the idea of the person who produced it. Insofar as Thoreau believed his book to be about himself, a "sincere account of his own life," it is not surprising that he should promote an attentive, high-minded, and decorous mode of reading. Conceiving of his text as a reflection of himself, Thoreau might well prescribe that a book be "read as deliberately and reservedly as [it was] written" (92). Still, such a prescription did not keep him from imagining the voracious and indiscriminate readerly appetites of uncongenial hordes.

Challenges to Friendly Reading

By the last two decades of the nineteenth century, the interpretive norm of "friendly reading" was threatened from several directions. The practice of reading for the author had required that a text be perceived as an expression of an authorial personality. But it had required at the same time that certain boundaries, a kind of reserve or "common courtesy," should guide all acts of reading and interpretation. Melville and Thoreau well knew that there were many kinds of readers and many ways to read, but they could still affirm the value and importance of reading for the author, a mode of appreciation they both craved for themselves and sought to bestow on (selected) others.

Toward the end of the century, however, it became increasingly difficult for a writer to conceptualize his or her reader as a familiar acquaintance. For one thing, the reading public itself had grown exponentially and had become far more heterogeneous in the process. During the 1880s, as the "Great Immigration" brought new waves of foreigners to America from eastern and southern Europe, the problem of diversity became a cause of concern for many people who were already troubled by what seemed to them an increasingly fragmented society. Although the idea of an American "melting pot" retained its viability in public discourse into the late 1880s, the official welcome extended to immigrants coexisted with mounting anxiety about the impact of "aliens" on the cultural coherence of American life.[51] Such anxiety was evident not just in the urban centers where growing slums absorbed many new arrivals, but in communities across the nation.

At the end of the century, writers, reviewers, and publishers were preoccupied with the fragmentation and diversity of the reading public. As Brander Matthews put it in 1902, there was no such entity—only "multiple publics."[52] Under these conditions many writers, especially upper-class eastern writers, grew increasingly uncertain about whom they were addressing and what their work was revealing to a diverse and far-flung readership. After visiting New York in 1905, Henry James expressed concern for the fate of the English language itself. Owen Wister decried the "hoardes [sic] of encroaching alien vermin that turn our cities to Babels" and make "our citizenship" increasingly "mongrel" and "hybrid."[53] As we shall see, James and Wister would each find a different solution to the problem of addressing an unknowable reading public, but one thing was sure: it was increasingly difficult to stabilize a sense of who one's readers were.

The illusion of writing for a community of like-minded peers was further threatened by the transformation of the publishing industry.[54] With the rise of a managerial elite and the proliferation of mediating figures—editors, literary agents, and others—authors found the route from manuscript to print increasingly impersonal and cumbersome. As the publishing bureaucracy developed, the image of the reader receded from the author's field of vision. An article in *The Dial* of 1895 evokes a ghostly image of the publisher as coming between the writer and the page; a discussion in *The Critic* speaks of "the great number of intermediaries" between "the message and its hearers."[55] In 1899 William Dean Howells pronounced the distance between authors and readers an unbridgeable "chasm."[56]

As the sense of distance between writers and readers increased, a new figure loomed over the divide: the author-celebrity, now considerably larger than life and already cut loose from the text itself. The marketing of authors had begun to emerge as a new ploy at midcentury. In the 1850s the publisher James T. Fields projected an image of Hawthorne's "reclusive" personality as a promotional strategy worthy of Barnum.[57] Yet the inviolability of Hawthorne's "private life" was precisely the point to be advertised. It was only toward the end of the century that the practice of marketing the author's life along with the book became a common practice.[58] At that point the marketing of authors had a far-reaching impact on reading conventions.

The publishing history of *Little Women* (1868) affords an early example of a text advertised by an image of its author. The promotion of Louisa May Alcott as the reader's "friend" explicitly affirmed reading as contact with an author while emphasizing the autobiographical overtones of the story.[59] The author thus came into focus as a sharply delineated image in its own right; but it still was firmly anchored in the text. The imaginative merger of the author with the fictional heroine sold books; yet the evocation of Alcott as "the children's friend," supported by pictorial images of Alcott reading to children, did not point away from the text itself. Rather, such representations of the author reinforced the many scenes of reading within *Little Women*, where reading emerges not merely as moral education but also as meaningful human connection (see figure 2).[60]

If antebellum readers and reviewers had believed that "a poet's life is in his work," this had meant mainly that a sense of human character, an author's "individuality," was an inextricable component of the text. By 1900, as new marketing techniques made authors available for consumption in an escalating variety of forms, the figure of the author was no longer evoked with a few strokes that pointed right back to the work, and an author's personal life was by no means off-limits. Biographical facts about writers were now used on a new scale to market fiction; authors' lives became a source of fascination in themselves.

Toward the end of the century, as Daniel Borus points out, widespread interest in the private lives of writers sustained "a flourishing cottage industry."[61] Many publications catered to the reading public's wish to "know" authors by providing new modes of access to them. "All lovers of books like to know something about the writers of books," notes the preface of a work titled *Authors and Authorship* (1882). Stressing the reader's natural and "harmless appetite for personal information" about authors, the preface observes that "we cannot help feeling an interest in those whose works have delighted and instructed us, and we value even the smallest details that throw a light upon their character and mode of living."[62] The proliferation of books about writers "at home" elaborated the image of the author with details about his or her appearance, house, garden, and neighbors. It increased the imagined distance between author and fictional text by turning "the author" into an independent object of attention.

Soon photographs, interviews, and "at home" books were seen to represent

FIGURE 2. "'Louise Alcott' The Children's Friend." Lithograph by Lizbeth B. Commins, used as a frontispiece in Ednah Dow Cheney, *Louisa May Alcott: The Children's Friend* (1888). *Courtesy of the American Antiquarian Society.*

authors more fully than their own writing. An introductory note to Jeannette Gilder's *Authors at Home* (1888) explicitly makes this point: "In reading the following pages one gets a closer and more intimate view of the authors sketched than their writing could possibly afford." Such a notion did more than foster the growing demand for biographical particulars; it also implied that *only* through such "personal information" would "our author" come to life.[63] As Borus notes, "The well-informed knew all there was to know of Mark Twain's Tiffany decorations, William Dean Howells's cigars, and James Whitcomb Riley's porch and rocking chair" (124). The very abundance of detail itself raised doubts as to whether it was the author's written work or "personal situation" that more faithfully represented the individual whom a reader might wish to "know."[64]

The growing public interest in the home life and work habits of well-known authors also elicited resistance, of course. As Hippolyte Taine put it in his influential *History of English Literature* in 1883: "If we give our works to our readers, we do not give our lives. Let us be satisfied with what Dickens has given us. Forty volumes suffice, and more than suffice, to enable us to know a man well; moreover, they show of him all that it is important to know."[65] Taine's formulation still assumes that an author is immanent, and accessible to his readers, in his works: Dickens's novels are said to represent "Dickens" in ample detail that enables us to "know [him] well." At the same time, however, by insisting that Dickens's forty volumes "show of him all that it is important to know," Taine proposed that what is left out is not "important." In other words, it was not the reader's business either to seek "Dickens" outside the text or to probe the text for the authorial secrets it might be made to yield.

Toward the end of the century many discussions of books and reading insisted (like Taine), that fiction reflected all that it was "important to know" about the life or personality of an author. Such assertions, however, could not by themselves constrain reading practices. Widespread curiosity about the private lives of writers persisted and impelled many people to try reading around or through the work to an author's private life. The imagined unity of author and text was threatened from several directions. Another contributing factor that should be mentioned in this context is the copyright debate.

The problem of copyright was a focus of attention both before and after the passage of international copyright legislation in 1891. By figuring the writer as producer and the text as a product, like a table or suspenders, the arguments over copyright further distanced the idea of a book from that of a person speaking through it. In many formulations, the imagery of mechanical production replaced the rhetoric of books as living creatures intimately linked with their authorial creators. The idea of a book as intellectual property became familiar to readers all over the country. Imagined as property, a book was not merely an inanimate thing; it was an object independent of its author.

A discourse of books as things soon appeared in many contexts. The same newspapers and journals that printed fiction, essays, and reviews drew attention to the proliferation of literary agents and editors, technical innovations and word counts.[66] Authors in the 1880s and 1890s were often seen as "vendors," "piece workers,"[67] or "fiction-mills."[68] When books were depicted as mechanically generated objects—"the spawn of the press," as Charles Dudley Warner put it—the figure of the author could appear almost extraneous to the process of creation.[69] The indefatigible press with its bottomless "maw" was figured as a kind of sorcerer's apprentice, with a near-demonic life of its own.[70] Amid growing uncertainty about what a book is, the discourse of friendly reading was replaced by a more threatening range of images.

The copyright debate contributed to mounting confusion about how to conceptualize the relation of a book to author and reader. Is a book a child, a second self, "the pretious [sic] life-blood of a master spirit" (see figure 3), or is it merely a "dumb object"?[71] Is an author creator, progenitor, craftsman, or owner of goods?[72] "Many people," Howells complained in a popular lecture, "read your book without ever looking at the title page or knowing who wrote it, or caring. [They] . . . do not know apparently how books come to be, or how they differ in origin from the products of the loom or the plow."[73] The sense of a book as a living thing, gestated and in some way *inhabited* by its author, vied with the sense

FIGURE 3. Milton's words, set over the portal of the main reading room in the
New York Public Library (1911), expressed and promoted the long-standing
identification of an author with his or her book. *Photograph by Karen S. Frieder.*

of a book as an inanimate object, quite separate from its creator. The figure of
the author, the place of the author in the reading process, became a highly unstable factor in discussions of books and reading, exacerbating doubts about
whether reading is a kind of human interaction or something else entirely.

Just when the copyright debate was combining with marketing strategies of
the period to create a new sense of disjuncture between author and text, literary discourse began to conceptualize the separation of the author from the
work as an aesthetic ideal. While many reviewers went on affirming authorial
presence *in* the text, proponents of realism generated grounds for taking the
writer *out*. The narrative strategy of authorial self-effacement, a vital component of the realist aesthetic, served to bolster the idea of the text itself as an independent object that would represent reality, virtually without the author's
mediation. As W. R. Thayer wrote (disapprovingly) in 1894, "The Realist . . .
was impartial; he eliminated the personal equation; he would make his mind as
unprejudiced as a photographic plate."[74]

By giving formal expression to the removal of the author from the work, the
realist goal of authorial invisibility capped the process of differentiation which
had already begun to undermine the notion of a book as a friend and reading
as a mode of human intercourse. Affirmations of authorial objectivity and

impersonality only compounded the problem of how to conceptualize an author's place in the fictional text. If a book is not identified with human presence, the question arises, where *is* the author in relation to the work? If a book is *not* a friend, if a reader does not "confer with [an author] through his book,"[75] then what *is* the reader's relation to the text and its author? Conversely, how is an author to imagine his or her relation to the reader?

By banishing narrative intrusions, the authorial voice, and the first-person pronoun itself, realist writers attempted to establish "professional" distance, not only between themselves and their material but also between themselves and their readers. It was as if they believed that to control narrative rhetoric was also to limit a reader's access to "the man behind the pen." But the professional neutrality of the realists could neither transform the expectations and desires with which a reader approached a text nor eliminate their own anxiety about what a writer's work might reveal to the public at large.

At the end of the century, legal debates about the right to privacy raised additional questions about how firmly one person could limit another's access to letters, photographs, and other products or representations of the self. For Warren and Brandeis, as Brook Thomas suggests, "a work of art was . . . simultaneously a potential piece of property and an expression of its creator's innermost self."[76] Not only questions about the boundary between the self and what it makes, but also questions about the gap or continuum between private person and public persona, are directly relevant to the question of how to conceptualize the relation of a writer to both text and reader. Two formulations that do not directly address either the idea of a right to privacy or the problem of fictional rhetoric are illuminating in this context.

In his *Principles of Psychology* (1890), William James emphasizes the blurry line that divides what is from what is *not* the self by using the example of an author whose manuscript is destroyed. "There are few men who would not feel personally annihilated," James writes, "if a life-long construction of their hands or brains—say an entomological collection or an extensive work in manuscript—were suddenly swept away." James accounts for the inevitable "depression" that would result by suggesting that in this case one would experience "a shrinkage of . . . personality, a partial conversion of ourselves to nothingness."[77] In this scenario, an author's manuscript is treated as a literal extension or an integral part of the person.

Writing in 1911, Georg Simmel represented the relation between self and work in different but related terms: "The claim that we can recognize the person in his works holds true only with very powerful reservations. Sometimes we are more than our work. Sometimes—paradoxical as this sounds—our work is more than we are. Sometimes one is remote from the other, or they coincide only in fortuitous respects."[78] Unlike James, who stresses an author's underlying belief that a part of oneself is all but literally deposited in one's manuscript, Simmel stresses the disjuncture between self and work. If "we" are sometimes more and sometimes less than our work, what makes the difference? Both of these formulations point to the unstable boundaries between a writer and his or her book, implying that authors have only a limited control over their presence in the writing they themselves have produced.

At the turn of the century, many writers came to feel that rhetorical strategies could neither enforce the boundaries of self-representation in writing nor effectively control reading practices. Neither rhetorical nor philosophical sophistication could protect a writer from the sense of having deposited or revealed too much "self" in his or her book. Even worse, there was no way of knowing what the reading public would make of the authorial image inscribed in the work. In 1893, when Stephen Crane sent Hamlin Garland a copy of his new novella, *Maggie: A Girl of the Streets*,[79] he added the following inscription:

> It is probable that the reader of this small thing may consider the Author to be a bad man, but, obviously, this is a matter of small consequence to
>
> > The Author.

Crane's dismissal of what readers might assume about him—his assertion of indifference—suggests that he, like many writers of his generation, rejected this way of reading altogether. Yet these lines also reflect Crane's assumption that readers would nonetheless draw inferences about his moral character after reading his book. As Crane very well knew, a considerable gap remained between the realist ethos of the absent author and the reading habits of numerous people.

By 1900, realist writers had acquired a solid place in the newly emergent culture of professionalism. The impersonal voice had become a sign of authority and value not only in American literature and criticism but also in history, ethnography, medicine, and other fields. Schoolchildren were encouraged to replace the first-person pronoun with the impersonal "one" in their compositions and creative writing. By the same token, the interpretive convention of reading for the author had been stigmatized as a naive and uncultivated practice. Those who renounced this way of reading acquired an imaginative foothold in the burgeoning "high" culture of letters.

Still, reading habits were slow to change. The tendency to equate a text with an authorial personality persisted, even among professional readers.[80] As we shall see, many of the same novelists who advocated authorial invisibility in their own work suspended their critical principles when reading for pleasure themselves. Professional as well as nonprofessional readers, men and women, continued to read for the author. The interpretive practice of linking the words of a text with the idea of an authorial person survived in the face of the most strenuous attempts to challenge its conceptual viability and moral authority. Indeed, in many quarters it is alive and well today.

2

The Erosion of "Friendly" Reading: The Realist Challenge

Appreciation of literature is the getting at an author.
Samuel Crothers, "The Gentle Reader" (1900)

Late nineteenth-century discourse reflects the radical changes in the way authors and readers imagined one another and their relation to the words of a book. For readers in the middle years of the century, as we have seen, an image of the author seemed a natural concomitant of fiction reading; a sense of connection to authors was considered an inevitable, legitimate, indeed desirable part of the reading process. After the Civil War the assumption that reading was a human transaction, a kind of virtual friendship, received formal expression in many discussions of how to choose a book and how to read it. Human connection and exchange between author and reader were often singled out as valuable goals. "Effective reading," Noah Porter wrote, "depends most of all on the relations in which the reader finds himself, with respect to his author." In an extreme formulation of a widespread assumption, Porter compares the situation of the captivated reader to that "of the most confiding friend and enraptured lover."[1] But the recurrent and explicit emphasis on reading as rapport and dialogue in the 1870s, 1880s, and 1890s already testifies to the growing instability of what I have called "friendly" reading. The idea of a book as a catalyst for proto-personal exchange or intercourse between writer and reader was steadily eroded toward the end of the century. Precisely when a variety of forces began to threaten this reading convention, its governing assumptions were insistently affirmed.

Anxiety about reading practices played a formative role in shaping the realist aesthetic, particularly its emphasis on authorial invisibility as the sine qua non of narration. In this chapter I examine how realist writers came to imagine the reading public at the end of the nineteenth century. I propose a direct link between the realists' ambivalence about their readers and the emergence of authorial self-effacement as their rhetorical ideal. Increasingly uncertain about who was reading fiction and why, the realists devised a narrative discourse that challenged widespread and long-standing reading habits. In addition, the realists' mounting discomfort about who their readers were and how those readers read was displaced onto a range of motifs—dystopian scenes of reading—which reflect an adverse relationship to readers, a relation born partly of thwarted desire.

By the end of the century, the feeling that a text at once invites and frustrates access to its maker pervaded novelistic and critical discourse. In Henry James's short story "The Private Life" (1892), the work of the novelist Clare Vawdrey stirs in his readers a passionate desire for contact with the man who wrote the book. The implacable readerly wish to get at the author persists, even though Vawdrey himself "disappoints every one who looks in him for the genius that created the pages they adore." Listening attentively as the writer reads aloud from his own work, a character in the tale sums up the irreducible paradox. "Do you know what was in my mind last night and all the while Mr. Vawdrey read me those beautiful speeches?" Blanche Dabney asks. "An insane desire to see the author."[2] Blanche is exasperated as she listens to Vawdrey declaim his own "beautiful speeches." Even as the author stands before her, Blanche feels that she does not "see" him.[3] Here as elsewhere in James's artist tales the desire for an author is doomed to frustration. "Real" authors never live up to the figures imaginatively extrapolated by readers from the texts they read.

The disjunction between the authorial persona and "the man behind the pen" had already been a focus of interest at midcentury. "On a personal interview," Melville noted in his discussion of Hawthorne's "Mosses," "no great author has ever come up to the idea of his reader" (1032). In the 1890s, however, the image of an author pursued, but also misperceived, by benighted readers became a recurrent emphasis of literary discourse. In his popular 1899 lecture "Novel-Writing and Novel-Reading," William Dean Howells offered a sardonic view of readers "who amiably confuse you with some brother author, and praise you for novels you have never written."[4] James's artist tales proliferate absurd and even bizarre variations on the theme. Authors flee from their readers, put on disguises, seek the protection of intermediaries, literally split into two people.[5] For many of the realists, the idea of the reader was accompanied by a deepening sense of threat.

Reimagining the Reader: The Text as Refuge

Toward the turn of the century, writers such as William Dean Howells, Henry James, and Edith Wharton, as well as other contributors to the magazines in which they published, had come to see the reading public as a fragmented and faceless mass from which they felt increasingly divorced. The American reading public of the 1890s included a large proportion of new readers: immigrants, first-generation emancipated African Americans, and others to whom the language of these authors did not come easily. Neither the socioeconomic nor the ethnic composition of this diverse public was generally alluded to in the discussions of books and reading that regularly appeared in journals such as the *Atlantic Monthly* and the *North American Review*. Yet "the reader," whom educators and reviewers had once imagined as the writer's "most confiding friend" and even lover,[6] was now represented as a novice, an outsider, in need of direction and instruction. A terminology of readers proliferated. There were said to be "lay readers," "literary beginner[s],"[7] professional readers, and scholars—all in all an "enormous multitude reading,"[8] such as "never before in the history of the world."[9] Many "professionals" seized the opportunity of providing services to this disparate population with its growing appetite for books. Chautauqua courses and reading clubs offered guidance, encouraging readers not merely to read but to count hours and pages in a regular regime.[10] New literary journals promoted "the reading habit," encouraging widespread systematic consumption of literary works.[11]

While promotion of "the reading habit" (see figure 4) became an avowed goal of teachers, librarians, and literary journals, many writers and critics viewed this phenomenon, and the omnivorous reading public itself, with suspicion. As Amy Kaplan has suggested, "genteel" upper-class authors such as Howells and Wharton were especially uncomfortable as they contemplated the reading public from across class lines.[12] Such writers were deeply ambivalent about the widespread emphasis on cultivating the reading habit as a social asset for the upwardly mobile. The idea of reading as a daily regimen—healthy diet, hungry or not—became a particular target of attack, especially in the older, well-established journals.

Writing in the *North American Review* in 1903, Edith Wharton castigates what she calls the newly emergent "vice" of reading and its concrete embodiment, the "mechanical reader." Wharton's ideally conceived "creative" reader (a phrase adapted from Emerson) is said to read "as naturally as he breathes"—by intuition, never "by rule." Wharton's "mechanical reader," however, reads out of "duty," reads everything that is "talked about," but succeeds only in becoming "a slave of his bookmark."[13] In a similar turn-of-century formulation, the benighted modern reader is envisioned as an "eager devourer of fiction" who "goes to a book just as he goes to a department store" for a "neat parcel," a "literary 'quick lunch.'"[14] Such allegedly insensitive readers are repeatedly evoked in literary essays of the period, represented as hurried consumers, voyeurs, or professional grinds and characterized by absolute indifference to "the flavor of [an author's] individuality." They are sharply contrasted with that responsive soul of "a generation or two ago" for whom the act of reading was directly associated with "human companionship."[15]

Many writers shared the belief that a significant change had taken place in the character, tastes, and expectations of novel readers. This alleged change is

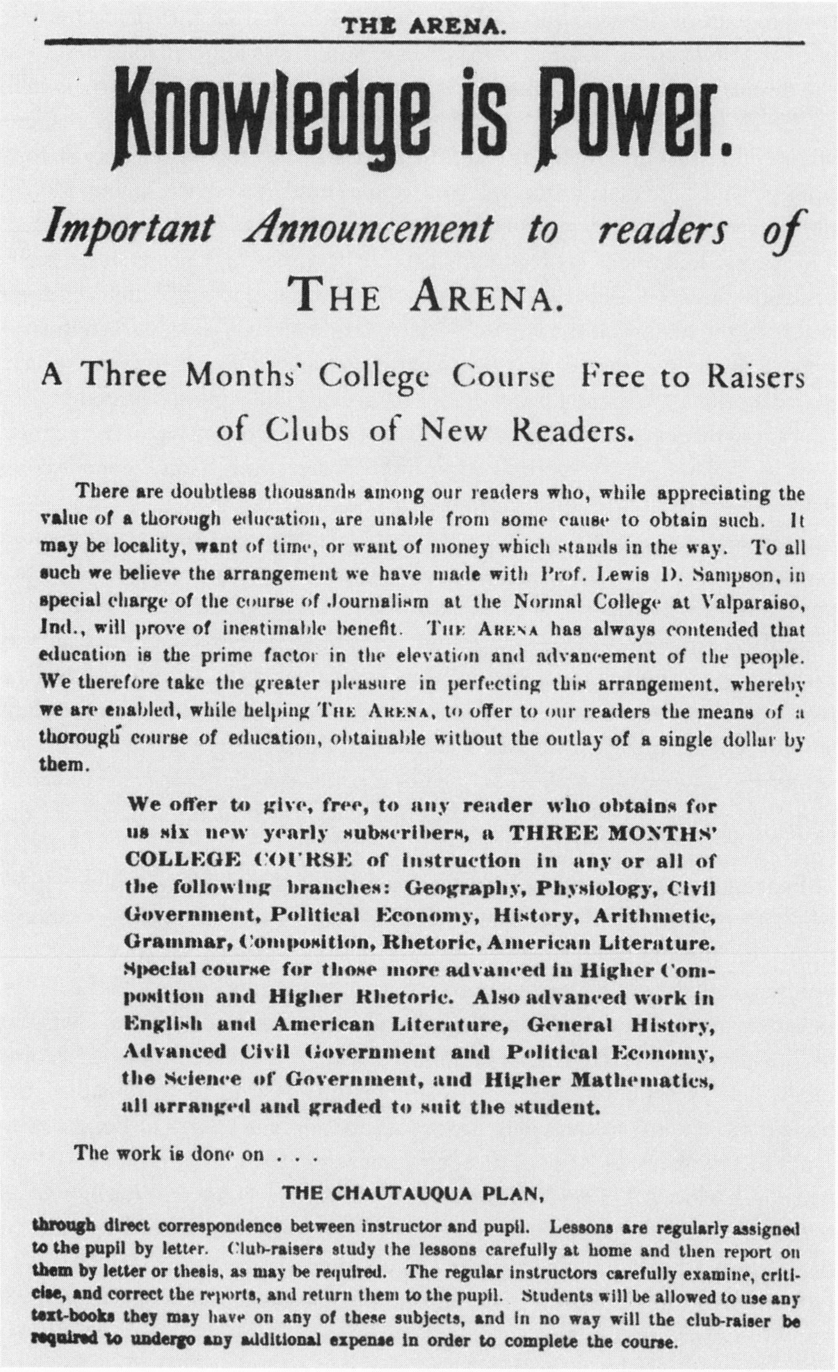

FIGURE 4. This oft-reprinted ad, facing the contents page of *The Arena* (May 1898), promotes the journal while encouraging "the reading habit."

explicitly thematized in fiction that represents mindless, pretentious, or otherwise obtuse readers, appropriating books for all the "wrong" reasons. Silas Lapham, proudly employing an architect who will include a library in the design of his new home, is a relatively benign version of the motif.[16] More emphatic and grotesque images of grimly determined or vulgar consumers of printed matter appear in many contexts. In one recurrent scenario, a reader's preoccupation with a living author effectively displaces the reader's ability to make "contact with an author's mind" via the literary work.[17]

The same qualities that Wharton attacks in "The Vice of Reading" are exemplified by the characters in her short story "Xingu." Although the women in the tale's cultural "Lunch Club" lionize a famous author, they read without pleasure or understanding—only with determination. "Nothing would induce me, now, to put aside a book before I'd finished it," says Mrs. Plinth, "just because I can buy as many more as I want."[18] Similarly, Frank Norris's "Dying Fires" presents a group of culture vultures who revere the latest author without the slightest comprehension of his work. Like some of the characters in "Xingu," these "readers" praise books they have not understood.[19] In James's story "The Figure in the Carpet," the woman who fills her home with weekend guests to entertain her favorite writer does not have "a line of his writing" in the house.[20] Thus, while authors are pursued as a living idols—and often destroyed in the process—books appear as discounted, lifeless objects. The possession of books (and authors) is figured as cultural capital; but reading is doggedly purposive work,[21] as far as can be from a reciprocal interchange of thought between writer and reader.

The heightened discomfort about who was reading fiction and why was a prime motivating force behind the realist aesthetic of authorial invisibility. Beneath the claim of scientific accuracy and professional impartiality lay the desire of many turn-of-century novelists to maximize the distance between themselves and their imagined readers by depersonalizing their narrative discourse.[22] All authors write for readers, both real and imaginary. Although authors may have little or no direct access to the readers they write for, some conception of a reader is necessary to every act of composition, be it a love letter, novel, or critical essay. As Walter Ong puts it, an author fictionalizes himself in the rhetoric of narration and by doing so defines a "reader role" for the consumer of the text.[23] Conversely, an author's prior image of his or her readers inevitably informs the author's rhetorical style. What Erwin Wolff calls "the intended reader" is present to an author's imagination in one form or another before composition begins.[24] This intended reader is shaped by historical and cultural norms as well as personal preoccupations. Partly derived from the wider cultural field inhabited by the author, the imagined or intended reader is a composite figure that makes its way more or less obliquely into every text. This figure can be shaped by anxiety as well as by desire.

The marketing of authors in the late nineteenth century triggered in many writers a fear of being consumed—not only bought but also eaten alive.[25] This anxiety was only exacerbated by the changes that many authors believed were taking place in the composition, taste, and expectations of the reading public. A perception of the reader as hurried consumer, aggressor, or machine rather than friendly collaborator influenced how the turn-of-century realists fictionalized *themselves:* as neutral, scientific, personally effaced. In this sense, the depersonalized authorial persona was not only a reaction to but also a kind of mirror image of the projected reader who was perceived as increasingly cold and distant on the one hand but, paradoxically, intrusive and all *too* personal on the other.

What Frank Norris called the "suppression of the author's personality" in fiction[26] was affirmed in principle by most of the writers whose work would come to constitute the literary canon for the period. James and Wharton, among others, repeatedly stressed the importance for fiction of effacing authorial presence and letting "situations speak for themselves," as James put it.[27] This self-effacement eliminated the digressive authorial persona whose proto-personal narrating "I" was reaffirmed by the responsive participatory "you" often inscribed, in various forms, within the text itself.[28] Even a novelist like Dreiser, who persisted in providing commentary on events of the plot, tended to do so in the guise of historian or philosopher-scientist, not as the reader's trustworthy, familiar companion.

The transition from a personal tone of direct address, evident in numerous novels at midcentury, to the more neutral "objective" narrative mode adopted by many fiction writers in the 1880s and 1890s, reflects the changing idea of the imagined reader and his or her relation to the author of the book. Whatever its aesthetic or ideological rationale, the practice of authorial self-effacement, a hallmark of American realism, was also a defensive response to frightening new images of a reading public that seemed to be "growing like Topsy" in more ways than one, a public that seemed increasingly invisible as well as unknowably "other." If, as a reviewer of Wordsworth's memoirs had declared in 1851, "a poet's life is in his works,"[29] it is not surprising that the growth of an increasingly heterogeneous reading public made many authors feel isolated and exposed. In this context, authorial self-effacement was a kind of safety net for writers who were exhilarated by the new opportunities for professionalism, celebrity, and profit, and who often contributed to their own "packaging,"[30] but who were uncertain of the outcome, fearful lest the "flavor" of their "individuality" be consumed too indiscriminately by a growing mass of invisible strangers.

"Don't talk to me about living in the hearts of my readers," one novelist character says to another in Wharton's early story "Copy" (1901). "We both know what kind of a domicile that is."[31] Written as a dialogue, Wharton's story itself has no narrator, no pervasive, sustaining authorial voice. As many writers grew increasingly skeptical about their readers, they adopted various modes of self-distancing narration, techniques that seemed to afford rhetorical shelter in impersonality. Once imagined as a ground of self-presentation and potential give-and-take, the work of fiction had become a place to hide.

Realist Theory: Between Author and Reader

The question that bears further scrutiny in this context is how the uncertainty about reception that afflicted particular writers in the 1880s and 1890s came to shape not only their own theory of narration but also the interpretive conventions of their readers, and in turn the values that would guide the study of fiction throughout much of the twentieth century. If we focus on the difficulty of addressing an audience perceived as increasingly fragmented and unknowable, we can see how depersonalized, objective narration could be used as a kind of defensive strategy. By asserting the writer's separation from the written work, the rhetorical stance of authorial self-effacement seemed to encourage imaginative distance between author and reader. But there is always a gap between theory and practice. The realist goal of taking the author out of the text was more easily said than done. Many novelists spoke about authorial removal from the work as if this could be accomplished as easily as erasing a comma; and any reviewers responded in kind, protesting the withdrawal of authorial "personality" as if it were a palpable ingredient of every book worth reading. Yet the attempt to restructure conventional expectations with regard to the presence or absence of the author also served to underscore the problem of just where in the text "the author" was to be located in the first place.

The narrating "I" of the authorial persona had reinforced the interpretive convention of identifying the written work with an image of the person who spoke through it. In antebellum America, as we have seen, literary quality was often figured in terms of an author's human attributes. A range of works by a single author was believed to provide an account of the writer's life and spirit.[32] Thus, for the anonymous Hawthorne reviewer discussed in chapter 1, *The Scarlet Letter* raised the question whether Hawthorne's "spirit had suffered . . . material injury" from his Custom House experience. "Of that, however, we have no means of judging, except by comparing this book of recent production with his former writings" (138). An author's moral, spiritual, and intellectual qualities were felt to be visible in his or her work. "No American, perhaps no English reader, needs to be told who and what Mr. Emerson is," states a review of Emerson's *Representative Men* in 1851. "In poetry and in prose, by spoken discourse and by written books, he has stamped his personality too deeply to be effaced upon the literature and speculations of the age."[33]

By scorning the narrating "I" that speaks directly to a "you," realist works presented a challenge to deeply rooted reading habits. Walter Ong and others have taken the awkwardness of the "dear reader" convention as a sign of authorial discomfort with print culture in general and the constraints of the novel form in particular.[34] Such discomfort, however, may be more characteristic of twentieth-century academics than nineteenth-century readers. At a time when letter writing and reading was a common activity for thousands of Americans, when letters, like novels, were often read out loud, and when reading aloud was a staple of elementary education, the narrating voice that struck a proto-personal note through direct address could be welcomed into many middle-class households on familiar terms.

In *Gendered Interventions,* Robyn Warhol distinguishes between two modes of direct address in fiction. She stresses the "embarrassment" generally felt by modern critics when encountering this practice in any form; but her main concern is to differentiate more finely within the mode by paying attention to gender. Thus Warhol makes a distinction between "engaging" and "distancing" narrators—those who make an emotional appeal through exhortation and those who, while using the first-person pronoun and addressing the reader as "you," rely on self-reflexive and meta-fictional digressions.[35] During most of the nineteenth century, however, both modes of direct address, "distancing" and "engaging," promoted a sense of collaboration between author and reader. Whether rooted more in sentimental appeals or in irony and intellectual game-playing, the convention of direct address contributed to a sense of common ground and shared values. Speaking to a "you," a narrating voice sounded "personal," and made it all the easier for contemporary reviewers to group books by the same author together in terms of a real-life author figure.[36]

In 1860 Hawthorne had expressed his admiration for "quite another class of novels than those which I myself am able to write. . . . [T]he novels of Anthony Trollope . . . precisely suit my taste; solid and substantial . . . and just as real as if some giant had hewn a great lump out of the earth and put it under a glass case, with all its inhabitants going about their business, and not suspecting that they were being made a show of."[37] Hawthorne's image of the fully inhabited segment of earth, preserved under glass, pleased Trollope himself and has received considerable attention as a figure for realism. According to Walter Kendrick, the image "describes how a realistic novel ought to be regarded by its reader. . . . There is no novelist in the business: the giant is nowhere to be seen."[38]

Hawthorne's evocation of the unseen giant anticipated that authorial removal from the represented world of the text which twenty years later would attract growing numbers of proponents, including one of the most influential advocates of authorial absence, Henry James. As the idea of impersonal narration was refined with increasing precision toward the end of the century, however, Trollope began to seem the very antithesis of a self-effacing author. From this point of view James's own essay on Trollope presents a sharp contrast to Hawthorne's comment. "Certain . . . novelists," James writes, using Trollope as his central example, "have a habit of giving themselves away which must often bring tears to the eyes of people who take their fiction seriously. . . . In a digression, a parenthesis, or an aside, [the novelist] concedes to the reader that he and this trusting friend are only 'making believe.' He admits that the events he narrates have not really happened, and that he can give his narrative any turn the reader may like best."[39] Taking Trollope's "digression" or "aside" to his "trusting friend" the reader as a fatal concession, James attacks a key element of the narrative mode that had fostered friendly reading at midcentury. The friendly author/narrator, such as Eliot, Trollope, Thackeray, or Stowe, provided a running commentary for the reader that could include moral reflections as well as a (more or less ironic) consideration of aesthetic obstacles encountered and choices made in the course of narration.[40] Although James criticizes Trollope for undermining his own illusion of fictional reality and "giving himself away" as a mere writer of fiction, it is precisely this confessional tone (or meta-fictional gamesomeness) that had long certified the author as the reader's winsome companion and confidant.[41]

A fundamental sign of the author-book-reader connection in nineteenth-century fiction was a narrative style that allowed readers to identify a story-telling voice with a real, individuated, even fallible author, while simultaneously attributing to that author unlimited knowledge about the represented world and its "people." The author/narrator's free access to the thoughts, feelings, and motives of the characters (along with his or her readiness to evaluate the action in moral terms) became a mark of the teller's authority. At the same time, the willingness to digress and reflect on aspects of the storytelling process itself (behind the back of the characters, so to speak) endorsed the author/narrator as the reader's trusting friend.

At midcentury the link between the narrator and a particular biographical figure had been generally implicit even when not expressly underscored (as in Hawthorne's preface to *The Scarlet Letter* or Stowe's "Concluding Remarks" to *Uncle Tom's Cabin*). Pointers to an author's real existence fostered the sense of the author/narrator as a mortal being inhabiting the same world as his or her readers. When *Ruth Hall* sold fifty thousand copies in eight months of 1855, *Harper's* proudly noted, "It has sold universally . . . and that profoundly interesting question whether Ruth Hall is Fanny Fern has been debated from the Penobscot to the Mississippi."[42] Indeed, the use of pseudonyms (and the practice of anonymity itself) only reaffirmed governing assumptions about the vital bond between author, text, and reader. Although the convention of anonymity served to endorse cultural assumptions both about the autonomy of ideas and about authorial modesty, writers, publishers, and readers all employed strategies for undermining anonymous postures and encouraging speculation about authorial identity.[43] The eventual disclosure of the author's "true" name only confirmed the existence of a real person behind the printed page. In a similar way, the editorial "we" and the unsigned reviews of well-established journals such as the *Atlantic* paradoxically affirmed a sense of community, as if authors and readers were already familiar to one another, which made introductions superfluous.[44]

Susan Fay has proposed that etiquette guides provide a key to conventions of authorial anonymity and unmasking in antebellum America. They do so precisely because writing and reading fiction were themselves experienced as social transactions. In this context, a fictional narrator who could merge with both the author and the characters became a particular favorite. Imagined as an inhabitant not only of the represented world within the text but also of the world outside it, such a narrator was a fertile source of reader identification—a composite human figure, exemplary but not distant.[45] One of the most popular novels in the second half of the century was *Little Women,* which became not just an unanticipated success in its own time but an enduring classic. As Barbara Sicherman has suggested, the inexhaustible popularity of the book can be partly attributed to the way it has allowed women readers to identify both with Louisa May Alcott herself and with Jo, her chief representative in the text.[46] Women who were disappointed by the text's ultimate recovery of the rebellious tomboy Jo for domesticity could imaginatively conflate the heroine with the author, a woman who remained unmarried and became a professional writer. Moreover, since *Little Women* has been generally perceived not as serious, highbrow literature but as a "girl's book," generations of admirers continue to read it "for the author" even today.

Authorial narrators such as Stowe, Thackeray, Trollope, and Alcott were rejected on aesthetic grounds with increasing vehemence by the most "serious" turn-of-century American writers. In his lecture of 1899, Howells discusses the "great impure and imperfect" narrative form, the "sort of novel whose material is treated as if it were real history" (33). Howells labels this form "impure and imperfect" because, while the novelist implicitly claims to be "narrating a series of [real] events,"

> he dwells in a world of his own creating, where he is a universal intelligence, comprehending and interpreting everything . . . without accounting in any way for his knowledge of the facts. The form involves a thousand contradictions, improbabilities. There is no point where it cannot be convicted of the most grotesque absurdity. . . . [T]he novelist . . . has the intimate confidence of his characters in the hour of passion, the hour of remorse, the hour of death itself. (33)

Howells articulates a rhetorical problem here that he himself does not solve. The "improbabilities" and "contradictions" that bother him arise because the novelist seems to know more about his characters than he possibly could if he dwelled on the same plane of reality as they. If the narrator "has the intimate confidence of his characters" even in "the hour of death," it is obvious to Howells that the teller of the tale can only be one person: the novelist who has authored the story in the first place. The inescapable presence of this omniscient figure creates absurdity by destroying the illusion that the world and its characters are real. James would formulate the influential solution to this problem: the separation of the narrator from the novelist.

In the preface to *The Golden Bowl*, James explains that in his shorter fiction he often employed "the impersonal author's concrete deputy or delegate" for the purpose of narration, "a convenient substitute or apologist for the creative power otherwise so veiled and disembodied." Reflecting on the difference between the author and the narrating figure within the text, James insists that "anything, in short, I now reflect, must always have seemed to me better— better for the process and the effect of representation, my irrepressible ideal— than the mere muffled majesty of irresponsible 'authorship.'"[47] By representing events through the consciousness of a particular character (or characters), James eliminated the "grotesque absurdity" that troubled Howells and others. Events were now to be reflected through the mind of a character whose sources of information would never exceed what could reasonably be expected of either a participant in the action or an observer of it. There would be no knowledge of the future, no revelation of another character's inchoate desires, no authoritative account of deathbed regrets.

For the purposes of the present argument, the most significant consequence of this innovation was that (theoretically) it expelled the figure of the author from the reading experience. Later, when the idea of a narrative voice became a staple of narrative theory, it set a kind of professional seal on the withdrawal of the imagined author from a situation of exchange with the reader.[48] Once fiction is, in James's formulation, told by "the impersonal author's concrete deputy or delegate," the author himself is imaginatively displaced from the discourse—all the more "muffled," "veiled and disembodied."

The radical division between author and narrator, the elimination of the figure of the author from the reading process, the notion that "great" works of literature find a rhetorical solution to the problems that bothered Howells and James—these assumptions about narration, already partly in place by the turn of the century, would become categorical with the New Criticism.[49] Yet even as new ground rules for the rhetoric of fiction were being adopted by many writers, the rewards of friendly reading were still emphatically affirmed in critical essays, reviews, and books—all the more so, in fact, as fiction withheld the familiar pleasures. Toward the turn of the century, as the "remote[ness]"[50] of the author became an explicit goal of realism, many writers and critics not only continued to praise authorial personality in fiction but also went on recommending works by the traditional "friendly" writers for study, self-culture, inclusion in public and private libraries. Thus, after drawing attention to the problem of imprecise, inconsistent narration, Howells himself proceeded to praise the very kind of novel whose "impurity" he had exposed. Although this form "involves every contradiction, every impossibility," Howells notes, it "is the only form which can fully represent any passage of life in its inner and outer entirety" (34). Howells's brief list of preferred examples includes *Don Quixote*, *Middlemarch*, *Bleak House*, *Uncle Tom's Cabin*, and *The Scarlet Letter*, all novels that foreground the process of narration one way or another, often addressing the reader with an "I" or a "we" that can be taken as referring to the author of the text.

Resistance to the Model

The realist goal of maximizing the distance between the author and the work elicited powerful negative responses at the turn of the century. This part of the realist controversy is rarely recalled today, perhaps because the author has disappeared so effectively in the interim that the very notion of authorial presence in a text seems naive. But the authorial persona was not removed from fiction without a struggle. When the aim of self-effacement began to be formulated, it was attacked quite as vehemently as realism's "low" subject matter, desultory plotting, and proliferation of detail. The newly "objective," self-consciously "impartial" mode of narration associated with realism was experienced by many readers and reviewers just as it was presented: as a radical withholding of the author. Since contact with an author's "personality" had long been seen as a prime reward of fiction reading, the new mode of narration only heightened in many readers the desire for authorial presence of one sort or another. "The more [the writer] differentiates himself from his story," Norris insisted, "the more remote his isolation[,] . . . the more will his story seem to have a life of its own."[51] Norris, James, London, and others explicitly affirmed the value of a text that could make its reader "forget the author."[52] For many readers, however, forgetting the author was precisely the problem. Many believed that in fiction the result of authorial removal was not more "life" but less. Turn-of-century editors, educators, and reviewers felt left in the lurch, alone with a "blur of printed paper" rather than a human voice made accessible through fiction.[53]

Writing in the *Atlantic* in 1900, Samuel Crothers expressed a common belief: "[L]iterary values inhere not in things or even ideas, but in persons." Like many commentators of his generation, Crothers makes it clear that what he calls "literature" is a "kind of picture of a man's own disposition."[54] In her "Plea for the Shiftless Reader," Martha Baker Dunn embraces a book as a "good companion," insisting that in "literature, as in life, one has a right to choose one's own friends."[55] But these defenses of reading as an "interchange of thought" between writer and reader already constitute a rear guard action, a nostalgic evocation of dying interpretive conventions. After the end of the century, one emerging condition for imaginative entry into the newly consolidated "high" culture of letters was, for the writer, to renounce the "old-fashioned intrusion of the author among his puppets"[56] and, for the reader, to eschew the practice of reading for the author.

By 1900, the chatty, self-reflexive authorial persona had encountered so much disapproval in critical discourse that the taboo on the first-person pronoun was ripe for parody.[57] In *The Lost Art of Reading* (1902), Gerald Stanley Lee, a frequent contributor to the *Atlantic,* attacks the convention of authorial objectivity by lampooning it. Proposing to admit "the worst . . . at once," Lee confesses that he intends "to say I—a little—in this book" (24). In his "Parenthesis to the Gentle Reader," he asserts his right to speak in his own name, "right here in my own book at least" (24). "I have tried other ways," he admits.

> I have tried calling myself he. I have stated my experiences in principles—called myself it, and in the first part of this book I have already fallen into the way—page after page—of borrowing other people, when all the while I knew perfectly well . . . that I preferred myself. At all events this calling one's self names—now one and now another,—working one's way *incognito,* all the way through one's own book, is not making me as modest as I had hoped. (24–25)[58]

Parody is possible only when its object is fully familiar to its audience.[59] Lee's comments effectively confirm that the self-effacing author had won the field—at least in circles where the craft of fiction was analyzed, debated, and considered a serious matter.

Yet for many realist writers themselves, the victory was a pyrrhic one. Insofar as the strategy of authorial self-effacement seemed to create a greater sense of space between author and reader, it also exacerbated the feeling of anonymity and isolation that already beset many novelists of the period, writers for whom (as for Mrs. Dale in Wharton's "Copy") the idea of "living in the hearts of [one's] readers" was nothing but a joke. When readers are imagined with distaste, for whom does one write? Indeed, why write at all? One recurrent scenario in fiction of the period answers this question by imagining not publishing as a triumph.

Wharton's "Copy" reaches its logical conclusion when the story's two writer protagonists burn a collection of love letters that each of them had contemplated publishing. The moment of withholding material from public consumption is the climax of the story. The refusal to publish is linked to a renewal of spontaneous feeling, a fleeting return to "the old days" when Mrs. Dale and her lover were "real people" (104) and "a signature wasn't an autograph" (117). At stake here is the gap between "real" person and authorial persona. But just how different is a "signature" from an "autograph"? To what extent is any person represented by his or her written name?[60] Does the first-person pronoun—do written words in general—project or conceal the individuality of the man or woman behind the pen? "Copy" implies that if the process of writing and publishing is not experienced as a circuit of communication, it may be nothing more than a mode of self-embalming. "Before long I shall become a classic," says Mrs. Dale in Wharton's story. "Bound in sets and kept on the top bookshelf—brr, doesn't that sound freezing" (113). Collapsing the space between self and work with her use of the first-person pronoun (I shall become a classic), Mrs. Dale's formulation still reflects the common identification of an author with his or her book. Becoming "a classic" turns into a terrible fate because it means being relegated to "the top bookshelf," far from all revitalizing human warmth.[61]

Like the miniature action of "Copy," Jack London's novel *Martin Eden* (1909) projects a dynamic in which the act of writing, bound up at first with ardent desire for a reader/beloved, creates in the author a deep sense of isolation and dissociation. Martin's ambition to be an author takes shape when, after eight months at sea, "tortured by the exquisite beauty of the world," he decides to describe to Ruth, the woman he loves, "many of the bits of South Sea beauty." Soon he is impelled to "recreate this beauty for a wider audience than Ruth."[62] But Martin's literary production does not elicit the response he had anticipated, either from Ruth or from the editors to whom he sends his work. He even comes to "doubt that editors were real men. . . . If he had received one line, one personal line, along with one rejection . . . he would have been cheered. But not one editor had given that proof of existence" (160–61).[63] Later Martin's unexpected popularity makes the lack of a human and "personal" response all the more disorienting. "Where does Martin Eden and the work Martin Eden performed come in all this?" Martin asks himself once he has become a celebrity (450). Unable to answer this question, he soon disavows not merely public performance but all performance. Having once believed that "my desire to write is the most vital thing in me" (329), he now finds it incomprehensible "that men found so much to write about" (477). His experience suggests that to give up the desire for a responsive reader is to give up the possibility of writing altogether.

Reading continued to be conceived as a reciprocal activity even after the idea of the writer-reader relationship began to look dubious—or treacherous. Realist writers themselves could not write without imagining their relations with the reader, "gentle" or otherwise. The very authors who spoke most effectively for authorial removal and the transparent text often violated their own rules of impartial narration. They also generated recurrent motifs that reveal the wish to be present in the text as strongly as the fear of being consumed there. Realist texts abound with surrogate figures for the author engaged in some kind of transaction with the reader.

Some of the most thoroughgoing advocates of the neutral voice in fiction smuggled themselves into their discourse "incognito" (to use Lee's term), adding a kind of personal signature, which may have gone unperceived by most readers but which can nonetheless be taken to signify a wish for what F. Scott Fitzgerald would call his own *"personal public."*[64] Charles Norris suggests that his brother Frank slipped an image of himself into a description of a mining office in *McTeague,* where an unidentified character with "surprisingly gray" hair is found playing with a Great Dane puppy. "Nothing could be more characteristic of the whimsical humor of Frank Norris," Charles wrote in a biography of his brother, "than this casual introduction of himself into his story."[65] Kate Chopin creates a similar sense of veiled self-representation in *The Awakening,* where recurrent references to her namesake the composer raise questions about the relation of audience to performer. Yet the link to Kate Chopin herself is never directly indicated.[66] R. W. B. Lewis and Amy Kaplan have suggested that Edith Wharton herself "is" the lady shopper in "Bunner Sisters."[67] As Michael Fried has shown, Stephen Crane repeatedly sneaks his initials into his work.[68] Such strategies, often spontaneous, sometimes unconscious, could nonetheless serve as oblique invitations to those who might recognize the authorial "person" behind the writer's mask.

In many novels of the period, as we shall see, the motif of stage presence becomes a trope through which authors explore the idea of being directly visible and physically present to an audience. The culturally volatile image of a woman onstage repeatedly becomes a stand-in for the figure of the writer in turn-of-century fiction, and it does so precisely because of the questions under discussion here: questions of self-representation, relations with the public, authorial presence versus invisibility. In the work of Henry James, Edith Wharton, Willa Cather, and others, the woman onstage is a recurrent motif. Only partly protected by the frame of stage or podium, the actress is vulnerable to the gaze of spectators who might seek to violate what Cather called "the hard, glittering line . . . [of] the footlights."[69]

Insofar as an author is imagined as partly hidden within a text, a great deal comes to depend on how the reader and the act of reading are imagined. Some essays and reviews of the period continued to represent reading as an opportunity for a meeting of minds or "best selves."[70] Increasingly, however, especially in realist fiction, the idea of reading as a productive transaction, a shared "labor"[71] or writer-reader interchange was replaced by negative evocations of the reader and the reading process. Many late nineteenth-century texts envision the reader's relation to author and book as highly destructive.

I have already noted that the image of readers who seek authors *outside* the text became a recurrent fictional motif at the turn of the century. Projections of hurried, insensitive, or otherwise inadequate readers in pursuit of a receding author figure appeared in a variety of contexts and only intensified the feeling that written works were no longer adequate sites of connection between author and reader. As many readers continued to harbor the desire for an author, the strategy of circumventing the text altogether was complemented by another— a way not of dispensing with the text but of reading through it to the author hidden behind or within. A shift of critical vocabulary toward the end of the century exemplifies this mode of reading. For many writers and reviewers, the notion of conversing with an author through his book had become an anachronism. It was replaced by the concept of "getting at" an author, a phrase that in itself implies obstacles, distance, and aggression.

Getting at the Author

In *The Aims of Literary Study* (1894), Hiram Corson speaks of "get[ting] at" an author in order to argue for reading as a kind of communion of spirit. From Corson's point of view, "to get at the being of a great author" is a benign enterprise. It is "to come into relationship with [an author's] absolute personality[,] . . . the highest result of the study of his works."[72] Elsewhere in the 1890s, however, "getting at" an author is explicitly presented as a futile and destructive approach. Many of James's artist tales clearly thematize the negative consequences of this mode of reading. In "The Figure in the Carpet," the narrator's decision to "get *at*" the novelist Vereker sets off a process that effectively destroys the narrator's pleasure in the text.[73]

As "The Figure in the Carpet" begins, the narrator is enjoined by his friend Corvick to write about Vereker's new novel (358). "For God's sake try to get *at* him," Corvick says. Accepting the challenge, the narrator begins to read an advance copy of Vereker's "last" (358). "I sat up with Vereker half the night," the narrator notes—by which he of course means he was reading Vereker's book. The idea of having sat up with a novelist half the night epitomizes friendly reading: at this stage of the story, the narrator sees the author as the text and vice versa: "If I always read him as soon as I could get hold of him, I had a particular reason for wishing to read him now" (357).

When the narrator-reader turns from Vereker's text to the author himself, however, he becomes involved in "an experiment that [brings him] only chagrin" (375). After the narrator's first conversation with Vereker, he is determined to find "the figure in the carpet," the "buried treasure" in Vereker's work (374, 380, 384). In the process he seeks confirmation of the author in the text and confirmation of the text in the living author. Shuttling from the one to the other without satisfaction, the narrator begins to feel that the author has tricked him—"made a fool of me"—with a "bad joke" and "a monstrous *pose*" (370). Conceived as "antagonist" (376), the author, like the work, becomes a source of pain to the once devoted reader: "Not only had I lost the books, but I had lost the man himself: they and their author had been alike spoiled for me" (378).

The animus implicit in the narrator's way of reading makes him a character-istic reader figure in realist fiction of the period. But the narrator's aggressive reading practices are also complemented by his reticence as an author in his own right. For him, as for the narrator of James's earlier *Aspern Papers* (1888), the reading of an author's work becomes inseparable from the desire for access to the writer himself. (The narrator of *The Aspern Papers* is determined to ac-quire a dead poet's love letters, virtually at any price.) Both narrators therefore know only too well how dangerous it can be to encourage in one's readers the interpretive practice of "getting at" the author. This is precisely what they seek to forestall when "writ[ing] out" their own "little history" ("Figure," 400 389). Neither the narrator of "Figure in the Carpet" nor the narrator of *The Aspern Papers* reveals his name to the readers of the tale.[74] Still, particularly in *The As-pern Papers*, the pose of cautious anonymity repeatedly comes into conflict with an impulse toward self-revelation. The storyteller's discourse is pervaded from the start by a tension between the wish to confide in the reader (right down to "the worst thing I did") and a fear of revealing too much, a resistance to "the last violence of self-exposure" (123, 108). The work of many turn-of-century re-alist writers is characterized by a similar tension: the commitment to authorial self-effacement repeatedly clashes with the authorial desire to be present in the text, one way or another.

Serialized in the *Atlantic, The Aspern Papers* were flanked by articles that im-plied growing uncertainties about author-book-reader relations. Discussions of books and authors in the *Atlantic* of 1888 reflect two approaches to reading that vied with each other throughout the fiction and criticism of the period. One approach still represented a book as a kind of living thing: "A Word for Silent Partners," for example, evokes the various "voiceless," often "neglected," partners who participate in all our lives, concluding with an image of the in-dispensible and often unappreciated "silent partners" on our bookshelves.[75] Such formulations suggest that the image of an author, embodied in a book, is sufficient unto itself. In this perspective, books are "like people"—in fact, they virtually *are* people (silent partners, friends, lovers, soulmates). The opposing notion, however, suggests that the author may be hidden in the book. This ap-proach invites a reader to go through or behind the text to excavate the figure of the author, probing personal life, work habits, perhaps love letters. Like the narrator of *The Aspern Papers*, many commentators in the same volume of the *Atlantic* gave the biographical figure of the author as much attention as his or her work.

Well-established periodicals of the day tried to hold the line for the idea of community and virtual friendship in and through literary discourse, maintain-ing what Christopher Wilson calls the tone of "after-dinner conversation" and emphasizing decorum in reviewing even after the turn of the century.[76] Yet the growing attention to writers' notebooks, letters, and diaries, in the *Atlantic* and

elsewhere, only furthered the erosion of friendly reading conventions, legit-
imizing the attempt to go around or through the text. Many writers believed
that readers were ever more determined to seek "the man behind the pen" as if
the experience of reading could no longer provide a satisfying sense of contact.

Turn-of-century writers felt increasingly uncomfortable with the conception
of reading implicit in "getting at" authors; such discomfort leaves multiple
traces in realist texts of the period. Late nineteenth-century fiction is full of
characters who, like some of those we have already seen, are non-writing, non-
publishing, or otherwise reticent and nameless writers. Throughout Howells's
Hazard of New Fortunes, Basil March takes notes for sketches he intends to
write but never does. In Norris's *Octopus,* Presley is in a similar position during
most of the novel. When he finally publishes not the "epic of the West" he had
intended but a poem (under a pseudonym), he releases the violence that is repeatedly linked in turn-of-century texts with the act of writing, publishing, and
especially being read.

From this perspective, "The Yellow Wallpaper" by Charlotte Perkins Gilman can be understood as a brilliant nightmare version of a characteristic late
nineteenth-century conception of reading. Like many of James's artist tales,
"The Yellow Wallpaper" begins with a writer whose name we never learn. Although the narrator's lack of a name has clear implications for a feminist reading of the story,[77] this aspect of "The Yellow Wallpaper," like many others, takes
on a different emphasis in the present context.

The tale begins by emphasizing the narrator's need to write and her difficulties in doing so; but the narrator's involvement with the act of writing is dissi-
pated by the middle of the text. In the course of the story, the focus on writing
is displaced by a focus on reading: the narrator becomes a close, indeed obsessive, reader of the paper on the walls that surround her.[78] She is far more determined as a reader than she has ever been as a writer, and her commitment to
reading only grows stronger as the story unfolds. Early in the tale, her greatest
desire is to be released from her prison; later she insists that nothing will induce
her to leave before she has finished puzzling out the pattern in the paper. "I
WILL follow that pattern to some sort of conclusion,"[79] she declares. Soon she
locks herself into the room with the wallpaper and refuses to open the door.
Studying the pattern day and night, she is "determined that nobody shall find
it out but myself" (27).

Most significant for our purposes is the fact that what this narrator-reader
finally discovers as she studies the lines of the printed pattern is the figure of a
woman. The narrator's growing commitment to getting at this woman—the
woman behind the printed pattern, the woman in the "sub-pattern" (18)[80]—has
some devastating results at the level of the plot, as well as additional implications for the idea of reading. That the woman in the paper is also identified as

the narrator herself points in a distorted way to the long-standing argument against fiction reading by educators and reviewers. At this level the narrator enacts the merger between reader and fictional creations which many critics of the novel-reading habit had attacked for decades. The collapse of self into other in "The Yellow Wallpaper" is an act of total identification, a loss of borders, very different from the nineteenth-century norm which conceived of reading as a kind of conversation with the author.[81] The blurring of boundaries enacted literally in "The Yellow Wallpaper" is the antithesis of such a give-and-take: both reader and text are destroyed in the process.

The narrator of "The Yellow Wallpaper," stripping layers of paper off the walls in order to get at the woman in the subtext, represents an extreme dystopian version of a paradigmatic turn-of-century scenario. Like the recurrent figure of the woman onstage, images of the hesitant writer and aggressive reader reflect a changing conception of what an author is and how his or her relation to book and reader can be understood. Many texts that on the face of it have nothing to do with either writing or reading reflect their author's preoccupation with the danger of being read. Like Theodore Dreiser's novel *The Financier* (1912) in which a lobster devours a squid in the glass tank in a fish market window, many fictional texts of the period contain oblique and fanciful vignettes in which a beleaguered figure, defended only by a "cloud of ink," is gradually devoured by another creature who never removes his "beady . . . eyes" from the first.[82]

In due course I will look more closely at how the writer-reader interchange was imagined by realist writers, and will trace authorial ambivalence not only about being exposed in one's text but also about being concealed there. We turn first, however, to some of the writers who scorned the realist aesthetic outright, and who continued to promote the idea of reading as a kind of conversation with an author. While proponents of realism theorized authorial invisibility as a goal of narration, the idea of an author as a precious acquaintance was still affirmed by many writers and reviewers as a criterion of value in literature.[83] Indeed, the most popular fiction even after the turn of the century continued to foster the image of a benignly accessible author, and many readers went on expecting such a being to emerge whenever they picked up a book.

3

Refusing Authorial Self-effacement: Popular Fictions at the Turn of the Century

> **There are too many "yous" and "yours" in it; you ought to say "one" now and then, to make it seem more like good writing. "One opens a favorite book;" "One's thoughts are a great comfort in solitude," and so on.**
>
> Kate Douglas Wiggin, *Rebecca of Sunnybrook Farm* (1904)

The split between popular and serious fiction at the end of the nineteenth century widened partly along the lines of what narration implied about the writer-reader transaction. In both realist and popular works,[1] the implicit exchange between writer and reader served as a model for social relations. The debate over modes of address in fiction of the period grew partly out of anxieties elicited by an increasingly fragmented and uncertain world. The desire for a stable community (and the difficulty of imagining it) informed not only the realist strategy of authorial self-effacement but also the friendly narration of numerous best-sellers.

The impartial, nonintrusive narrators of realist texts offered little personal commentary and few moral reflections to offset the harsh sense of social disjuncture and individual isolation projected by novels such as *McTeague, Sister Carrie,* and *The House of Mirth.* By contrast, the friendly authorial narrators of much popular fiction, addressing the reader as a familiar acquaintance, implied that a reliably centralizing consciousness could always be trusted to explain and evaluate the unfolding events of a story. In popular fiction of the period, events confirmed what narration implied: that moral clarity, meaningful choices, and enduring human relationships were possible.

By rejecting the personal tone in narration, the realists alienated many people for whom the sense of being in touch with an author's individuality remained one of the prime pleasures of reading. While proponents of realism sought to differentiate as sharply as possible between the narrating voice in the text and what Frank Norris called "the man behind the pen," other contemporary novelists continued to conflate the two by employing an "authorial" narrator who shared his or her views of life and art with the reader while telling the story. Even after the turn of the century, many reviewers warmly praised the digressive, expansive, morally normative narrators of Owen Wister, Winston Churchill, Francis Marion Crawford, and others. The question that deserves consideration here is what made friendly narration so popular in late nineteenth-century America? As Pierre Bourdieu points out, to persist in the use of a literary convention that has come under attack is already to give it a different meaning.[2] In this chapter I ask what fears were neutralized, what desires fulfilled, and what social issues engaged by novels that rejected the impersonal voice which was every day becoming more familiar in the culture of professionalism.

I suggest that toward the end of the nineteenth century, some of the most popular American novels addressed problems generated by a changing social reality—many of the same problems addressed by the realists—but they did so by displacing these problems into a foreign locale, into another time frame, or into the realm of "innocent" childhood. As in dreamwork, such displacements effectively obscured the relation between the images of the text and the difficult issues they raised (and seemed to resolve). Couched in the friendly terms of authorial narration, some of the best-loved novels of the period implied that despite the pressures of industrial society, mass culture, and an increasingly heterogeneous population, fiction could still foster a sense of reading as a benign, proto-personal transaction predicated on common assumptions—a kind of conversation between author and reader.

Many popular novels at the turn of the century self-consciously affirmed and enacted just the sort of bond between writer and reader that the realists refused. Kate Wiggin's *Rebecca of Sunnybrook Farm* (1904) is typical in this respect. The narrator often addresses the reader directly and refers to herself in the first person.[3] The heroine, by contrast, painstakingly learns to say "one" in her compositions and poems "to make [them] seem more like good writing" (112). Her efforts to follow this recipe are represented as poignantly comic. "It is horrid!" Rebecca exclaims, after reading one of her poems to some friends. "I ought not to have put that 'me' in. I'm writing the poetry. Nobody ought to know it *is* me standing by the river; it ought to be 'Rebecca,' or 'the darker maiden'" (123). These lines gently make fun of Rebecca as she struggles with the absurdities she has been taught. To her it is self-evident that the speaker of a poem is the writer herself. How is she to disguise such a plain fact? The barb is directed against the aim of depersonalized, objective, "literary" discourse.

The personal tone of narration that characterized many popular works of the period implied a shared understanding, a community of values, between reader and author which must have been particularly reassuring in the face of rapid social change. In novels such as Owen Wister's *The Virginian*, Winston Churchill's *Richard Carvel*, Francis Marion Crawford's *A Roman Singer*, and George Du Maurier's exceedingly popular *Trilby*, meta-fictional and other digressions lent support to the theme of coherence and stability in the self, in language, and in social relations.[4] To judge by the sales figures, there was considerable appeal in speakers who addressed the reader as a knowing ally with shared assumptions. A tone of wise consensus based on life experience reinforced the sense of solidarity between author and reader. As Willa Cather put it, describing her response to *Trilby* in the *Nebraska Journal:* "Always you feel behind the book the strong, tender personality of a man who has seen much of love and sin and suffering and who has not at all solved the riddle of it all. That is the great charm of [*Trilby*], the wise, gentle, sympathetic man, whom every sentence brings you closer to."[5] The pleasure Cather takes in gaining access to a "strong, tender personality" through reading is echoed in many other reviews of the period. Just as Cather praises *Trilby* for bringing the reader "closer" to the "wise, gentle, sympathetic man" who wrote the book, so Ouida says that "to read [Francis Marion Crawford's] books was to feel in the company of a well-bred man of superior gifts."[6] The "company" of Norris, Crane, the late James, or the young Cather herself did not elicit such responses.

Realist texts tended to thrust their readers, unaccompanied, into a chaotic, sometimes violent space, generally that of a contemporary American city, where an increasingly diverse population struggled for equilibrium. In the fictional world of Howells, Wharton, and Dreiser, some characters challenged class distinctions; others fought to maintain them. Realist works provided no solutions to the social problems they explored. But, as Amy Kaplan has suggested, they did attempt to project a renewed sense of common ground—of community—within a changing social reality.[7] They did so partly by representing populations previously excluded from serious literature.

In recent years realism has been much taken to task for reappropriating and subordinating the "other" populations that it claimed to depict for democratic purposes.[8] But if we examine popular romances of the period with an eye to their underlying attitudes toward social diversity, we gain a wider perspective on the realist project. Popular fiction sometimes spoke for "democracy," or for what is referred to in *The Virginian* as "this land of equality."[9] But the novels of Wister, Churchill, Crawford, and others unabashedly endorsed an image of small and stable—indeed, exclusive—communities that kept otherness firmly at bay. The reassuring voice of an authoritative narrator was a crucial element in legislating and sustaining benign imagined worlds for which writer-reader relations themselves became the model. Paradoxically, of course, these select "societies" were open to anyone who could read.

Walter Benn Michaels has suggested that unlike the major works of American realism, other texts of the Progressive period (such as the novels of Thomas Nelson Page and especially Thomas Dixon) were "deeply concerned with questions of racial national identity."[10] The writers we will be looking at in this chapter were preoccupied with related questions. Contemporaneous

with Page and Dixon but more popular than they, Wister, Churchill, Crawford, and others did not directly engage the issue of racial purity; but they projected an image of America as a homogeneous entity, sometimes imagined as a
family. Moreover, by repeatedly exploring the problematic of a marriage that
was to be made in the course of the action, these novels raised questions about
the extent to which America could or should assimilate foreign others into itself. This relatively oblique brand of xenophobia, with its vague sense of a "generalized foreign danger" (in the words of John Higham),[11] appealed to readers
by the hundreds of thousands.

The popularity of fiction that stressed an ethic of exclusion is a paradox that
repays close attention. Unlike the white supremacy of a novel such as Dixon's
Clansman, the exclusionary emphasis of Wister's *Virginian* or Crawford's *Roman Singer* was indirect (or ambivalent) enough to enlist the sympathetic interest of a wide variety of readers. Questions about the cohesion or fragmentation of society were of concern to many—both insiders and outsiders—who
wondered where they stood as they contemplated the increasingly corporate
America of the 1890s, with its growing urban centers, its manifest poor, and its
massive waves of immigrants from eastern and southern Europe. Many novels
of the period became best-sellers partly because the seemingly open invitation
issued to all comers by the friendly authorial narrator subsumed and offset the
exclusionary, xenophobic, even racist assumptions inscribed in the plot. The
fiction of Wister, Crawford, Churchill, and others was sold to a large, heterogeneous reading public. These popular writers had no way of knowing who
their readers were, any more than did the realists themselves. But whereas realist writers constructed their readers as strangers and took refuge in a discourse
of impersonality, popular novelists of the period constructed their readers as
intimate friends. It would seem that a great many people were prepared to play
this role.

The Cultural Work of Friendly Narration in *The Virginian*

Unlike realist and naturalist texts, popular novels of the period were generally
set in an imagined world at a considerable remove from turn-of-century America. The appeal of these romances has often been explained as that of vicar-
ious adventure, contact with foreign places or bygone days. But whether set in
the prerevolutionary colonies, Renaissance Italy, mid-nineteenth-century England, or the sheltered space of childhood, the specific context of the action
may well have mattered less than the opportunity to include the reader in a
small, homogeneous world where the pressing difficulties of contemporary life
(including the problem of the author's relation to a mass audience) were elided.
In the represented world of popular fiction there were always problems to be
overcome, cowards and villains (often foreign ones) to be destroyed or expelled.

But a small core of loyal, virtuous, right-minded people were invariably on hand to do that job, often by banding together. I suggest that the sense of community within this represented world was a crucial element in the success of many best-sellers. The sense of community was reinforced, moreover, by a mode of narration that created a "community" of narrator and reader.

The Virginian (1902) exemplifies some of the contradictions characteristic of many popular works at the turn of the century. Through plot, structure, and narrative discourse, *The Virginian* seems to affirm the closing of social gaps created by birth and education. The novel projects several optimistic messages about the benefits of individual autonomy and American democracy. Most directly at this level, Wister depicts a world of open possibility: the "ungrammatical son of the soil" (10) not only becomes a trusted foreman (and finally "an important man, with a strong grip on many various enterprises" [434]); he also wins the hand of the refined eastern schoolteacher who is descended from generations of "gentlefolk." (Molly Stark Wood "could have belonged to any number of those patriotic societies of which our American ears have grown accustomed to hear so much" [76]). The Virginian woos the genteel New Englander in part by borrowing books from her and learning to discuss Shakespeare, George Eliot, and Browning. Yet he asserts his own independent standards of literary taste from the start, teaching Molly the relative unimportance of the "slips in his English" (310),[12] as of other conventional proprieties. Finally Molly comes to recognize his value, what critics of the novel have variously called the Virginian's "inherent superiority" or "categorical authority."[13] As the narrator puts it toward the end of the novel: "Her better birth and schooling . . . had given way before the onset of the natural man himself. She knew her cowboy lover, with all that he lacked, to be more than ever she could be, with all that she had" (386).

Molly Stark Wood herself has not been much appreciated by readers of *The Virginian*. Wister's mother did not like her; Henry James criticized Wister for uniting the Virginian with "the little Vermont person."[14] Nor has Molly fared much better in more recent discussions. Yet at one highly dramatic juncture "the schoolmarm" shows her independent spirit, rising above her decorous upbringing, "the pale decadence of New England" (298). When she finds her lover badly wounded five miles from the nearest house, Molly transcends herself, so to speak, by behaving like a hero—like a man ("You have got to be the man all through this mess," the Virginian tells her [284]). Molly soon shows herself to be "a rebel, independent as ever" (287), indeed a "revolutionist" (290). These terms project a powerful sense that for Molly, as for the Virginian (as, implicitly, for anyone with enough character and determination), anything is possible. Yet at the same time the very terms applied to Molly here underscore her heritage: "[un]watered . . . good old Revolutionary blood" (298). The climactic chapter itself is titled "Grandmother Stark," and throughout the book this woman, whose image in "a colonial miniature" (115) hangs on the wall of Molly's cabin, becomes a touchstone for values. As Marcus Klein has shown, *The Virginian* places considerable emphasis on who one's ancestors are and how far back they go.[15] Despite its democratic affirmations, the novel asserts cultural difference in the strongest, indeed in exclusionary, terms. These contradictory messages enabled it to speak to different groups of readers at the same time. If we look at these tensions more closely, we see how they are reenacted at the level of narration and, beyond that, how similar tensions informed other popular works of the period.

Set in the West, and the past, *The Virginian* draws its characters from several regions: Molly Stark Wood is from Vermont, the Virginian is a southerner, and the first-person narrator introduces himself as an East coast "visitor" (56), "descend[ing], a stranger, into the great cattle land" (2–3). Thus the novel underscores the notion of diversity, though this diversity is kept within strict limits. In the second chapter, the narrator and the Virginian find themselves looking for lodging in the town of Medicine Bow, where the last beds have been taken by some "drummers": "two Jews . . . one American . . . and a Dutchman" (12). The clear distinction between the "American" and the others already anticipates one way in which the novel will qualify the ideas of democracy and equality for which it seems to speak. *The Virginian's* ethos is emphatically essentialist: it relies on the notion that people always "naturally" find their "own level" (125). As the narrator explains in one of the best-known passages of the book, "true" democracy creates a kind of natural "aristocracy"; in fact, "true democracy and true aristocracy are one and the same thing" (125).[16] The novel's "democratic" credo—"Let the best man win" (125)—also reflects the novel's sense of gender relations. In the Virginian's encounters with both men and women, his superiority remains unchallenged.

The Virginian is singled out from the start by his desire to learn ("I ain't too old for education," he reflects [115]). Indeed, the novel devotes considerable attention to the education of the "cowboy." It was partly this emphasis that allowed Wister's novel to be read—like *Rebecca*—as a paean to the possibilities for social and economic opportunity in America ("I am the kind that moves up," the Virginian tells Molly in an early scene [123]).[17] What was widely referred to as "the reading habit"[18] is a linchpin of the Virginian's education. With Molly's help, and winning Molly as a central goal, he learns to spell, to express himself in writing, and to read—primarily Shakespeare and a great many novels. Yet the Virginian's desire to learn, like his ability and even his opportunity, only becomes additional proof of his "natural" superiority. Not surprisingly, the Virginian turns out to be as talented a reader as he is a foreman, politician, storyteller, and lover. He knows by instinct that Shakespeare is the greatest poet; even his assessments of novelistic structure and narrative method are in line with the dominant interpretive conventions of late nineteenth-century high culture. He approves of the ending of *The Mill on the Floss,* but he thinks that the book talks too much ("It will keep up its talkin'. Don't let you alone" [118].) He is therefore not surprised to discover that its author is a woman (118). In writing *The Virginian,* Wister was careful not to "talk too much" himself; that's what his narrator was for. Yet he could not or would not, like the realists, sustain a self-effacing narrative stance.

At the level of narration *The Virginian* defies the imperatives that Howells, James, and others were formulating at the turn of the century. Emerging conventions of "serious" fictional narration were well known to Wister; in fact, he was somewhat defensive about the inconsistencies of his own narrative discourse. He wrote to his mother that the narration of *The Virginian* was like that of *Madame Bovary,* where "the first person 'simply dissolved away into the third.'"[19] Yet this formulation misrepresents the case. The eastern stranger who begins to tell the tale is indeed superseded by a disembodied voice; but that voice is displaced in its turn by the reappearance of the narrating "tenderfoot." The result is not a single shift (from "the first person . . . into the third") but a recurrent oscillation. The story is told sometimes by the tenderfoot, sometimes by an omniscient narrator who frankly merges with the figure of the author. From the point of view of James or Howells, as we have seen,[20] such blurring of the boundaries between narrator, character, and author made for sloppy, inconsistent, flawed narration. Yet for many turn-of-century readers, it was precisely such blurring that offered a reassuring sense of one's author as a trustworthy, comprehending human presence in the text.

Throughout *The Virginian,* the unmarked movement back and forth between first-person character-narrator and omniscient authorial narrator creates obvious "impossibilities" and "absurdities" (to use Howells's terms). The easterner often tells the reader things he could not possibly be expected to know: Molly's private thoughts ("what she wondered on her pillow" [115]), the content of the Virginian's letter to his future mother-in-law, events during the married couple's honeymoon, and so on. Throughout the story, the narrating tenderfoot intermittently asserts his personal presence in the represented world, only to disappear again for long stretches of the discourse.[21] In the middle of the novel he is present as a character—sleeping in the Virginian's cabin, chatting with the Virginian from his bed. Yet the narrator-as-character is not heard from during the sequence of events that includes Molly's visit to Vermont, some of the Virginian's adventures as traveling foreman, Molly's rescue of the Virginian, her betrothal, and her nursing the Virginian back to health. Only after the Virginian recovers his strength and sets off again "into lonely regions" does the narrating character reintroduce himself: "That errand took [the Virginian] far . . . into the borders of East Idaho. There, by reason of his bidding me, I met him, and came to share in a part of his errand" (321).

Readers of *The Virginian* could easily identify both the embodied and the disembodied narrating voices of the novel with the figure of Wister himself. The authorial persona first appears in the introductory material that precedes the story, and its functions are established there. The dedication in the 1902 edition emphasizes Wister's debt to Theodore Roosevelt, an early reader of *The Virginian:* "Some of these pages you have seen, some you have praised, one stands new-written because you blamed it; and all, my dear critic, beg leave to remind you of their author's changeless admiration." These lines represent Wister not only as a professional author but also as a member of a select circle. The preface ("To the Reader") extends both of these emphases,[22] but it also implies that the reader is already part of the community to which Wister himself belongs.

Reflecting on the disappearance of the horseman and his "historic yesterday," Wister notes in the preface that "a transition has followed . . . a condition of men and manners unlovely as that bald moment in the year when winter is gone and spring not come and the face of Nature is ugly. I shall not dwell upon it here. Those who have seen it know well what I mean" (x). These lines evoke a group of discriminating, like-minded readers—readers who will immediately recognize the "unlovely" condition of men and manners in contemporary America. These readers are presumed to share the narrator's regret for a receding past, before the horseman and his pasturing cattle had vanished—a time when it was easier to imagine the nation as a community, if not a family,[23] and when authors might still have had a clear sense of who their readers actually were. Yet Wister's preface also suggests that, even in 1900, a novel could become the catalyst for meaningful dialogue between author and reader.

"Sometimes," Wister notes, "readers inquire, Did I know the Virginian?" (x).[24] In citing this question, Wister asserts the ongoing reality of the writer-reader interchange (readers "inquire" and he responds). By asserting that he knew the Virginian "as well, I hope, as a father should know his son" (x), Wister foregrounds another aspect of his authorial function: he implies that the Virginian may be his own "creation" rather than a historical reality. Because Wister leaves open the question of whether he "knew" or invented his hero, it becomes all the easier for readers to associate the author of the introductory material with both subsequent narrators of the tale.

Implicitly decent, sane, well-bred—and unnamed—the narrating tenderfoot is (like Wister) an easterner gone west. At times he even refers to himself as the "novelist" (372), and expresses opinions like Wister's, as stated in the preface. The narrator echoes the author's remarks to the reader by expressing amazement at the changes taking place in America (36; cf. 126). Against this background of change, the narrator's intermittent appeals to the reader in the course of the story take on a characteristically friendly function: they become reassuring moments of human connection that provide a kind of refuge from social transformations beyond anyone's control.

Writing in *The Nation*, one contemporary reviewer gave *The Virginian* high praise: "This is not a book but a man," he wrote.[25] Although the reviewer refers here to the character of the Virginian (not to Wister), this formulation is in harmony with the widespread and persistent reading practice that had associated a book with a person throughout the nineteenth century. Although that way of reading generally linked a book to an originating author, identifying a book with its main character was another way of experiencing the reading process as a kind of human intercourse.

Unlike realist texts, many popular novels of the period centered on characters with sharply etched personalities whose ultimate triumph gave reciprocal support to the authority lodged in the friendly authorial narrator. Such novels often took their titles from the name of the hero or heroine: *Rebecca of Sunnybrook Farm*, *Little Lord Fauntleroy*, *Hugh Wynne*, *Richard Carvel*, *Marietta, Maid of Venice*, *Trilby* (*Trilby*, with its defeated heroine, is an exception in this context that will deserve special attention). The anchoring of both narration and action in strong-minded, highly integrated (but never isolated) personalities served to bolster both the belief in effective, autonomous selves and the faith in enduring interpersonal relations, two beliefs that—like the idea of a homogeneous society—were badly threatened in the diverse, sprawling, and increasingly impersonal society that America had become at the end of the nineteenth century.

Best-selling Narration: "Strictly between Ourselves"

In the last line of the *The Virginian* the narrator confides that "strictly between ourselves, I think [the Virginian] is going to live a long while" (434). Whether the "I" who thinks and speaks here is identified with the narrating character, the omniscient narrator, or the author, the formulation takes leave of the reader in an intimate mode ("strictly between ourselves"). We shall now take a look at some other popular turn-of-century novels that used friendly narration to make the writer-reader interchange the model for a close-knit, like-minded community. In order to consolidate that community, some of these works go well beyond *The Virginian* by actively expelling racially, ethnically, or morally "impure" characters from the represented world of the text. Nonetheless, as in the case of *The Virginian*, the popularity of these works suggests that "tremendous numbers" of readers were able to cast themselves in the role of the "happy few."[26]

Winston Churchill's *Richard Carvel* (1899) is a good example of a novel that foregrounds the value of a small, stable, homogeneous society by making the hero the narrator and casting the reader in the role of someone who is about to participate in family tradition. Just when Edith Wharton, Frank Norris, Jack London, and others were projecting a vision of publication as an inhuman process that was likely to exploit, isolate, or destroy the author, *Richard Carvel* makes publication itself a family affair. The novel addresses the general reader as if he or she were already part of the family, but the plot emphatically underscores that family's revolutionary heritage. Thus *Richard Carvel*, like *The Virginian*, projects a double message: on the one hand, the reader (*any* reader) is warmly invited into both the represented world and the experience of reading; on the other hand, through its emphasis on birth and qualities "bred into the bone,"[27] the text designates certain characters (and, by implication, readers) as more qualified than others to participate in the projected community. But since novels (unlike membership in patriotic societies)[28] are open to the entire reading public, the most homogeneous, even exclusive community that is projected in and through a text has highly porous borders.[29] Although *Richard Carvel* asserts its confidence in the presence of reliably like-minded readers (imagined as a group of blood relatives), the novel also extends an open invitation to anyone who is prepared to engage in imagined relations with the narrating hero.

Written in the form of a memoir, *Richard Carvel* is presented as the hero's recollections, recorded for his children and "never intended . . . for publication" at all (vii). In the foreword, Carvel's grandson remarks that his own "sons and daughters have tried to persuade me to remodel these memoirs of my grandfather into a latter-day romance. But I have thought it wiser to leave them as he wrote them. Albeit they contain some details not of interest to the general public, to my notion it is such imperfections as these which lend to them the reality they bear. Certain it is, when reading them, I live his life over again" (vii). Thus the reader of the text is invited into the family circle not merely to live Richard Carvel's "life over again," but to do so in spite of the fact that certain aspects of his experience may not even be "of interest to the general public." Carvel's grandson has not taken his children's advice—"to remodel these memoirs of my grandfather"—but nonetheless the text begins with a focus on the children's response to the idea of publication. The emphasis on storytelling by and for the family intermittently informs the ongoing narrative as well. "Those times, my children, are not ours," Richard exclaims, early on (2). And again: "Though you have often heard from my lips the story of my mother, I must for the sake of those who are to come after you, set it down here as briefly as I may" (7). Finally, he says that "it is time, my children, to bring this story to a close" (536).

In *Richard Carvel*, as in *The Virginian*, the reader is invited to be part of a small inner circle that harks back to America's revolutionary beginnings. Whoever the reader may be, he or she is invited to know the narrating Carvel as he would like his children and grandchildren to know him.[30] Implicitly Carvel's character and experience deserve attention outside the bounds of the family as well. One could aptly apply to the figure of Carvel the words of Churchill's dedication (to James E. Yeatman): "An American Gentleman Whose Life Is an Example to His Countrymen." This dedication suggests that all of Yeatman's "countrymen" are free to follow his life of "Example." Fearless, upright, and "straight-dealing" (524), Carvel too is represented as an inspiration to all men.[31] But if Carvel's virtues (like the Virginian's) are implicitly fit for imitation, they are also seen to be natural, inborn, his by right of birth. And when "the author" appears in the "Afterword," addressing the reader directly and offering "humble apologies to any who have, or think they have, an ancestor in this book" (537), he reasserts the reality of a small and stable world in which readers could understandably make the error of believing that they have been reading about their own ancestors. At the same time Churchill's parting comments in the "Afterword" make the existence of an honest, accountable, and human author the final affirmation of the text.[32]

Realist writers on the whole did away with elaborate dedications, prefaces, forewords, and afterwords—those extended, illusion-breaking asides to the reader at the beginning or end of a book. Despite the emerging self-consciousness about narrative modes and levels of reality in fiction, however, many popular novelists of the period persisted in using these tokens of sincerity, connection, and exchange between writer and reader. Novelists such as Wister and Churchill, who occupied the same literary field as James and Howells, were well aware that by the end of the century, realist imperatives such as authorial objectivity and a consistent narrative perspective had become sure signs of high literary sophistication. Wister's comment about the narration of *Madame Bovary* reflects his own sensitivity to questions of voice that he effectively disregards in *The Virginian*.[33] Other popular novels of the period inscribed the debate about narrative perspective right into the fictional text. But these meta-fictional digressions constituted an endorsement of friendly narration in and of themselves.

Francis Marion Crawford's novel *A Roman Singer*, first published in 1884 and reprinted fourteen times by 1896, provides a particularly clear example of the deliberate resistance to realist narration which contributed to the popularity of many novels even after the turn of the new century.[34] Crawford's narrator, like Wister's tenderfoot, has unrestrained access to the intimate feelings and private experiences not only of the hero but of the hero's beloved and others as well. Yet this narrator (unlike Wister's) repeatedly justifies his narrative practices. "You must not wonder that I can describe some things that I did not see," the narrator tells us, "and that I know how some of the people felt; for Nino and I have talked over the whole matter very often."[35] Despite such gestures toward consistency and verisimilitude, the narrator repeatedly renders the thoughts and emotions of characters who would have been highly unlikely to report them with the detail he provides. In this sense, the narrator of *A Roman Singer*, like the eastern stranger of *The Virginian*, often functions as an omniscient teller whose intimacy with his characters is essentially that of the author, and whose habit of directly addressing the reader promotes the effect of a writer-reader relationship.

For the narrator of *A Roman Singer* the process of narration itself is a source of considerable drama. The narrator's most salient characteristic is his attention to his own prerogatives and his concern with the obstacles he encounters in getting his story told. "I cannot be interrupted by your silly questions about the exact way in which things happened," the narrator says. "I must tell this story in my way or not at all; and I am sacrificing a great deal to your taste in cutting out all the little things that I really most enjoy telling" (74).[36] Throughout *A Roman Singer* such passages foster the illusion of intimate (which is not to say frictionless) relations between narrator and reader. Anticipating, though not necessarily fulfilling, the reader's presumed expectations and desires, the narrator acknowledges the realist taboo on narrative intrusions ("all the little things that I really most enjoy telling") only to defy them.[37] He alternately badgers, baits, and placates the reader ("I am not taking all this trouble to please you, but only for Nino's sake" [106]). Despite the belligerent tone, here as elsewhere, the narrator's vocative "you" can be taken up by any reader. Indeed, as Irene Kacandes has emphasized, the "irresistible invitation" of the second-person pronoun has a compelling appeal of its own. It creates the sense that a relationship is being forged in the very act of reading.[38]

The narration of *A Roman Singer* reinforces a governing theme (also central to *The Virginian* and *Richard Carvel*):that personal relations can be sustained despite obstacles and across significant gaps of time and space.[39] The relationship between narrator and reader in *A Roman Singer* is itself the model for a resilient, enduring relationship. The friendly mode of telling combines will the plot, implying that social harmony can be achieved by transcending individual differences. The narrator himself helps the Italian peasant boy attain his goal: Nino marries the beautiful German countess despite her father's opposition. But in *A Roman Singer,* as in many popular works at the turn of the century, the goal of personal happiness and social harmony can be achieved only by removal of the "foreign" other.

In best-selling fiction of the period even relatively benign "outsiders" were repeatedly expelled from the community constituted by narrators, readers, and heroes,[40] while the friendly relationship between the reader and the authorial narrator deflected attention from the harshest exclusionary implications of the story. Moreover, the problems of class and ethnicity engaged by the plot were generally placed at a considerable remove from the contemporary social reality of America. On the face of it, as I have noted, such fictions were not about America at all. By locating the action in the past or across the Atlantic, they smoothed the way for a variety of readers to project themselves into stories that associated "foreignness" with evil and brought it to a bad end. Because these

novels never mentioned American society, they made it all the easier for readers who may themselves have been outsiders of one sort or another to identify
with the privileged insiders of the imagined world. At the same time, this distancing mechanism also enabled progressive middle-class readers, who would
not have affirmed an end to immigration or a strict separation of races, to delight in the defeat of foreign characters who were expelled or destroyed for the
good of the community and the benefit of true love. Many readers who would
not have accepted the explicit racism of *The Leopard's Spots* (1902) or *The Clansman* (1905) could respond to the xenophobia of Wister, Churchill, or Crawford without directly relating the fear of otherness to contemporary American
issues.

As we have seen, the friendly narrator of *A Roman Singer* makes the reader
an ally in his campaign to marry the hero to the woman he loves. The alliance
of narrator, hero, and reader gains additional support from the negative char-
acterization of the heroine's father. Count von Lira is defined largely by his
"foreign" accent and his inability to speak the language of the dominant culture.
He is said to be "a foreigner of rank . . . [who] speaks Italian intelligibly, but
with the strangest German constructions, and he rolls the letter *r* curiously in
his throat" (43–44). If the count's oft-cited "German constructions" make him
a comic figure, his opposition to the love between Nino and his daughter makes
him a villain. The count's own candidate for his daughter Hedwig's hand, however, is both more villainous and more "foreign" than he himself. Benoni the
wandering Jew is vain, pleasure-loving, and nihilistic; he has nothing but con-
tempt for the "entire human race" (174), and proudly admits that he has often
"amused [himself] by diabolically devising plans for [the] destruction [of love]"
(319). Benoni turns out to be a madman who spent "many years [in] . . . a
private lunatic asylum in Paris" (320). But first and foremost he is "foreign," and
frequent assertions that "foreigners are different" (51) combine with the extreme negative portraits of von Lira and Benoni to reinforce the supposed ho-
mogeneity of the reading community implied by the text.

At one level *A Roman Singer* (like other works by Crawford) applauded individual initiative and the desire to cross cultural boundaries. Hedwig's own
otherness (not only her German origins but her aristocratic ones as well) presents no real problem, partly because, like Molly in *The Virginian,* she can adapt
herself totally to her lover's mode of life,[41] and partly because Nino (like the
Virginian) turns out to be a kind of "natural" aristocrat himself.[42] On another
level *A Roman Singer,* by resoundingly defeating the more intransigent "others"
in the represented world of the text, emphatically affirms the value of small,
stable, homogeneous communities. As we have seen, this value was often re-
confirmed at the level of narration. The narrators we have already considered
were as exclusionary as they were friendly, and were also (like their heroes) pa-
ternalistically authoritative.

I have suggested that the sense of a "universal intelligence" constantly "comprehending and interpreting" which was so offensive to Howells was an inducement for many other readers. Novels such as *The Virginian* and *A Roman Singer* created a reassuring sense of certainty in an unstable world not only by rewarding initiative, perseverance, and romantic love, but also by endowing a clearly individuated, presumably fallible character with the prerogatives of omniscience in narration, the ability to see not just into human hearts but behind closed doors and sometimes into the future as well.

There is a big difference between a first-person narrator with intermittently omniscient powers and one who is confined to the same mortal limits as every other character in the represented world. James himself often used first-person narrators in his short fiction, though he emphatically rejected the autobiographic form of the full-length novel. Unlike the narrators of Wister and Crawford, however, James's tellers never break frame: their knowledge of people and events never exceeds what is appropriate for their character and situation. When restricted to the fallibility that characterizes the rest of us, a first-person narrator underscores the limits of our capacity to know anything for sure—an effect that the writers of popular romance generally sought to avoid. Whereas James radically circumscribed not only the epistemological but also the moral authority of his first-person narrators, popular writers of the period made friendly narration the guarantee of moral order, social harmony, and effective human agency. Such a guarantee had a wide appeal for middle-class readers threatened by class conflict and social change. But insofar as the friendly narrator also seemed to endorse the aspirations of struggling outsiders, many people who were outsiders themselves could be drawn into the imagined community of the text.

We Pay Special Attention to *Trilby*

The voice of a friendly authorial narrator is even more pervasive in *Trilby* than in the other novels we have considered, and was probably a significant factor in the novel's success. *Trilby* created a popular rage in America of the 1890s.[43] Written by George Du Maurier, the British author and well-known illustrator of *Punch,* this novel may seem a peculiar touchstone for American fiction and American social reality. But it was precisely *Trilby*'s foreign flavor that made it such an effective vehicle for engaging sensitive questions about contemporary American culture without seeming to do so. In *Trilby,* as in the other popular works we have looked at, friendly narration served to create and reinforce a sense of family, community, and coherence in a society deeply threatened by otherness.

According to the narrator, *Trilby* was written for just such "respectably-brought-up old Briton[s]" as himself.[44] Obviously, the book could not have been as popular as it was in America had it appealed only to the population for which it claimed to speak. I have already noted the paradox by which works with exclusionary emphases became best-sellers. I look more closely at *Trilby* now to isolate some grounds of its appeal. Dominated by an extremely obtrusive narrating presence, this novel provides a particularly interesting contrast to realist works at the level of narration while reflecting a range of issues—involving otherness, performance, and authorship—that were of vital concern to realist writers as well.

Trilby begins with what sounds like an omniscient narrator (referred to only as "the present scribe" [27]); but it proceeds to individuate that figure, often stressing his direct participation in the represented world while maintaining his privilege of knowing things he could never have known if he were entirely confined to that position. This narrator often asserts his presence on the Champs-Elysées or in the painters' studio; but he is more than just a character within the represented world. As a declared Englishman who speaks fluent French, a self-proclaimed writer and artist, the narrator invites the contemporary reader to identify him with George Du Maurier, author and illustrator. At the same time, the narrator's discourse promotes the illusion of a friendly, even intimate transaction with his readers, many of whom in fact deluged him with mail.[45] It was not only Willa Cather who felt that to read *Trilby* was to come closer to "the wise, gentle, sympathetic man" who wrote the book.

This "wise, gentle" man recounts a devastating tale. More emphatically than the work of Wister, Churchill, or Crawford, *Trilby* demonstrates that no outsiders are to be incorporated into the homogeneous community that bonds the narrator, the reader, and the benign (always British) characters. "Pauvre Trilby," with her lower-class background, her beautiful voice, and her essential goodness, was an object of fascination and sympathy for contemporary readers, especially American readers. Yet the seductively poignant figure of this heroine constitutes a special problem, for Trilby is resolutely denied a place within the dominant community of the text. Although Trilby and the upper-class British painter Little Billee fall passionately in love, Trilby is so emphatically "other" that virtually all the "respectable" characters in the novel join forces to defeat her. Only under the shadow of death can Trilby be reinstated as a legitimate object of affection for Little Billee, the narrator, and the readers.

Trilby's otherness and her exclusion are multiply grounded. To begin with, she is poor, French, and of dubious origin. Moreover, when the novel begins, she has been earning her keep by posing as an artist's model—"for the altogether," as she puts it (17). Even worse, she has had sexual experience. In short, as Little Billee's mother concludes, Trilby is not "a lady." Therefore, not only from the point of view of Little Billee's mother but also from the perspective of Little Billee's friends—and of course that of the narrator—marriage between the lovers is out of the question. Little Billee's mother accomplishes the separation of the pair by appealing to Trilby's "higher" nature. But—partly because she is a woman—being a "natural aristocrat" cannot help Trilby as it does Nino and the Virginian. Although Trilby even turns out to be related to a duchess ("on the wrong side of the blanket," the narrator notes [402]), this revelation comes too late to make any practical difference. It does, however, help to legitimize the tears that flow so freely on Trilby's behalf before she dies.

The final wash of tears and absolution at the end of the novel effectively divert attention from the stubborn facts of class, background, and especially experience that have led everyone in the book to agree that Trilby must not marry Little Billee. Trilby's fatal illness becomes the occasion for a renewal of generous feeling all around. Little Billee's love now becomes permissible; even his mother is won over to Trilby in this context. Once Trilby no longer threatens middle-class morality and decorum, she is reinstated in everyone's good graces—so much so that it is easy to overlook how firmly she has been excluded.

The separation of Trilby and Little Billee becomes absolutely irreversible only when Trilby throws in her lot with Svengali, at which point any chance of rehabilitating Trilby for normative middle-class life is eliminated. Hypnotized by the evil musician, enslaved to a man she has hated and feared,[46] Trilby becomes a singer who enchants all of Europe. The sustaining presence of the friendly narrator serves an especially important function when Trilby's bizarre and demeaning relations with Svengali come to the fore. The pervasive presence of the narrating voice—bantering, ironic, but always authoritative, upright, confidential, and reassuring—goes a long way toward offsetting the horrific potential of Trilby's story. Narrated in a different register, Trilby's history could well take on the uncanny power of *Frankenstein.*

Trilby's experience dramatizes the destructive force of dislocation and alienation from one's self, one's origins, one's mother tongue, and the people one has cherished. By contrast, the discourse of the narrating voice is informed by a premise of integration and continuity not only within the authorial self but also between that projected self and a community of readers. Cultured, gently ironic, and firmly centered in time and space, the narrator of *Trilby* (like the narrators of *Richard Carvel* and *The Virginian*) reaches out to a reader cast in his own image. His mode of narration, his casual, confident use of several languages, and his essential, unshakeable, morally rigorous character all serve as a buffer against the problems implied by Trilby's fate.

Unlike the narrators of *The Virginian* and *A Roman Singer,* the narrator of *Trilby* assiduously differentiates himself from his heroine, and by doing so he reaffirms his bond with the reader of the book. The implied grounds of connection between narrator and reader are numerous. The teller of the tale makes an ongoing effort to bring the reader into a shared world, but from the beginning it is presumed to be *already* shared. Like Nino, Crawford's Roman singer,

Trilby herself is represented as if already familiar to the reader. The assumption (the fiction) throughout both books is that the reader knows from the start that the hero or heroine will achieve fame at a later stage of the narrated events. In *Trilby* this strategy shapes not only the representation of Trilby but also that of Little Billee and the other painters, whose art is said to be on display in the National Gallery, where every "cultivated" reader can see it (208–9). "Lorrimer, Antony, the Laird and Little Billee made those beautiful chalk and pencil studies of [Trilby's] head which are now so well-known" (392).[47] Even Svengali's fame is presumed to extend well beyond the pages of the book into the "real" world—as, indeed, it subsequently did. (Ask educated people about Svengali today and you will find a great many who believe he once existed.)

Trilby is informed throughout by passing reference to knowledge that "we" all share. That knowledge, moreover, goes beyond people, performances, and works of art to social norms that are taken for granted. The reader of *Trilby*, like the reader of *A Roman Singer*, is encouraged to participate not only in the narrator's easy familiarity with "culture" (music, painting, foreign languages) but also in his absolute sense of moral imperatives. The narrator repeatedly reminds us that Little Billee's mother, Mrs. Bagot, had "right on [her] side" in preventing the marriage of Trilby and her son (192).[48]

Du Maurier himself was somewhat bewildered by the extravagant success of *Trilby* in America.[49] Against the background of the other best-sellers we have considered, however, some possible sources of its appeal should be clear. Insofar as *Trilby* offered readers the chance to identify with characters who were prepared to violate class distinctions and other conventional boundaries in the name of love and self-fulfillment, it could be read as if it affirmed traditional American values—life, liberty, and the pursuit of happiness. Indeed, given the anomalies of the heroine's position, the popularity of the book could even be taken, in the words of one contemporary reviewer, as an indication of "the increasing tolerance of our moral judgements as a people."[50] At another level, of course, readers who were aspiring "upward" themselves could identify deeply with Trilby, suffering with her in defeat. Nevertheless, like *The Virginian* and *A Roman Singer*, *Trilby* also spoke to the worst fears of those who were anxious about immigration, "licentious" women, and cultural diversity. By bringing otherness to a bad end, *Trilby* neutralized such fears. By setting the entire drama in England and France, it did so without implicating America. And finally, by inviting readers to share the cultural superiority of a cosmopolitan narrator who is at home with foreign languages, poetry, and art, the book had considerable snob appeal. One could skip the French and Latin passages and still feel right at home with the friendly spokesman for a self-contained "high-class" community. Throughout, the narrator's all-embracing vocative "you" offered free entry to all.

The inviting tones of the friendly narrator were deceptive, of course. The

FIGURE 5. "Et Maintenant Dors, Ma Mignonne!" In George Du Maurier's *Trilby,* Svengali becomes a lightning rod for the distaste and even disgust associated with all "outsiders."

dangerous seduction of otherness is a recurrent emphasis in *Trilby,* reasserted by the narrator at every opportunity. Because Trilby's marriage with Little Billee is prevented and Trilby dies a beautiful death, her own otherness is finally glossed over. But the feelings of revulsion, fear, and outrage that are kept in check and finally dispelled in relation to Trilby's otherness are given free rein in relation to the figure of Svengali. Svengali is presented as vile from the very beginning. His foreignness is explicitly responsible not only for his inability to speak good English (or indeed any other language) but also for his moral failings: "being an Oriental Israelite Hebrew Jew," the narrator explains, Svengali "had not been able to resist the temptation of spitting in [Little Billee's] face" when they met again in Paris toward the end of the novel (356).

From start to finish, the figure of Svengali becomes a lightning rod for the distaste and even disgust associated in *Trilby* with every outsider (see figure 5). Placing Svengali beyond the pale of the civilized human world, moreover, only brings the narrator, the reader, and the virtuous characters closer together. In *Trilby* the "*fin-de-siècle* reader" (170) for whom the narrator claims to tell his tale is repeatedly embraced as a peer and soulmate. Explicitly identifying himself as a member of the British "higher middle class," the narrator says he is "writ[ing] for just such old philistines as himself. . . . Alas! all reverence for all

FIGURE 6. "Three Nice Clean Englishmen." Writer-reader relations are consolidated by making the text itself the site of an exclusive, cultivated, and homogeneous society.

that is high and time-honoured and beautiful seems at a discount" (151–52; cf. 170, 320). Writer-reader relations are thus consolidated by making the text itself the site of an exclusive, cultivated, and homogeneous society. The one indispensable entrance requirement for membership is literacy.

The bond between writer and reader in *Trilby* obliquely but powerfully proclaims the anathema of otherness and raises the question of who is left out (see figure 6). The implicit harmony between the narrator and the novel's English-speaking readers is reinforced through parodic citation of French discourse, facetious definition of foreign terms, and deprecatory humor against foreign customs and tastes. By implication the narrator and reader share a secure place in the same community, one that extends beyond the text and is continuous with it. The narrator even invites the reader to provide emendations to the narrative: "Should any surviving eye-witness . . . read these pages, and see any gross in accuracy in the bald account of it, the P. S. [present scribe] will feel deeply obliged to the same for any corrections or additions" (370).

Despite the alleged concern with accuracy and "truth" here as elsewhere, such digressions with regard to the process of narration function primarily as playful confidences that reaffirm the bond between writer and reader. The narrator's repeated references to his rights and duties as the author of a fictional work unabashedly highlight the very thing that outraged Henry James (but delighted many others): that the narrator "and his trusting friend [the reader] are only making believe.[51] Shared ground rules are indispensable to game-playing. Apologies to "the casual reader" for "the length and possible irrelevancy of . . . digression[s]" (98),[52] or the single comic footnote that suddenly appears after 296 pages,[53] rely for their effect on the "cultivated" reader's familiarity with critical and literary conventions. They project a common vocabulary and promote an imagined community, a sense of belonging. As I have been suggesting, this sense of belonging derived not only from the moral vision upheld by plot and structure, but also from an ideal of cultural cohesion that many feared was disappearing in late nineteenth-century America. Within the novel this cohesion is most concretely embodied by Little Billee and his fellow British artists, even (or especially) when far away from home. It is reinforced by the rhetoric of narration: consistently reliable in its values and commitments, self-reflexively playful in the telling of the tale.

One additional aspect of *Trilby* deserves attention in the present context. The novel elaborates a recurrent motif in realist works of the period: the figure of a woman onstage. We have seen that the voice of the friendly narrator provides a contrast to Trilby's moral and social experience; but it provides an even sharper contrast to the figure of Trilby as a stage performer. Like many women onstage in realist fiction, the image of Trilby—her relation to voice, self, and public—indirectly raises difficult questions about the figure of the novelist and the writer-reader interchange. The model of the artist-audience connection implicit in the stardom of "la grande Trilby" is diametrically opposed to that suggested by the narrator's relations with the reader. Thus *Trilby* provides a useful transition to many realist texts where, in the absence of a friendly authorial narrator, the woman onstage becomes a highly charged figure for authorship: desirable but also isolated, vulnerable, and dangerously exposed.

As we have seen, the narrating rhetoric of *Trilby* implies a benign set of assumptions about the relation between "I" and "you" (self and other, performer and public, author and reader). The experience of Trilby herself provides a very different version of these relations, especially once she becomes famous.[54] Trilby is a great singer only when she is hypnotized by Svengali. After his death, Trilby cannot even remember her singing self. For Trilby, then, the split between "private woman" and "public stage" is absolute.[55] Unlike Nino, the operatic performer of *A Roman Singer*, whose real identity is triumphantly revealed when he finally appears onstage, once Trilby becomes a singer, she finds herself in a position that is self-alienating and ultimately fatal. Both her extreme self-division and her amazingly expressive voice make Trilby an evocative figure for the novelist, whose words are addressed to a large "mass of unseen people,"[56] but whose mode of narration circumvents the problems implied by the equivocal position of the heroine.

Trilby's voice itself is a recurrent focus of interest in the novel.

> How can one describe the quality of a peach or a nectarine to those who have known only apples?
>   Until La Svengali appeared the world had known only apples—Catalanis, Jenny Linds, Grasis, Albonis, Pattis! The best apples that can be for sure—but still only apples! . . . The like of that voice has never been heard, nor ever will be again. (307; cf. 392, 415)

Absolutely enthralling to its listeners, Trilby's voice is an asset any author might envy; it brings crowds to their feet, applauding and weeping. But precisely what or who is represented by Trilby's voice remains a mystery; the source of its power is suspect. Despite an extraordinarily subtle and vibrant speaking voice, Trilby is tone-deaf. When she sings for Little Billee and his friends at the beginning of the novel, she cannot tell one note from another. Five years later, when Little Billee and the others see her onstage, staring vacantly but singing beautifully, they are at once moved by the performance and plagued by uncertainty about whether the singer is Trilby or not. Thus a clear contrast emerges between Trilby before and after she has been transformed by Svengali into a European star. But an even sharper contrast is implicit in the difference between Trilby the great singer—divided against herself, estranged from friends and lovers, oblivious to the audience—and the benign model of relations between performer and public provided by the figure of the friendly author-narrator directly addressing a cozily receptive reader.

Elsewhere in the literature of the late 1890s and the early years of the twentieth century, as the figure of the friendly narrator disappears, the image of a woman onstage acquires a different emphasis. In novels by James, Wharton, Dreiser, and others, the vulnerable position of the stage performer provides not a contrast but an analogue to that of the novelist. This analogue reflects growing uncertainty about the grounds of relation between the author and the expanding, fragmented, heterogeneous reading public. In the absence of a benign narrating presence, the woman onstage becomes a highly charged image of public performance—and of authorship.

As a recurrent motif in fiction of the period, the woman onstage often points to the figure of the novelist by emphasizing the dissociation between words and the voice that articulates them. The image of actress, public speaker, or singer raises questions not only about authority (Whose voice is speaking? Where does it originate?) and self-display (What is being revealed to whom?) but also about interpersonal relations (Where does the audience come in?). These questions are loosely analogous to the very questions about the relationship of author to text and reader that became central in discussions of narration at the end of the century and beyond. Many questions about making and selling fiction are refracted through the motif of stage presence; some of these are provisionally resolved at the turn of the century through the separating out (in theory) of author, text, and reader.

Both the authorial narrator and the image of a collaborating reader gradually disappear from the self-consciously serious works of fiction that would later constitute the literary canon for the period. Evaporated into a disembodied narrating voice, however, many a novelist is symbolically displaced onto the image of a vulnerable, visible woman in a problematic relation to her public. As we shall see, when both the figure of the author and that of the reader disappear from the rhetoric of narration, the recurrent juxtaposition of the highly visible woman onstage and the indistinct audience in the darkened hall disclose growing authorial uncertainty about self-representation and radical doubts about reading practices.

4

The Return of the Author: The Realist Writer as a Woman Onstage

> How I wish I belonged to a plastic race and drew beautiful hieroglyphs with my person instead of having to depend on dull old words.
>
> Edith Wharton, letter to Bernard Berenson (March 14, 1912)

Authorial remoteness or removal from the text was not only a difficult but also an ambivalent enterprise, even for writers wholly committed to it in theory. Theodore Dreiser liked to quote the advice he was given as a young reporter: "All the facts, you know, just as far as they will carry you."[1] Turn-of-century reviewers often took the realists at their word and, grouping them together, condemned their "elimination of the personal equation";[2] yet many readers still assumed that every work of art "instantly involves the personality of the artist."[3] In 1899 William Dean Howells developed the figure of a "family likeness" among books by the same author. "All Mr. James's books are like Mr. James," Howells wrote; "all Tourguenieff's books are like Tourguenieff; all Hawthorne's books are like Hawthorne. You cannot read a page in any of them without knowing them for this author or that . . . through this sort of blood relationship."[4]

Believing that it was all too easy for readers to expose the represented reality of a text both as a making believe and as the subjective projection of a particular person, many writers felt incompletely hidden by objectified narrative discourse. Even the noncommittal narrative voice that stuck to "the facts" could be read as suggestively personal. No one knew this better than Henry James: "M. De Maupassant is remarkably objective and impersonal," James wrote, "but he would go too far if he were to entertain the belief that he has kept himself out of his books. They speak of him eloquently, even if it only be to tell us how easy . . . he has found this impersonality."[5] Given certain ways of reading, neutrality itself exposed a subjectivity behind the pen.

At the turn of the century many writers (and readers) continued to think of reading as a human, proto-personal interaction. Although the young Wharton sardonically dismissed the notion of "living in the hearts of [her] readers,"[6] her most direct attack on turn-of-century reading habits, "The Vice of Reading," also contained her vision of the antidote: "creative" reading as a spontaneous and intuitive mode of exchange in which writers and "born readers" could still make "contact" with one another through a book. Along similar lines, Howells expressed his sense of fiction as a ground of responsive connection. While his popular lecture "Novel-Writing and Novel-Reading" evoked the unbridgeable "chasm which parts authors and readers," it also asserted his conviction that "nothing good that the author puts into a novel is ever lost. Someone sees it, feels, loves it, and loves him for it."[7] Despite their commitment to a "professional" model of authorship, Howells, Wharton, James, and others were deeply ambivalent about taking "themselves" out of this imagined circuit of communication, this implicitly reciprocal human transaction.

We have seen that realist writers began to develop the idea of a remote or invisible author toward the turn of the century, amid growing uncertainty about how to conceptualize the relations between authors and books. Although many popular novelists of the period continued to construct the reader as a friend, affirming (or trying to create) a like-minded readership, the realists took the opposite tack. Depersonalizing their narrative discourse, James, Wharton, and others sought to eliminate, or at least distance, their personal selves from their publications. But a book without an author was not so easy to imagine. The attempt to regulate the reader's access to the author through the rhetoric of narration only intensified questions about just where within a text an author resides. At this point the author reentered the text, not as the narrating persona who, like every novelist, tells the story, but rather as a different kind of performer for a different kind of audience.

The figure of the woman onstage—seductive, exposed, and in one degree or another always representing herself—repeatedly makes her way into realist texts. Appearing in public, performing for an audience, the figure of actress, orator, or singer suggests a range of threatening and yet tempting possibilities associated with the act of writing and reading fiction at the turn of the century. In realist works, the difficulties implicit in the situation of the woman onstage are not offset, as in *Trilby*, either by the amnesia that dissociates Trilby from her own performing self, or by the pervasive presence of a reassuringly normative and culturally secure authorial persona telling the tale.

Popular writers such as Wister, Churchill, and Crawford, whose work consistently provided right-minded, experienced, cultivated narrators, relied on the fact that their readers would accept the prescribed reader role of bonding with the spokesman for middle-class norms who told the story. Such fiction, set far from contemporary America in time or space, offered tantalizingly facile solutions for difficult contemporary problems without even referring to them.[8] *The Virginian, Richard Carvel, Trilby,* and other popular novels offered unambiguous ground rules for inclusion in or exclusion from the dominant social reality of the text, be it primarily a community of two or an explicit microcosm, say, of the early American republic. As we have seen, the implied consensus of reader and authorial narrator provided the paradigm for these harmonious imagined worlds.

We have also seen, however, that many authors of the period felt increasingly vulnerable, as if on display and for sale to a heterogeneous mass of invisible yet intrusive readers. These writers sought protection in a discourse of impersonality, but they also projected images of contemporary society that, if not entirely representative of turn-of-century America, were far more diversified than those of popular romance. The authorial condescension, even revulsion, implicit in Norris's Maria Macapa and Zerkow, in Crane's ethnic immigrants, in some of Cather's stranded European exiles, or in Wharton's Rosedale are as nothing when compared with Du Maurier's Svengali or Crawford's Benoni. It is paradoxical but not surprising that the very writers who entertained the idea of so much otherness among both their readers and their characters were also frightened by it. It is precisely the uncertainty that realist writers felt when contemplating "the chasm which parts authors and readers" that made the actress such a resonant figure.

As feminist critics have shown, women have been particularly dependent for their own sense of themselves on their reflection in the eyes of others.[9] Such gender-specific vulnerability was isolated and writ large in the figure of the actress.[10] At once visible to but separate from her audience, the actress was disguised and celebrated but also exposed and vulnerable. Her very inaccessibility could serve to heighten the desire for intimacy or possession on the part of those who watched her from afar. Thus the woman onstage exaggerated and epitomized certain features of women's existence in general. But the situation of the actress simultaneously reflected many aspects of an author's position in relation to the turn-of-century readership.

The situation of the woman onstage, speaking, acting, or singing in public, implied the self-effacing realist's uneasy relation to his or her own audience in part by highlighting the problem of bodily presence to others. Both the extraordinary success of certain singers and actresses of the period and the controversy surrounding suffragettes and other women who spoke in public helped make the figure of the woman onstage a particularly rich vehicle for exploring (or deflecting) certain highly charged aspects of authorship.[11] Physical visibility, potential intimacy, but also danger and ambiguity were inextricable components of the relationship between performer and public imagined in the context of live female performance.

Throughout the nineteenth century, appearing in print was a complex and ambivalent enterprise, one that changed along with the cultural context of production and reception. As Mary Kelley has shown, Catherine Sedgwick's bid for authorship, like that of other antebellum women writers, was complicated by her "perfect horror at appearing in print."[12] Richard Brodhead has taken Hawthorne's "Veiled Lady" in *The Blithedale Romance* as a figure for midcentury authorship generally. Contextualizing Hawthorne's Priscilla within the developing American entertainment industry of the 1850s, Brodhead asserts that "the Veiled Lady is a victim of her display. In celebrity she is only exploited. . . . A Priscilla who took pleasure in performance or its rewards would be someone else."[13] Such a Priscilla might well be, as Brodhead suggests, one of the newly celebrated women authors of the period, women who, unlike Priscilla, seemed to relish the publicity they received in spite of their own pseudonymic and other veils (54–55).[14] By the end of the nineteenth century, as well-publicized performance (including novelistic performance) became a national phenomenon on a grand scale, both men and women writers were increasingly prepared, as one commentator put it, to "luxuriate" in their "first taste of type" and their own public visibility.[15]

"I was to appear in print!" are the words with which (after thirty-five years) Edith Wharton recalls the excitement she felt when she first learned that Scribner's would publish her poems. "As long as I live I shall never forget [the] sensations [of that moment]."[16] Recapturing those sensations in *A Backward Glance,* Wharton renders her dawning awareness that anyone might enter a shop and ask for a book by her name, and "the clerk, without bursting into incredulous laughter, would produce it, and be paid for it, and the purchaser would walk home with it and read it, and talk of it, and pass it on to other people to read!" (113). "The truth about any girl," Wharton wrote in *House of Mirth,* "is that once she's talked about she's done for."[17] In *A Backward Glance* (and in her life) Wharton revised that truth by delighting in a projected authorial self that anyone, in principle, might discuss. Yet Wharton's exhilaration about her own public visibility and accessibility in print is the other side of a hesitation about self-exposure, a fear of "incredulous laughter," an uncertainty about the implications of exhibiting oneself to the public in and through representation.

Wharton's delight as well as her doubts about being accessible in a book are at once deeply personal and culturally typical. While her intense pleasure at appearing in print provides a particularly sharp contrast to Catherine Sedgwick's "perfect horror," she had her own reservations about being visible, on display, and for sale to the public through her books. Many turn-of-century writers resented both the intrusive public and the popular image of the author as "rich man's jester,"[18] circus performer, or actress.[19] Like the sequence of barroom singers in Stephen Crane's *Maggie: A Girl of the Streets,* many of the author figures evoked in literary discourse of the 1890s seem to appear each time with a slightly shriller song and a little "less gown."[20] In 1929, when Fitzgerald wrote to Hemingway that "the *Post* now pays the old whore $4000 a screw,"[21] he was only intensifying a familiar trope, making explicit the implications of erotic

exploitation, self-exposure, and self-hatred that had long informed the performance motif—for men as well as women. As the disadvantages of celebrity
came to outweigh the benefits, many authors decided to add a disappearing act
to their bag of tricks.

Representing Oneself: Wharton's Lily Bart and the Writer-Reader Interchange

At a climactic (and much discussed) moment in Edith Wharton's *House of Mirth,*
Lily Bart appears onstage, dressed as a figure in a painting by Sir Joshua Reynolds
(see figure 7). In evoking this moment, Wharton underscores the difference between Lily's aims and those of the other women in the performance. There was,
we are told, no doubting the "preponderance of personality" in Lily's appearance
onstage (141). Lily herself has "not an instant's doubt" that the enthusiasm of the
audience is "called forth by herself and not by the picture she impersonate[s]." Indeed, she particularly relishes the distinction. The other actresses, however, exemplify an antithetical approach. They "had been cleverly fitted with characters
suited to their types. . . . Indeed so skillfully had the personality of the [actresses]
been subdued to the scenes they figured in that even the least imaginative of the
audience must have felt a thrill of contrast when the curtain suddenly parted on
a picture which was *simply and undisguisedly the portrait of Miss Bart*" (141; my
emphasis). The opposition between Lily and the other performers here is the
very clash that informs turn-of-century debate about "suppression of the author's
personality" in fiction.[22] Unlike Lily, many novelists, including Wharton, were
increasingly uncertain about the extent to which they themselves were present
and accessible to readers in their work. Ambivalence heightened uncertainty; the
desire for self-disclosure could be as strong as the wish for concealment. The figure of Lily points to both sides of this conflict.

When the curtain goes up on Lily, decked out as a figure in a painting but in
fact representing nothing more dramatically than the minimally concealed figure of Lily Bart herself, it is both her greatest moment and her greatest debacle. As Amy Kaplan puts it, "At the moment that [Lily] is most fully transformed into art, she is also most fully exposed."[23] Here as elsewhere in the
novel, Lily's behavior and her person elicit diverse reactions from observers.[24]
The conflicting responses to Lily's appearance onstage underscore her precar-
ious social situation; but Lily's participation in an evening of tableaux vivants
also highlights several issues that were directly cogent to Wharton's position as
a novelist. By foregrounding the role of audience response in establishing the
meaning of performance, this episode raises the question of reading habits. Despite the disparate reactions elicited by Lily's appearance onstage, all the characters share one basic unspoken assumption: that Lily Bart is "simply and
undisguisedly" representing herself.

FIGURE 7. Sir Joshua Reynolds's portrait of Joanna Leigh, *Mrs. Lloyd*, is the painting through which Lily Bart represents herself in the tableaux vivants scene in *House of Mirth*. © *Royal Academy of Arts, London / Private Collection.*

Both the most sublime and the most vulgar responses to Lily onstage completely discount the performance as the representation of an object outside Lily.
Some of the spectators see her physical beauty, others her compromised moral
position; still others, including Lily, see the elusive configuration of her "essential" self. But no one (least of all Lily) reflects on the performance as a representation of a Reynolds painting. There is plenty of disagreement over the implications of Lily's self-projection: what it reveals about her body, her moral
standing, her place in society, her future. But everyone agrees that first and
foremost, the performance represents Lily Bart herself—whoever she is.

Like James's Miriam Rooth, Dreiser's Carrie Meeber, Cather's opera
singers, and other stage presences in realist fiction, the figure of Lily as she appears in tableaux vivants reflects the novelist's own dilemma of representation.
Is the "self" of the author, like the "personality" of the actress, ineluctably intertwined with his or her text? And if so, will the result be the reader's "contact
with the author's mind" and "an interchange of thought between writer and
reader,"[25] or simply indiscriminate consumption, voyeurism, and misunderstanding?

Discussions of *The House of Mirth* have often pointed to the difficulty of separating the "real" Lily from her own representations of herself.[26] It is clear
throughout the novel that most of Lily's actions are calculated: "the feeling for
effect . . . never forsook her" (18). Lawrence Selden, observing Lily, repeatedly
draws attention to her histrionic gift. Selden is Lily's most highly valued spectator; he observes her "premeditated" effects with respect and fascination (69,
70).[27] Selden's responses, however, are not necessarily to be trusted. At the start
of the novel, when Selden finds Lily unaccountably at loose ends in the train
station, his reaction is to test her with a little act of his own. Pretending not to
have noticed her, he walks by to give her the chance of revealing herself to
him—or not. Selden's ruse immediately makes it clear that Lily's apparent in-
decision is far from being "the mask of a very definite purpose" that Selden has
suspected (3). Moments later, Selden wonders whether Lily's hair is "ever so
slightly brightened by art" (5). Thus the opening sequence clearly suggests that
Selden himself is preoccupied with the question of artifice. When he subsequently tells himself that "even [Lily's] weeping was an art" (75), we should recall that Selden's perceptions, like those of any reader, are colored by his own
assumptions and preoccupations.

To recognize that Wharton casts doubt on Selden's interpretive acumen,
however, is not to discount his importance to Lily. Lily's craving for a responsive audience is one of her defining characteristics from the outset; nothing
gives her more pleasure than to see aspects of herself reflected back to her in
Selden's eyes. But the status of Lily's "real" as opposed to her projected self remains deeply ambiguous, at least until she visits Selden for the last time and

unobtrusively burns the packet of letters with which she might have saved herself economically and socially.

Lily's letter burning has been the source of much critical speculation.[28] This small drama is enacted under Selden's very nose, but so discreetly that Selden remains permanently unaware of Lily's action. By dropping the packet of Bertha Dorset's letters into the fire, Lily renounces not merely her own material advantage but also her long-standing need to be affirmed by others. As we have noted, being watched, especially by Selden, is from the start the virtual condition, if not for Lily's existence, at least for the existence of "this real self of hers," the self that is "so little accustomed to go alone" (99).[29]

Lily's destruction of the letters constitutes a climactic renunciation of her need to perform. In the course of the novel, Selden's participation is repeatedly required to bring "the real Lily" into focus. But when Lily silently drops the letters into Selden's fire, she seems to be representing—for her *own* benefit—"the Lily Bart [that Selden] knew" (325). By investing herself in a dramatic act without an audience, Lily becomes her own audience and lays claim to herself. By burning Bertha's letters, however, Lily also destroys the only possible basis for telling "her story" convincingly to the public at large.[30] She thus enacts a refusal of representation that amounts to self-destruction.

Many links can be drawn between Wharton and the heroine of her first novel. From her cultural context to her name, Lily is a partial projection of Wharton herself.[31] But no ground of analogy between Lily and the novelist is more cogent to the present argument than Lily's relation to herself through her relation to an audience. If Lily's experience seems to suggest that *all* representation is self-representation, it also suggests that to remain silent and to renounce even one's most coveted audience is to court death.

The vexed question of whether Lily's effects are premeditated or spontaneous—"herself" or merely an "act"—is a question even Lily cannot answer, and one that reflects Wharton's uncertainty about what is revealed by her own writing. Describing Lily's preparation for her tableau vivant, the narrative voice notes that Lily "had shown her artistic intelligence in selecting a type so like her own that she could embody the person represented without ceasing to be herself" (141–42). Yet despite this apparent authorial endorsement of Lily's aesthetic practices, Lily's audience, as we have seen, discounts the representation of otherness altogether and reads the performance mainly as a kind of striptease. Wharton herself well knew how wide the gap could be between rhetorical intentions and fulfillment. "I dream of an eagle and I give birth to a hummingbird," she wrote, evoking the disjunction between the conception and execution of *The House of Mirth* itself.[32] Wharton's uncertainty about production is matched by her anxiety about consumption. Knowing that one cannot control one's own discourse, one may well wonder what it inadvertently exposes.

At a certain point in Wharton's short story "Copy," the former lover of the novelist Mrs. Dale confronts her with the charge of disingenuousness, of being a more "accomplished actor" than himself. "Oh, I'm a novelist," Mrs. Dale replies. "I can keep up that sort of thing for five hundred pages" (116). Yet as it turns out, even Mrs. Dale, veteran novelist, cannot consistently separate her "self" from her performances. The dialogue reveals that many words once expressed by the author-lovers in private have made their way into their own publications. Precisely for this reason they are irresistibly impelled to burn the letters that, if published, would only expose the link between public discourse and private experience.

"Copy," and *The House of Mirth*, like other stories that Wharton wrote in the same period, express her mistrust of her audience while dramatizing not only the risk of self-disclosure but also the difficulty of even *knowing* where to find oneself within one's own representations.[33] Through the letter-burning episode in particular, *The House of Mirth* implies that Wharton (like Lily, and like Mrs. Dale) was quite prepared to imagine the delights of jettisoning her audience altogether. But at the same time Wharton was also deeply invested in the idea that responsive, "creative readers" could still engage with an author in a reciprocal and proto-personal interchange.[34]

"The Vice of Reading," published two years before *The House of Mirth*, conceptualizes the writer-reader relationship as a creative or destructive but always uniquely active interaction that continues long after the reader has closed the book. The liberating potential of such give-and-take stands in stark contrast not only to most of the personal relationships depicted in Wharton's work, but also to the nightmare vision of authorship as isolation (or violation) implicit in "Copy" and other early Wharton stories.[35] In "The Vice of Reading," Wharton anticipates some of the vocabulary adopted by reading theorists over forty years later. Representing the act of reading as a transaction or "interchange of thought between writer and reader," Wharton stresses the "reciprocal adaptability" of reader and text.[36] She claims that "if the book enters the reader's mind, just as it left the writer's—without any of the additions and modifications inevitably produced by contact with a new body of thought," it has been read to no purpose (513). Shifting from the notion of "interchange" to that of "intercourse between book and reader" (514), Wharton's language repeatedly reflects her sense of a writer's personal—almost physical—presence within her own text.

Writing in *The Atlantic* in 1906, Henry Dwight Sedgwick stressed the value of authorial "personality" in fiction. Reading the novels of Mrs. Wharton, Sedgwick notes, gives "the most casual investigator" access to "that special possession which in creative art is of the first importance—human personality. . . . [T]he more fiction is interpenetrated by the author's personality the more interesting it is."[37] To some degree Wharton too took for granted the idea that her own individuality was present in the text. If her exuberant "I was to appear in print!" implies an identification of self or body and printed page at a radical level, the desire for some such seamless amalgam is still more remarkably expressed in the letter to Bernard Berenson from which I have taken this chapter's epigraph: "How I wish I belonged to a plastic race and drew beautiful hieroglyphs with my person instead of having to depend on dull old words."[38]

Seen in this context, the implicit give-and-take between Lily and her spectating audience evokes the dynamic reciprocity in the creation of meanings that for Wharton constituted not only the greatest danger but also one of the greatest pleasures of being read by others. In 1903 Wharton could still imagine the rewards of making contact with a "creative reader" through her work. It is not surprising then that Wharton was prepared to take the one risk that Lily Bart finally refused: the risk of telling a version of her story in public.

Reading through, or Getting at, James's Women Onstage

Like Wharton's evocation of Lily in tableaux vivants, James's portrait of the actress Miriam Rooth in *The Tragic Muse* underscores the difficulty of separating the aesthetic and rhetorical effects of the actress from her own personality and physical presence. For James, perhaps even more than for Wharton, "the constant effort . . . of the novelist" was precisely "to convey the impression of something that is not oneself." Yet James was keenly aware that the effort to represent otherness could well prove "delusive" for novelist and actress alike.[39]

The Tragic Muse (1890) presents Miriam Rooth's situation in the characteristic terms of the nineteenth-century debate about actresses. At the heart of that discussion was the question whether an audience, watching an actress, is looking at a physical body or at an "idea."[40] Whereas Gabriel Nash, the novelist in the story, thinks of Miriam "as a producer whose production is her own person" (376), Miriam herself insists, on the contrary, that "the famous 'person' . . . the great stick they beat us with," is in fact only "the envelope of the idea, . . . our machinery, which ought to be conceded to us" (474). The argument about authorial self-effacement is once again restated here.

Miriam Rooth insists that if *any* "idea" at all is to be represented onstage, the spectating audience must do precisely what Lily Bart's audience fails to do: it must "forget" the actress, especially her body.[41] "In proportion as the idea takes hold of us," Miriam says, "we become unconscious of the clumsy body. Poor old 'person'—if you knew what *we* think of it! If you don't forget it, that's your own affair: it shows that you're dense before the idea" (474). Within *The Tragic Muse*, however, the interpretive convention of "reading through" the performer proves difficult to adopt. Peter Sherringham, for one, never manages to separate Miriam's histrionic effects from her person. Indeed, Sherringham falls in love with Miriam as a direct result of her representations onstage. He therefore seeks to claim the entire woman for himself, to remove both her "ideas" and her body from the theater. Like Lily Bart, Carrie Meeber, or James's own Verena Tarrant, Miriam Rooth becomes a vehicle for projecting uncertainty about what is on display and to whom in any act of public performance.

The recurrent link between physical presence and self-projection in James's portrait of Miriam (and elsewhere) grows out of his own conflict about self-disclosure. James's fascination with the possibility of being physically present—audible and visible—to a responsive public repeatedly surfaces in his work. Early in James's career, as we have seen, the idea of an author seemed inseparable from the experience of literature. James's review of Dion Boucicault's popular comic drama *The Shaughraun* has a somewhat fanciful but revealing emphasis in this context. Written for *The Nation* in 1875, the review reserves particular praise for the virtuoso stage performance of Boucicault himself: "The character of the Shaughraun is very happily fancied," James writes, "but the best of the entertainment is to see the fancy that produced it, still nightly playing with it."[42] James's enthusiasm for the stage appearance of the playwright himself provides a peculiar gloss on the novelist's own lifelong attempt to refine his idea of an author's position both in relation to the represented world of a text and in relation to the public.

To appear quite literally before one's audience in one's work is a pleasure necessarily denied to a novelist; James's desire for contact with his audience found expression more obliquely. From one perspective it colored his lifelong involvement with the theater itself and culminated in his own spontaneous appearance onstage at the worst possible moment of the *Guy Domville* debacle.[43] From another point of view, as we have seen, the idea of personal contact between writer and reader pervades many of James's artist tales.[44] Whereas a fictional text makes it impossible for its audience to "see the fancy that produced it," the figure of the woman onstage at once embodies and problematizes this option. Miriam Rooth insists that she can remain hidden even while physically displayed onstage; but throughout the novel both a rhetorical and a thematic concern with *in*visibility complicates Miriam's pragmatic approach.

Within *The Tragic Muse,* the novelist character Gabriel Nash never has a local habitation: none of the other characters seems to know where he lives. Fittingly, in this context, Nash has unaccountably disappeared from the represented world by the end of the novel; all that remains of him is his own painted image on Nick Dormer's canvas—and even the portrait itself has begun to fade. It is as if a kind of authorial recoil from the overexposure of imaginary footlights generates the figure of Gabriel Nash: the well-hidden or disappearing novelist and the visible, palpable actress are two sides of the same coin. Like Clare Vawdrey, the novelist character in James's story "The Private Life," the figure of Nash is in this sense both a concretization and a parody of James's dictum that "as a narrator of fictitious events [the novelist] is nowhere."[45] James was well aware that his own theories of narrative could have comic implications when taken too far or too literally. The motif of the absent or inaccessible author, like the recurrent figure of the actress, reflects a characteristic conflict about authorial positioning in relation to both text and reading public.

Early in his career, in a discussion of George Eliot, James had articulated the idea of reading as a reciprocal transaction not unlike Wharton's "interchange." In the dynamic and reciprocal "labor" of novel writing, James noted, "the work is divided between the writer and the reader."[46] This idea is an early expression of James's lifelong concern with the text as a basis for contact between unseen and distant partners in a shared endeavor. Although James was hardly complacent about the implications of such give-and-take, he never completely relinquished this model of the connection between writer and reader, even if the dangers of visibility and "presence" often threatened to overshadow the rewards of interaction, and the "ideal reader" came to be ever more firmly located in either the past or the future.

Over the course of the 1880s and 1890s, James came to feel increasingly skeptical about his grounds of connection to readers. *The Tragic Muse,* written four years after the disastrous commercial failure of *The Bostonians* (1886), can be seen as his swan song to the idea of writing and reading as proto-personal exchange. In *The Bostonians,* James had already projected his desire for visibility and contact with the reader through the figure of a woman onstage. When Verena Tarrant addresses an audience, she speaks (like a friendly narrator)[47] as if making a direct appeal to intimate acquaintances, temporarily fusing the motley group before her into responsive unity. The notion of Verena as a stand-in for the writer whose own words are aimed at a larger, less visible group of people is reinforced by the emphasis on voice that pervades the novel. Verena is an orator, not an actress; her effectiveness depends on her mesmerizing voice. Despite the difference between the visible, audible speaker and the silent, absent author, the focus on voice extends the analogy between Verena and her creator. *The Bostonians* repeatedly raises the question whether Verena herself is "conceal[ed] and effac[ed]" by her words—or whether, on the contrary, she "give[s] herself away," depleted as well as betrayed in a public act of self-projection. Miss Birdseye, the veteran public speaker in the novel, is said to have "given herself away so lavishly all her life that it was odd there was anything left of her."[48]

Like the figure of Miriam Rooth, that of Verena reflects James's own fear of being, like a vulnerable woman, converted bodily into an object of consumption—exhibited, bought, all but literally consumed. The plot and structure of *The Bostonians* explore numerous consequences of making one's expressive gift too freely available to one's audience. Verena herself, of course, is ultimately rendered both silent and invisible—despite, or indeed *because of,* her very power and irresistibility as a speaker. The beauty of Verena's person intensifies the problematic effect of her gift. That her voice is inseparable from her body only hastens her removal from the public arena.

The Tragic Muse reflects a newly assertive sense on James's part that the artist has the right to be separate, that his or her person need not necessarily be merged with the representation—even when, as in Miriam's case, the body it-self is the medium for the message. In *The Bostonians,* Verena proves unequal to the onslaught of those who are determined to get at the "charming creature" (53) represented by the red hair and spellbinding voice. Unlike Verena, Miriam Rooth successfully resists the suitor who would claim her as a private posses-sion and remove her from the stage. In *The Tragic Muse,* moreover, James's nar-rative discourse reinforces the thematic affirmation of distance between per-former and public.

The Bostonians explored the problematic of what Olive calls "a voice, a hu-man voice" (57) trying to reach an audience, and it did so by employing a nar-rator who (uncharacteristically for James) repeatedly addressed the reader, ap-pealing for help with the process of representation.[49] Like *The Bostonians, The Tragic Muse* employs the novelist's narrating "I," intermittently foregrounding the idea of reciprocity as an aspect of narration itself. But in *The Tragic Muse* the rhetorical stance that urges the reader to join in a shared creative effort is used far more sparingly than in *The Bostonians.* The authorial "I" is largely re-served for a few passages near the end of *The Tragic Muse,* as if to shore up the connective grounds of writer-reader interaction, just before the moment of separation.[50] Thereafter, the first-person pronoun on the part of the narra-tor/novelist is rarely used in James's work. From the 1890s onward, the autho-rial persona, encouraging the reader's participation in the narrative, progres-sively recedes, replaced by such fictional "reflectors"[51] as Fleda Vetch, Lambert Strether, Kate Croy, and Maggie Verver. During the 1890s, moreover, James makes increasing use of first-person narration. His artist tales in particular are often told by a narrating character with a clearly delineated personality. Such a narrator inevitably drives a wedge between the act of narration and the figure of the writer.[52]

I have suggested that the mid-nineteenth-century notion of fiction reading as a reciprocal exchange meant associating the voice of a narrator directly with the voice of the originating author. It was precisely this association that en-abled many nineteenth-century readers to experience fiction reading as an intense, virtually personal interaction.[53] But the link between narrator and novelist is immediately complicated by the device of first-person narration, particularly when a narrating character is sharply individuated and provided with moral or biographical characteristics different from those generally asso-ciated with the figure of the author. By the time James left the figure of the-ater behind as an organizing fictional theme, he had committed himself to a variety of self-effacing narrative strategies. He did so not just because at some level he had begun to despair of eliciting any "revitalizing" responses through fiction, but because he well knew how easy it was to "give oneself away" unwittingly in writing. One might say of James in his late phase what Ralph Touchett says of Isabel Archer after her marriage: "If she wore a mask, it completely covered her face."[54] By abandoning the woman onstage as a fictional motif, James replaced both the seductions and the dangers of physical presence, at least in theory, with the safety of invisibility, the severing of authorial person from representation.

Behind a Mask: Willa Cather's Actresses and the Price of Self-effacement

Severing person from representation, the ubiquitous figure of the woman onstage could point to both the difficulty and the price of this move. Like James, Willa Cather affirmed the seamless transmogrification of author into fictional artifact. From the start of her career, Cather was committed to subverting the interpretive convention of "reading through" the idea to its human generator, and she took the successful classical actress as a recurrent touchstone for this aesthetic aim. Many of Cather's early stories and reviews focus on actresses and singers. Her evocation of effective stage performance comes as close to an image of transmuted or inaccessible subjectivity as one could imagine without crossing the line that leads to comic figures as invisible as Gabriel Nash, or the authorial "half" of Clare Vawdrey in "The Private Life." Nonetheless, the figure of a woman onstage remains a paradoxical vehicle for conveying authorial absense.

Cather's first published story, "Peter" (1892), takes the figure of a certain kind of actress as a model of aesthetic transmutation and control while assiduously refraining from the leisurely, personalized mode of narration that Cather herself so admired in *Trilby*.[55] The narration of "Peter" is impressively cagey. The three-page story begins with ten lines of uninterrupted dialogue, the only narrative strategy that dispenses with a teller altogether. When the narrative voice subsequently begins to interject descriptive detail ("Antone pulled his ragged cap down over his low brow. . . . The old man . . . sat stroking his violin with trembling fingers",[56]) the authority of omniscient narration is unmitigated by personal opinion or individuating characteristics. Gender is unmarked, and the act of telling is not foregrounded as such.

The narrating voice of "Peter" is personified now and again only to the extent of being identifiable as that of the local community ("Antone was the acknowledged master of the premises, and people said he was a likely youth and would do well. . . . His corn was better tended than any in the county, and his wheat always yielded more than other men's. Of Peter, no one knew much, nor had any one a good word to say for him" [1–2]). "Embodied" only insofar as the narrator is familiar with what "people said," he or she discloses no additional identifying traits. When Peter's memories and longings are represented, the narrative voice unobtrusively merges with Peter's own consciousness:

> Long ago, only eight years by the calendar, but it seemed eight centuries to Peter, he had been a second violinist in the great theatre at Prague. . . . [o]nce, a French woman came and played for weeks, he did not remember her name now. He did not remember her face very well either, for it changed so, it was never twice the same. But the beauty of it, and the great hunger men felt at the sight of it, that he remembered. Most of all he remembered her voice. He did not know French, and could not understand a word she said, but it seemed to him that she must be talking the music of Chopin. And her voice, he thought he should know that in the other world. The last night she played a play in which a man touched her arm, and she stabbed him. As Peter sat among the smoking gas jets down below the footlights with his fiddle on his knee, and looked up at her, he thought he would like to die too, if he could touch her arm once, and have her stab him so. (2–3)

The narrative makes no attempt here to account for itself or its access to Peter's mind; the sequence assiduously deflects attention from the presence of any figure in the text outside Peter and "the French woman" (see figure 8). Thus, although the third-person pronoun always implies a teller, the passage effectively wards off questions about who the teller might be: the only subjectivity that comes into focus is Peter's own. After the statement about Peter's wish for death, the "communal" narrator reappears: "Even in those days [Peter] was a foolish fellow, who cared for nothing but music and pretty faces" (3). This opinion, cast as the conventional wisdom of a harsh midwestern prairie town, is clearly distinct from Peter's own perspective and, unless read ironically, equally distinct from Willa Cather's.

The impression that "the French woman" makes on Peter stays with him all his life. In particular, he never forgets her voice ("he thought he should know that in the other world"). By contrast, "he did not remember her name now. He did not remember her face very well either, for it changed so, it was never twice the same." The French woman's evocative power depends neither on her face nor on her name; so too Cather conceived of her own subjectivity as transmuted in her work. If the story makes it difficult for a reader to construct an individuated subjectivity for the narrator, it becomes still more difficult to conceptualize the figure of a clearly differentiated novelist.

Like the figure of "the French woman" in Peter's reverie, Cather herself is the impersonal vehicle for an evocative representation. The power to put an audience in touch with "beauty" and elicit "great hunger" in a mass of spectators—this is both the French woman's art and Cather's own model for aesthetic effects. In another early story about a stage performer, "Nanette: An Aside" (1897), Cather identifies "classical art" with the "conservation" of "emotional power."[57] Such art may at once "wring . . . your heart" and create "the

FIGURE 8. Sarah Bernhardt in Sardou's *Tosca* was Cather's model for "the French woman" in Peter's reverie. (According to one observer, the "electricity generated by one scene of this play would have been enough to light the streets of London" [Joanna Richardson, *Sarah Bernhardt and Her World* (New York: Putnam's, 1977), 126].) *Courtesy of ASAP / Hulton-Getty.*

impression of horrible reality" (88), but both effects depend on the radical transformation of the performer's own emotions. Only when the subjectivity of the actress is transformed does her work become "art exalted" (88).

Cather's "Peter" suggests that great acting turns the actress into an idea, à la Miriam Rooth, projecting or distilling subjectivity so thoroughly into representation as not to leave a trace. To be sure, "Nanette," like other Cather stories, clearly implies that such "conservation" or "hold[ing] back" of inner turbulence has its price ("Tradutorri is dying of it now, they say" [88]).[58] The subjectivity of the spectator, too, may be implicated to his or her cost. When Peter kills himself at the end of the story, he is *still* responding, at least in part, to "the idea" of "the French woman." One may question whether this idea is hers or his; either way Peter's response has no reciprocal impact on the actress.

It is worth recalling at this point that even while Cather was producing stories that exemplified the aesthetic value of emotional restraint and impartiality in narration, she was also writing book reviews that clearly affirmed the pleasures of "reading for the author." "Many books are read through curiosity," Cather wrote, reviewing *Trilby*, "but very few are widely read and read through real liking. That is Du Maurier's unpardonable crime; he . . . has become popular . . . by appealing to [people], warming them, going straight to their hearts." *Trilby*, Cather concluded, "has won for itself a place in the hearts of the people. Most of us would write books if we could do that."[59] Cather herself was already writing fiction by the time she wrote this review, but even in her earliest work her rhetorical strategy was diametrically opposed to Du Maurier's, with its elaborate construction of a humanly individuated, "likable" storyteller. The differences between Cather and Du Maurier are especially revealing in the context of Cather's own enthusiasm for *Trilby*.

Cather's praise of Du Maurier's most successful novel was by no means an anomaly. In essays and reviews of the period, Cather repeatedly asserted the value of likable, even "loveable" discourse.[60] In an enthusiastic discussion of a posthumous work by Eugene Field, Cather applauds an approach to books and reading that she never endorsed with her own fictional practice. Field's book *The Love Affairs of a Bibliomaniac* was one of the many turn-of-century volumes that celebrated books as friends and reading as a kind of conversation. In her review Cather emphasizes that Field "does not write of books as 'art,' but as personalities. He does not see them as studies in environment or character, but as trusty companions, and he speaks of them as 'a plain blunt man who loves his friends might speak.'"[61] What makes a book a "trusty companion," a friend? How can one reconcile these qualities with the idea of professionalism, "art," and greatness? Such questions are directly cogent to the contrast between the work that Cather read so enthusiastically and the kind that she herself produced.

It is precisely when the author is imagined as an actress whose mask completely covers her face, when authorial subjectivity seems to disappear altogether, that the writer-reader interchange is replaced by the unbridgeable "chasm that parts authors and readers."[62] The sense of self-division implied by such masking is reproduced by the sense of division between the self and others. "Coming Aphrodite," one of Cather's richest "performer" stories, addresses this issue in its final image: "Eden Bower closed her eyes, and her face . . . became hard and settled, like a plaster cast; so a sail, that has been filled by a strong breeze, behaves when the wind suddenly dies. Tomorrow night the wind would blow again, and this mask would be the golden face of Aphrodite."[63] The question of the relation between human face and plaster cast is central to "Coming Aphrodite," which depicts an encounter between two young, unformed artists, an actress (Eden Bower) and a painter (Don Hedger), who live for a short time on either side of a common wall in a New York apartment building.[64] Like many of Cather's early stories and theatrical reviews, the tale raises several kinds of questions about an artist-performer's relation to self, art, and others. Don Hedger first hears Eden Bower's "young fresh confident voice" (13) through the double doors that separate his room from the ones she is about to rent. Later, he spends many hours watching her naked body through a knothole in those same double doors. Eden Bower's New York interlude, a period before she achieves success as an opera singer, is a time for her to enjoy "the easy freedom of obscurity . . . [a] time to . . . watch without being watched" (42). Yet she is nothing if not watched from the moment she enters the room adjoining Hedger's, bringing both strangeness and desire into his life.

Once Eden Bower, with her "big, beautiful voice" (21) and her "blue silk dressing gown" (23), becomes Hedger's neighbor, "everything [is] different" (28) for Hedger. Eden Bower is the first tenant ever to object to Hedger's bathing his dog in the shared tub at the end of the hall. Watching the "single running line" of her "whole figure" (27), Hedger suddenly despises "the disorder of [his] place, . . . his old shoes and himself and all his slovenly habits" (28). Through these details and others the story repeatedly foregrounds differences of sensibility, gender, and class, all ultimately seen as unbridgeable distances and epitomized by the space between performer and spectator. In the course of the story many barriers, including the literal one of the double doors, temporarily open up between the two protagonists. But, like Eden Bower herself, Hedger remains alone. The thematic emphasis on distances, combined with the neutral, impassive tone of the narrative discourse, raises questions about the status of the text: is it a bridge or a chasm between writer and reader?

When the story begins, Hedger, the painter is at work on a "study of paradise fish at the Aquarium, staring out at people through the glass and green water of their tank. It was a highly gratifying idea; the incommunicability of one stratum of animal life with another" (13). In the final description of Hedger we are told that "we must leave Hedger thus, sitting in his tank with his dog, looking up at the stars" (74). The odd reference to the "tank" in which Hedger remains recalls his own "study of paradise fish" (and "the incommunicability of one stratum of animal life with another"). But the narrator's highly uncharacteristic "we" at this juncture is also worth pausing over. For one thing, it draws attention to the situation of telling and the existence of a reader. It also marks the difference between the novelist's mode of communication and that of both the painter and the actress in the tale.[65] In addition, the narrating "we" registers a certain resistance on Cather's part to the author's disembodied relation to her represented world—and her reader. The intimation of Cather's own presence is further betrayed at this moment in the story when the generally unobtrusive narrator adds that Hedger "pretended [the study] . . . was only an experiment in unusual lighting" (13). Such "pretending" on Hedger's part is a tactic that presumably goes unacknowledged by Hedger himself. It is privileged information, a communication from an authorial persona to the reader.

For Cather, as for many writers of the period, theatrical (and narrative) masks implied professionalism: they seemed to ensure objectivity and effectively lifelike representation. Yet the more fully transmuted the subjectivity of the actress, the more effective the projected illusion of a story without a teller, the more complete the isolation or desolation of the performer-creator. Toward the end of "Coming Aphrodite," the peculiar conjunction of the narrating "we" with the image of the painter in his "tank" suggests that for Cather, as for other proponents of authorial invisibility, any imagined intercourse or interchange between writer and reader was to some degree dependent on *incomplete* transformation, on the possibility of imagining at least the shadow of a human face behind the mask.

The Return of the Author

It is the failed or abrogated transmutation itself that makes for traces of human presence, the fleeting return of an authorial figure. In *A Backward Glance*, Edith Wharton uses the image of threads "on the wrong side of the tapestry" as a trope for the working procedures of the novelist.[66] Realist texts were repeatedly imagined as objective totalities, mirrors, windows, and other self-contained wholes. A glimpse of the threads on "the wrong side of the tapestry" implies the making process; it disrupts the self-containment of the finished work and destabilizes the illusion of transparency or represented reality. In realist texts, both the rhetoric of direct address (the authorial "I" or readerly "you") and self-reflexive elements such as discussions of aesthetic illusion (including stage presence) suggest that the language of representation can point to its own nature or its own methods of construction rather than to the represented world in the text.[67] Such moments generate flickering intimations of a novelist at work and foreground the existence of the writer.

Mark Seltzer has argued that in realist works, "narration . . . is everywhere threatened by [its] exposure as [a] mere . . . effect . . . of certain practices of writing."[68] But the exposure of "writing practices" is also the exposure of a writer. The threads revealed and perceived on the "wrong side" of the tapestry imply the presence of a maker. Realist writers were repeatedly impelled to offer glimpses of what went on behind the scenes of the finished work, even though such glimpses violated their aesthetic principles. James may have valued the "pudding," not what went on in the kitchen;[69] but late in his career he also invested a great deal of time and energy in writing prefaces that focus on both the "kitchen" and the writer while once again directly addressing the reader.

For writers of realism, self-disclosure was not just a danger but evidently a great temptation, as if only the projected presence of an author could engage the implicit reciprocity of a reader. Selden's belief that Lily Bart's performance in tableaux vivants has revealed her "real self" is exhilarating even for Lily, who knows it isn't so. For Dreiser's "Sister Carrie," too, there is no greater delight, no moment of intensity more absorbing or fulfilling than that which directly follows Drouet's appearance backstage to "buoy her up" in her representation of Augustin Daly's Laura.[70] Carrie's triumph in *Under the Gaslight* is arguably the most satisfying moment of her life. In *Sister Carrie,* as in fiction by James, Wharton, and Cather, the audience spurs the actress on to ever greater effectiveness, temporarily allowing her to discount her immediate social reality (and even "the clumsy body" itself). The performer's exhilaration is always accompanied by an intense experience of being connected to otherness. That experience paradoxically coexists with a unique sense of autonomy. Although both the sense of connection and the feeling of autonomy achieved onstage are fleeting and illusory, they are also unusually persuasive.

Carrie's performance as a humble and virtuous woman in *Under the Gaslight* creates a seductive illusion of intimacy for members of the audience who imaginatively cross the curtain line by discounting the representation as such. Sitting in the theater, watching Carrie perform, both of Carrie's lovers feel personally addressed;[71] making "strange resolves," Drouet and Hurstwood quite simply "read through" the play's lines as if they expressed Carrie's true sensibility. In the guise of Daly's Laura, Carrie is more desirable to her lovers than she has ever been before. As with Lily Bart and Miriam Rooth, so with Carrie: the thematic concern with "reading through" the script and the performance to the woman underneath signals anxiety about the writer-reader interchange.

The figure of theater allowed the realists to explore an artist's relation to the materials of self-projection and the idea of "person," both body and "self." At the same time, realist representations of stage performance stressed the function of response by underscoring the reactions of those who watch. When Lily appears onstage in *The House of Mirth,* Selden and Gerty imagine that they are in touch with her essence—"the Lily *we* know" (143). As Reynolds's "Mrs. Lloyd," Lily seems to be "divested of the trivialities of her little world" (142). But if Lily onstage temporarily becomes a sublime vision in Selden's eyes, she is by virtue of that same stage appearance nearly raped by Gus Trenor. The use of actress figures in realist texts repeatedly suggests that any representation depends on its audience for its meaning. Verena Tarrant, Miriam Rooth, and Carrie Meeber are never more fervently desired as sexual objects and as possessions than when they appear onstage. But in each case the question arises: Just who is being desired in this process? "It's myself, for the moment, whatever it is," Frank Norris's Laura Dearborn exclaims in *The Pit* as she plays Athalie and Carmen in turn.[72] It is precisely because incomplete transformations raise difficult questions about physical presence, representation, and interpretation that so many novelists who affirmed authorial disappearance in principle kept coming back to the motif of stage appearance as theme and trope.

Theatrical scenes repeatedly become scenes of reading in realist texts. The theatrical frame itself underscores the fact that all imagined meetings across the "hard glittering line of the footlights" are necessarily provisional and illusory. Yet the wish for a bond between writer and reader crept back into the work of the most fervidly impartial and impersonal turn-of-century authors. When the author-actress is desired by the audience only for his or her person rather than embraced as representation or idea, there can be neither aesthetic pleasure nor what Wharton called "real intercourse between book and reader."[73] When the mask completely covers the face, however, the author is unloved, anonymous, isolated.

For Cather, as for James, the aesthetic impact of fiction depended in theory on a projected illusion of life: narrative in this view was an "effect of representation,"[74] not intercourse. Both Cather and James sought to keep their readers at a distance, to make their narrative strategies proof against the practice of "reading through" the text and "getting at" the author. And yet for both these exemplars of representational opacity (or transparency) there was a big difference between their aesthetic goals and their own reading habits, a distinct difference between being read and reading others. "A great book is a creation, like a great man," Cather wrote.

> You can acknowledge its power and influence without cherishing any personal fondness for it. Many a great book and many a great man would be "ill to live with," as Carlyle's mother frankly said of her mighty son. But their greatness remains just the same and commands respect, not because it is good or bad, in the moral sense, likeable or unlikeable, but because it is mighty, a force, like the sea or a cataract, and thousands of other things that are not measured by their ethics or their amiability.[75]

The reader's love or the mantle of greatness: Which was it to be? The young Cather delighted in *Trilby* for its apparent revelation of "the wise, gentle, sympathetic man" who wrote the book; yet she tried to keep a personalized image of herself out of her own discourse. James too affirmed rhetorical distance and self-effacement as a novelist, and yet, like many other turn-of-century readers, he had a real weakness for texts that seemed to offer access to the "man behind the pen," texts that could be read first and foremost for the author.

James's susceptibility to the seductive, even coercive lure of authorial presence in the text is nowhere more visible than in his letters to H. G. Wells. James repeatedly states that the center of interest in Wells's work "was simply H. G. W. himself."[76] His letters to Wells criticize the latter's use of "autobiographic" narration while at the same time graphically revealing its captivating effect on James himself. After reading *The Future in America* (1906), for example, James writes his friend, "What primarily flies in my face in these things of yours is *you*" (113–14). James alternately "surrenders" to Wells and "absorbs" or "devours" him, reading through his prose to its author:

> I have read you, as I always read you, and as I read no one else, with a complete abdication of all those "principles of criticism" . . . which I totter . . . through the pages of others attended . . . by . . . but which I shake off, as I advance under your spell, with the most cynical inconsistency. For under your spell I do advance. . . . I live with you and in you and (almost cannibal-like) *on* you, on you H. G. W., to the sacrifice of your [characters]. . . . I see you "behave" all along, much more than I see them . . . so that the ground of the drama is somehow most of all in the adventure for *you*—not to say *of* you. . . . [Y]our "story," through the five hundred pages, says more to me than theirs. . . . I consume you crude and whole and to the last morsel, cannibalistically, quite, as I say; licking the platter clean of the last possibility of a savour and remaining thus yours abjectly. (166–68)

James's strikingly elaborate rendering of his pleasure and vulnerability as a reader of H. G. Wells casts James himself in the part of the "enthralled reader," an extreme version of a characteristic nineteenth-century reader role.[77] At the same time, however, this reader is represented as a voracious cannibal who literally consumes the author "crude and whole and to the last morsel." No wonder then that even while James repeatedly suspended his critical principles and broke his own theoretical rules as a *reader* of Wells, living "with . . . and in . . . and on" his literary friend, he sought to forestall any such approach to himself by becoming increasingly guarded as an *author*.[78]

By the turn of the century, authorial reserve and impersonality were well-established narrative conventions. As the authorial "I" and readerly "you" were expelled from the fictional text, those who still spoke of reading as "reciprocal adaptibility," an "interchange of thought," or "a kind of conversation" were increasingly embattled, already nostalgic. Still, just as James castigated the "autobiographic form" while intermittently "shak[ing] off" his own "principles of criticism" and advancing under the "spell" of H. G. Wells, so Cather took the transmuted subjectivity of the classical actress as her own aesthetic model while recurrently praising likeable, even "lovable" books. In theory, and as *writers,* James and Cather shared a commitment to authorial self-effacement. As *readers,* however, they sometimes delighted in the very authors whose work most flagrantly defied their own rhetorical goals.

Reviewing Wharton's *House of Mirth* in 1906, Henry Dwight Sedgwick stressed the importance of "human personality" in fiction and literary discourse. Yet he also felt the need to justify his reading habits, defensively drawing attention to his own anachronistic tastes: "Our generation, not yet wholly purged of the lingering effects left by the old Romantic individualism, cannot but feel that the more fiction is interpenetrated by the author's personality, the more interesting it is."[79] For many readers (and writers) at the turn of the century, the amalgam of authorial personality and text was no longer self-evident or harmonious, as it had seemed when friendly reading habits were the norm. Although many writers aimed at impersonal, objective narration, uncertainty about the relation of idea and person to novelistic performance fanned curiosity about the threads "on the wrong side of the tapestry." The desire to locate the traces of the author within the woven fabric was widespread.

We have seen that when the author was no longer represented as personable storyteller, he or she was often imagined as a public performer, sometimes as a naked one. But in many realist texts at the turn of the century and beyond, the author was embodied neither as a sociable figure conferring with a reader through his or her book, nor as a stage performer, on display and for sale. Rather, the author came to be seen as an increasingly diffuse and oblique kind of presence in the text. But with the author effectively hidden or collapsed into discourse, how was the reader to "get at" the author? Those who promoted authorial remoteness and the story that "tells itself" did not address the question of where the author was now to be situated; nor did they consider how the changing idea of the author's relation to the text would reciprocally influence the idea of reading itself. But many authors imagined that their readers were dismantling the text in the very act of reading and all but cannibalistically consuming them "crude and whole and to the last morsel." It is to this scenario that we now turn.

5

Getting at the Hidden Author in the Text

**He desired to be valued for himself, or for his work, which
was, after all, an expression of himself.**

Jack London, *Martin Eden* (1909)

In 1921 Percy Lubbock codified many of Henry James's ideas about narration in
The Craft of Fiction, a book that was to exert a powerful influence on the course
of literary studies. Lubbock's criteria—especially the value of "showing" over
"telling"—were soon firmly established for both fictional and critical discourse.[1] When E. M. Forster published *Aspects of the Novel* in 1927, he praised
Lubbock's professionalism, apologizing (somewhat disingenuously) for his
own informal, "talkative" manner, his use of "I," "you," and even "one."[2] But the
widespread emphasis on taking the authorial "I" out of critical discourse and
abolishing digressive interpolations in fiction only drew attention to the difficulty of controlling, or even deciding, what constitutes the traces of authorial
presence in a text.

In *The Writing of Fiction*, Edith Wharton upheld the standard set by James
and Lubbock and reaffirmed what by 1925 had become a familiar demand for
narration: no "old-fashioned intrusion of the author among his puppets."[3]
Twenty years earlier, when Frank Norris had asked, "How far is the author
justified in putting himself into his work?" he too had invoked a theatrical
metaphor, concluding quite simply that an author should never "take . . . the
stage."[4] What will come into focus in this chapter is how the act of reading itself was conceptualized when a text was no longer seen as a catalyst for writer-
reader interchange, and when an author was imagined neither as a narrating
presence nor as a stage performer but as someone hidden in the wings.

As a figure for the author, the image of the woman onstage had problema-
tized writer-reader relations, representing aesthetic performance as seductive
self-display and raising questions about the grounds for enthusiasm in the audience. As we have seen, many of the characters who watch Verena Tarrant,
Carrie Meeber, Lily Bart, and other performing women simply discount the

93

representation as such, reading through the performance to the "person-ality" of the performer. Although many writers recoiled from such reading practices, it was just this way of "reading through" a text to the human being at its source that made reading seem to many others like a mode of human interchange.

One of Lubbock's basic assumptions in *The Craft of Fiction* was that every reader tends to isolate the "people" in the text—and the "character of the author"—more quickly and easily than any other feature of the work. Lubbock's assumption was widely shared; the author's "personality" and the "reality" of the characters were fundamental reference points in book reviews of the period.[5] Lubbock's aim was to foster a new mode of critical reading, one that would replace the focus on "character" (both authorial and fictional) with consideration of a novel's "form."[6] Yet as we have already seen, there was a great deal of tenacity in the habit of identifying a book not only with the "people" in it but with the person who created it as well. This way of reading informs Forster's approach to the novel and partly accounts for his own sense of being "unprofessional." Forster's opening evocation of a scene in which his favorite authors are imagined as people, sitting in chairs around a large room, only reaffirms the association of a text with the idea of a human being in whom it originated and whom it represents.[7]

As the ideal of the unobtrusive narrator and invisible fiction writer gained currency, the notion of authorial personality was pronounced increasingly irrelevant to critical discourse; a reader's sense of human connection with an authorial figure was no longer considered a natural outgrowth of the reading process. Yet when the author was not embodied as a narrating persona, authorial figures reappeared in other forms.[8] Some reading theorists suggest that all language is associated with the idea of "a person who originated it."[9] Perhaps it is partly for this reason that the idea of a book without an author was so difficult to accept, especially for writers and readers who had themselves grown up at a time when another set of conventions prevailed.

Reading habits are slow to change. Even though the association of reading with human companionship was discouraged in much fiction and criticism after the turn of the century, many people continued to experience the act of reading as a mode of engagement with otherness. But when the "transaction" between book and reader was no longer conceived on the model of "polite intercourse" (a "kind of conversation"), or even as performance, with the author as the figure in the foreground, the writer-reader relationship was sometimes imagined instead as a strangely oblique, even hostile give-and-take. Many realist writers believed that their own "depersonalizing" narrative practices only fostered in their readers a redoubled desire to "get at" the inaccessible author. When the figure of the authorial storyteller exchanging ideas with the reader became unfashionable and "unprofessional," many authors imagined themselves in other guises, in a more highly charged relation to book and reader.

We will now consider three novels that foreground the issue of authorial invisibility and its implications for reading. Written in the years when the idea of authorial removal was being consolidated, *The Pit, The Financier,* and *The Age of Innocence* represent effective masking as the source of authorial (as well as social) power. Highly visible characters are represented conversely as flawed and threatened. Laura Dearborn, Aileen Butler, and Ellen Olenska, each in her own way, is flamboyantly conspicuous early in the novel; but each is removed from the spotlight by the end of the text. Like the women onstage I have considered, these characters could themselves be taken as figures for the author in the age of the writer-celebrity. In these works, however, the dramatically conspicuous woman is juxtaposed with more carefully concealed, assiduously masked figures, both male and female, who wield power more deviously, often more creatively, and whose methods are crowned with particular success. The point here is not simply that working behind the scenes is effective. The point is that these novels explore offstage performance and the gift of camouflage in detail, making the hidden manipulator rather than the thinly veiled stage performer a figure for the writer, and raising questions about the effect of authorial invisibility on the idea of reading. These texts often imagine the act of reading itself as aggressive behavior by readers who are impelled to unmask, dismember, or expose the veiled, disguised, or absent figure at the center.

Self-display as Self-destruction: Norris's "Unknown Bull"

Frank Norris's critical writing both affirms authorial self-effacement and exposes his ambivalence about it. Despite his own programmatic emphasis on the neutral voice and unobtrusive storyteller, Norris shared with other turn-of-century readers the sense that reading a book could generate the feel of a human relationship. Indeed, there was a kind of authorial presence in the story which Norris as a reader particularly relished.

In 1901, in the same essay that formulates his "theory of the suppression of the author's personality" in fiction, Norris praises "one of the best books of the last ten years," Frank T. Bullen's *Cruise of the Cachalot*.[10] Norris's pleasure as a reader (like that of Cather and James) often derived from the very qualities he rejected as a writer. The author's "individuality and the power to record it"— this is the primary appeal of the novel that Norris celebrates. Bullen, Norris says outright, "has recorded himself in *The Cruise.* . . . It is the mate himself, his ideas, his notions, his reflections, and the scant, scrimped, half-hinted-at autobiography that he occasionally permits to slip into his pages that holds one. The book is a human document. I know a new man now, have made a new acquaintance. . . . [T]hat's the thing to be thankful for" (54–55). Like many reviewers throughout the nineteenth century, Norris here asserts that the "individuality" of the author is the thing "that holds one" in reading. The author's "individuality" may be partly filtered through the central character, with the writer's "auto-biography" only "half-hinted-at"; but the book is "a human document" by virtue of the person, in this case the "new man," presented to the reader by the printed page (see figure 9).

Yet the pleasure of making "a new acquaintance" through reading in turn "suggests a question" to Norris: "How far is the author justified in putting himself into his work?" (55). In fiction, Norris answers, he "hold[s] with the theory of the suppression of the author's personality—so far as possible" (55). Like other writers of the period, Norris believed that the author's personality was most evident in digressions from the story line, and in the use of the first-person pronoun itself. At this level, traces of authorial "personality" could be easily suppressed, and Norris, like other realist writers, emphatically rejected the kind of authorial commentary that was still prominent in much popular fiction—what Lubbock would later call "telling." If a "story is not self-explanatory, it is a bad story," Norris writes (55). But for Norris, so long as authorial "personality" does *not* take the form of "intrusive" commentary, it constitutes an asset to the work. If "the point of view of the writer—his ideals, his ideas, *his personality, in a word*—does not appear in his work indirectly—mind I say indirectly—he had best give over the attempt to produce readable fiction; as well have the cinematograph and the phonograph" (55; my emphasis). Rather oddly for the man who became known as "the boy Zola," the "cinematograph and the phonograph" (presumed instruments of exact and objective representation) here become *negative* touchstones of novelistic appeal.[11] Authorial "personality" remains the sine qua non of "readable fiction." It is authorial individuality that creates a "human document"—so long as that "individuality" appears in the work only "indirectly."

"Art . . . instantly involves the personality of the artist," Norris wrote in another essay.[12] But in this formulation, an artist's "personality" would seem to make its way into the work will he nill he. At stake here is a question of control: How completely can a writer shape and limit the personality that will be visible to the reader of a text? In one of Norris's earliest stories, "The Jongleur of Taillebois," a murderer confesses his crime involuntarily when the instrument he chooses to play betrays him, and he ends up singing not "*his chosen composition*"[13] but one that reveals his inmost secrets. Numerous obsessive and self-destructive storytellers throughout Norris's work would seem to raise a similar question with respect to narrative itself: Is narration a crafted performance or an inadvertent act of self-disclosure?[14]

In "The Responsibilities of the Novelist," Norris speaks of the novel as a powerful "instrument," invoking the image of Ulysses wielding his bow as a figure for the writer. Ulysses is particularly suggestive as an authorial figure in the present context since the bow he takes up at a climactic moment of *The Odyssey* is an instrument of self-revelation. Odysseus' medium is disguise, craft, and

FIGURE 9. Illustration for Robert Louis Stevenson's "The Reader." For good or ill, the association of a book with a person remained widespread. In Stevenson's tale, a book that has offended its reader is angrily cast to the floor and reacts by advising the reader to blame the author, not the book. The fable relies on the reader's familiarity with the notion of an animated book, with reading as a reciprocal transaction, and with the question of whether or not a book embodies its author. From *Fables* by Robert Louis Stevenson, illustrated by E. R. Herman (New York: Charles Scribner's Sons, 1914). *Reprinted with the permission of Scribner, a Division of Simon & Schuster.*

storytelling even more than physical prowess throughout *The Odyssey*, but never more so than toward the end of the narrative, when, disguised as a beggar and undetected by his own wife, he orchestrates a sequence of recognition scenes. The culminating moment of these recognitions is the one that Norris refers to in "Responsibilities of the Novelist"—the moment of stringing the bow.[15] On this occasion Odysseus not only reestablishes his power, arming himself and beginning to kill his wife's suitors, but also reveals who he is, reclaiming his rightful place as ruler, father of Telemachos, and husband of the faithful Penelope.

When Odysseus wields his bow, he publicly reasserts his claim to the prerogatives of identity. Unlike Norris's "jongleur of Taillebois," whose instrument exposes and destroys him, Odysseus fully controls his instrument and its effects. Yet Norris was always aware that one's preferred instrument, like that of the jongleur, could take on an unexpected life of its own, causing the performance to reveal more than intended. If a novel can expose more truth about its author's individuality than the author means to reveal, questions about the reading public—who they are, how they read—become especially urgent.

Like many turn-of-century reviewers and critics, Norris believed that the American reading public was growing daily, its composition shifting and its consumption of printed matter on the rise. Seventy million Americans "have all at once awakened to the fact that there are books to be read," Norris wrote in 1902. "As with all things sudden, there is noticeable with this awakening a lack of discrimination. . . . It is a great animal, this American public, and having starved for so long, it is ready, once aroused, to devour anything."[16]

In "The American Public and 'Popular' Fiction," Norris argues for the value of "indiscriminate" reading. "Better bad books than no books," he writes; "do not spurn the 70,000,000 because they do not understand Henry James" (127). Yet while Norris here affirms his faith in the American reading public, his imagery of the "great animal," the "great brute" (127), conveys vividly negative overtones: "If the Megatherium has been obliged to swallow wind for sustenance for several hundred years, it would be unkind to abuse him because he eats the first lot of spoiled hay or over-ripe twigs that is thrust under the snout of him. . . . Once his belly filled, and the pachyderm will turn to the new-mown grass and fruit trees in preference to the hay and twigs" (127). Throughout Norris's fiction the idea of the "brute" is clearly associated with a range of implacable, subterranean, often violent needs and desires. To imagine one's audience as such a creature—a "great brute," a "great animal," an indiscriminate "pachyderm"—could well make one wary of one's mode of address and cautious of self-representation.

Norris repeatedly asserts that an author should stay out of his fiction. "The man behind the pen," he asked, "what has the public to do with him?"[17] But at the same time, Norris affirmed the presence of authorial individuality in theory and found numerous ways of inserting himself into his own work, "indirectly." As I have already noted, Charles Norris praised his brother's "whimsical . . . introduction of himself" into *McTeague* via an unnamed character who briefly appears in one scene.[18] In that moment, as in the use of autobiographical material that Norris adapted, especially for *Blix* and *The Pit*, Norris's own storytelling becomes a kind of game in which the possibility of self-representation, even self-revelation, is alternately entertained and resisted. But if Norris sometimes slipped oblique images of himself into his text on purpose, he also felt the potential danger of doing so inadvertently. The fear of involuntary self-revelation to an uncertain public partly explains Norris's determination to keep himself hidden behind his own words.

Written at the same time as some of Norris's most explicit formulations regarding authorial "remoteness" as narrative strategy, *The Pit* (1903) dramatizes the price of both self-representation and self-concealment by combining the motif of the actress with that of the financier. The figure of theater is cogent from the start of the novel both to the portrait of Laura and to Norris's depiction of the Board of Trade.[19] The very title of the book evokes a feature of the theater as well as of the stock exchange. Set directly in opposition to Laura's theatricality, however, is the invisibility of the financier, as he indirectly manipulates the price of wheat. In the course of the novel, actress and financier come to reflect each other as well as the figure of the author. But as the focus shifts to the financier, it is the absence rather than the presence of the performer that becomes the central feature of the act.

Whereas Laura Dearborn's impulse to perform is largely depicted in terms of her desire for self-representation, even exhibitionism, the financier Curtis Jadwin—the "Unknown Bull"—works in secret, carefully hidden behind the scenes. Jadwin thus becomes the counterpart of Laura, hell-bent on "display" of herself (404). This opposition reproduces the realist debate on authorial positioning: the financier—like the actress—projecting illusion, trying to sustain the confidence of an audience, dramatizing or obscuring his own visibility, provides another rich analogue and counterpoint to the figure of the novelist.

In the course of *The Pit*, the figure of Laura reproduces many of the issues raised by Lily Bart, Carrie Meeber, and other women onstage in realist texts. Here as elsewhere the difficulty of separating "idea" or representation from "self" is a recurrent focus. With her sense of herself as multiple selves, and her lack of security about where her roles end and she begins, Laura becomes a kind of nightmare version of the novelist, projecting himself into a variety of characters, struggling for the objectivity and distance that Norris repeatedly praised, the separation of author from both heroes and audience.[20]

It is from this point of view that Jadwin, in his greatest performance as the "Unknown Bull," suggests the other side of the coin. Like Carrie, or Lily Bart,

Laura indistinctly blends her "self" with every role she plays (representing the grief of Portia, Laura produces tears "as sincere as any she had ever shed" [295]). By contrast, Jadwin maintains an absolute division between himself and the appearance he projects in the theatrical arena of the market.[21] As the price of wheat begins to rise, and even once the existence of a grand manipulator becomes apparent to the public, neither Jadwin's wife nor his closest friends are aware of his central role in the drama. But with his "mask" completely covering his face, the strain on Jadwin of guarding his secret has disastrous consequences. At the level of plot it is partly responsible for the deterioration of his health and his marriage; it contributes (via his very success) to the ruin of many small farmers and businessmen. It causes the suicide of one of Jadwin's closest friends.

The analogy between the role-playing actress and the novelist may be more apparent than the link between novelist and financier.[22] But the details of Jadwin's dilemma in "the Pit" reproduce the emphasis on masking, distance, and isolation that characterizes many of Norris's evocations of authorship. With the realist imperative of authorial invisibility in mind, let us look at one climactic moment of the text to demonstrate how, for Norris, financier and novelist come to reflect each other.

I have noted how thoroughly Jadwin's identity is concealed from view as he works to consolidate his "corner." As Howard Horwitz puts it, only in the "climactic moment before his failure"[23] does Jadwin himself appear in "the Pit," venturing out onto the floor of the stock exchange at the moment of disaster. Jadwin's unexpected public appearance provides another version of the performance mode that has been typical of Laura throughout. But Jadwin's situation with regard to both his work and his audience also underscores Norris's own uncertain position in relation to text and reader. For Norris, as for James, Cather, and others, the reality of the represented world was directly dependent on authorial removal: "The more [the writer] differentiates himself from his story, the more remote his isolation[,] . . . the more will his story seem to have a life of its own."[24] Most of all, Norris insists, "when the catastrophe comes . . . we want to forget the author."[25] When the catastrophe comes in *The Pit*, however, the figure of Jadwin directly reverses this logic. The scene in which a broken, bewildered Jadwin is exposed to a raging audience is the prelude to chaos. A barrage of verbal violence accompanies personal humiliation and economic defeat. Having invisibly manipulated values on paper and enlisted public confidence in an illusion for too long, Jadwin is all but destroyed by the very public that he has deceived. When Jadwin's corner breaks, moreover, and Jadwin himself again disappears from public view, the "newspapers . . . of every city in the Union exploited him for 'stories'" (332).

If Jadwin may be seen as a figure for the writer, it is especially fitting that his final antagonistic relation to the public culminates in a moment of unmasking followed by the vengeance of the press. To be sure, Jadwin's experience (like Laura's) intermittently involves the exhilaration of performance, invention, and self-projection as well as disguise. But in this novel the distance from self-display to self-exposure and "exploitation of self" (404) is a short one, the difference between entertaining and coercing an audience is often unclear, and the enthusiasm of a crowd can become the antagonism of a mob.

Within *The Pit* the somewhat condescending and farcical perspective on turn-of-century reading habits that Norris projects through his image of the indiscriminate "pachyderm" is reproduced by the figures of Landry Court and Laura's sister Page (whose very name links her to bookish matters). "You are beautifully womanly," Landry tells Page as he takes leave of her one evening,

> "and so high-minded and well read. It's been inspiring to me, I want you should know that. Yes, sir, a real inspiration. . . ."
>
> "I like to read, if that's what you mean," she hastened to say.
>
> "By Jove, I've got to do some reading too. . . . I'll make time. I'll get that 'Stones of Venice' I've heard you speak of, and I'll sit up nights—and keep awake with black coffee—but I'll read that book from cover to cover." (222)

Like Wharton's "mechanical readers" who "*never skip a word*" but are ignorant of those more intuitive and spontaneous reading practices that Wharton sees as the only ground for "real intercourse between book and reader,"[26] Page and Landry constitute a parody of the drive for self-improvement that many turn-of-century writers saw as a threat to literary culture and "creative" reading.[27] Nonetheless, in *The Pit* the act of reading also becomes a recurrent trope for the idea of intimacy. Like many nineteenth-century readers, Page and Landry read aloud to each other, as do Laura and Jadwin during their best days. Indeed, when Laura and Jadwin abandon this long-standing practice, it becomes a sure sign of alienation and trouble between them. "How long is it since we've read any book together" (231) is a recurrent refrain when their difficult times begin (cf. 215–16, 231–36, 257, 262, 307).

Despite Norris's recurrent emphasis on the neutral voice and absent writer of the story, his conception of fiction participated in the same wish for some mode of human relationship through writing, and especially through reading, that we have seen elsewhere. Such a wish is implicit, for example, in Norris's well-known evocations of the oral storyteller spinning his yarn. Norris's yarn-spinner rhetoric is generally seen in terms of his disdain for "literariness," but it deserves further attention in the present context. The proximity of teller and listener implicit in the situation of an oral storyteller provides a sharp contrast to the professional writer of realist fiction who keeps himself, or herself, veiled and removed from text and audience. The very idea of a storyteller (like that of an actress) assumes a performer who is present and visible to others. Norris

often evoked an idyllic picture of the teller-listener situation: "young Greeks . . .
on marble terraces . . . listen[ing] to the thunderous roll of Homer's hexameter"
or "young boys" in "feudal castles" listening to the "minstrel [sing] of Roland."[28]
Whatever the historical status of such images, they suggest that Norris's repeated complaint over the lack of an American "epic," and his association of
novelist with oral poet, is also informed by nostalgia for the traditional relationship between listener and bard.[29] Similar concerns, as we have seen, informed
the work of many commentators of the period who mourned the "lost art of
reading," convinced that contemporary reading habits (like realism itself) were
eliminating "the personal equation" in writer-book-reader relations.[30]

To some extent the idea of reading as a catalyst for human contact, even intimacy, retains a foothold in Norris's last novel; but it is a tenuous and skeptical one. When *The Pit* first appeared (posthumously) in book form, it began
with the following words on the title page:

DEDICATED TO MY BROTHER
CHARLES TILMAN NORRIS
IN MEMORY OF CERTAIN LAMENTABLE TALES OF THE ROUND (DINING-ROOM)
TABLE HEROES, OF THE EPIC OF THE PEWTER PLATOONS, AND THE ROMANCE-
CYCLE OF "*GASTON LE FOX*," WHICH WE INVENTED, MAINTAINED AND FOUND
MARVELLOUS AT A TIME WHEN WE BOTH WERE BOYS.[31]

Recalling Norris's youth, when fictional worlds were mutually generated and
playfully shared, this elaborately personal dedication is anomalous for Norris.
Realist texts in general, as we have seen, tended to avoid such reminders of an
author's personal history.

Any dedication foregrounds the question of whom a text addresses. This
highly personal dedication to a brother, situated at the opening of a novel very
largely about siblings,[32] might seem to reconfirm that for Norris, as for other
readers of the period, the long-standing association of reading with proto-
personal intercourse was not easy to root out, however clearly conceptualized
the doctrine of authorial "self-suppression" and the fear of revealing too much
of one's self to the indiscriminate eyes of one's audience. Indeed, when I first
wrote the present chapter, this was just the point I meant to make. More recently, however, Bruce Nicholson has shown that the dedication of *The Pit* was
not written by Norris at all.[33] Instead, in keeping with the terse dedications of
Norris's other novels, *The Pit* was

DEDICATED
TO
MY DAUGHTER
JEANETTE WILLIAMSON NORRIS[34]

As Nicholson shows, the more elaborate sentimental dedication that has been
part of *The Pit* ever since it first appeared was written by Frank Norris's brother

Charles. This new evidence prevents me from taking the dedication as an additional sign of Frank Norris's ambivalence about professionalism and impersonality. But it suggests instead that we might take Charles Norris's insertion of himself into his brother's text as an extraordinary example of one contemporary reader's resistance to "objective" discourse. Although Charles Norris may have had many motives for rewriting the opening words of *The Pit*, one way of understanding this strange episode would be to see it as Charles Norris's effort to restore a sense of personal immediacy to his brother's most sophisticated and professional text.

The idea of a book as something shared by people is intermittently dramatized throughout *The Pit* via the two pairs of lovers who read. I would argue that Frank Norris did associate his writing with a more benign model of interaction and reciprocity than is suggested by the image of actress, financier, or self-effacing naturalist author. But as we have seen, Norris's last novel also implies a highly skeptical perspective on writing as public performance, representing an author's position as one of danger and exposure. When readers are imagined as undiscriminatingly voracious, or as an angry mob manipulated by an "Unknown Bull," the idea of reading as intimacy is relegated to the margins.

Something Fishy: Reading *The Financier*

Like Norris's "Unknown Bull," Dreiser's Cowperwood can be taken as a figure for the writer. Invisibly "manufactur[ing] fluctuations"[35] in the market, the financier is as dependent as the novelist not only on the public, with its pressures of supply and demand, but also on what Dreiser repeatedly calls the art of "illusion." Acting, dissembling, and stage presence are Cowperwood's own indispensable tools. In *The Financier* (1912),[36] as in *The Pit*, theatrical and financial arts (here consolidated in one figure) function together as governing metaphors. But Dreiser's scenes of reading in *The Financier* are at once more fearful and cynical than Norris's.

Unlike Norris, James, or Wharton, Dreiser published few theoretical or critical discussions of literary method. As George Becker remarks in *Documents of Modern Literary Realism*, "Dreiser was only incidentally a critic." Introducing a one-page article called "True Art Speaks Plainly," Becker comments that "the present selection states half of all [that Dreiser] ever had to say" about his aesthetic principles and practices. Dreiser's little essay says nothing about the reader or the position of the author in the text: it simply insists that the "sum and substance of literary as well as social morality may be expressed in three words—tell the truth." The novelist must "say what he knows to be true," Dreiser writes; this is the primary "business of the author," to express what he sees "without subterfuge."[37]

Here and elsewhere Dreiser's discourse of objectivity deflects attention from his rhetorical strategies and what Amy Kaplan calls his practice of "self-promotion,"[38] as well as from the fact that Dreiser's own particular form of truth-telling is fiction. Representing himself as a kind of reporter, recorder, or photographer, Dreiser takes a typical realist position. Yet with regard to the issue that has primarily concerned us here—the relation of author to represented world and reader—Dreiser is something of an anomaly as a realist. In theory he has virtually nothing to say about narration itself; he simply stresses the value of presenting "life as it is, the facts as they exist."[39] In practice, he often ignores the imperative of authorial invisibility as formulated by James, Norris, Wharton, and others.

The narrator of *The Financier* addresses the reader directly on numerous occasions, with limited assertions of commonly shared ground. Noting Frank Cowperwood's birth in Philadelphia, the novel begins by stating that "many of the things that we and he knew later were not then in existence—the telegraph, telephone, express company, ocean steamer" (5). Here Dreiser's communal "we" includes the reader in the narrator's perspective and experience. Elsewhere a more reflective, philosophical "we" also points to the presence of a governing intelligence, interpreting "the facts." These "'editorial' paragraph[s]," as Stuart Sherman called them in an early and influential attack on Dreiser's work, subvert Dreiser's claim to objectivity; they constitute a "coloring [of] the news."[40]

If both Dreiser's authorial "we" and his digressive intrusions make him something of an exception in the realist company, they by no means ally him with the popular "friendly" writers we have considered.[41] Unlike the inclusive, proto-personal "we" used by Wister, Crawford, and others, Dreiser's "we" never makes the reader part of the family. It never becomes a marker of shared moral norms or common literary tastes. It is far from cozy or reassuring. On the contrary. Either it is highly concrete and pragmatic (noting technological innovations, landmarks, and other historical phenomena "we" are aware of), or it becomes peremptory, assertive, even pugnacious. Dreiser's pronouncements about ethics, law, convention, science, and so on imply an uneven relationship between narrator and reader, an insistent assertion of the teller's professional authority. This writer-reader interchange is neither witty, casual, nor intimate.

Dreiser's narrative posture of wise omniscience is intermittently emphatic in both *Sister Carrie* and *The Financier*. But neither his repeated emphasis on "facts" nor his authoritative narration could ward off Dreiser's own sense of being inadequately concealed beneath his words, precariously situated as an author, both within his culture and within his texts. For Dreiser, the profession of authorship was fraught with hesitation. His background (lower class, midwestern, son of an immigrant) must have made his own sense of cultural authority and his relation to the novel-reading audience particularly uncertain.[42] Amy Kaplan has suggested that Dreiser's magazine experience taught him self-promotional techniques based on the premise that "men do not represent themselves directly in their writing."[43] Yet the question of where within one's work one's self resides was a pressing and unresolved question for Dreiser (as for Norris) throughout his career. Although he never confronted this issue explicitly when discussing his "art," recurrent motifs throughout *The Financier* project a fearful and embattled image of the writer, quite different not only from his purposively marketed authorial persona but also from the stolid authority of his narrative voice. At the same time, Dreiser's "editorial" passages constitute some of that theorizing on the nature of self-representation and reading that Dreiser never produced in the form of critical essays.

On the face of it, *The Financier,* based on the life of a rich and powerful historical figure, has still less to do with Dreiser's own professional experience than the story of Carrie Meeber. Yet finance itself is represented as an "art" from the beginning of the novel—particularly the art of illusion.[44] Throughout *The Financier,* Cowperwood is nothing if not a manipulator of appearance (it was always his "business and his intention to hide his real feelings" [388]). His "inscrutable" eyes (25) are only one recurrent sign that in every situation he himself remains hidden. The financier sees life as only "a play of sorts" (388), a "great dumb show" (242); "his policy [is] make-believe" (383). In this sense Cowperwood, like Dreiser, is an observer on the one hand, a creator of fictions on the other. Despite Dreiser's emphasis on his own lack of "subterfuge" as a writer, the figure of the masked financier bent on outwitting and duping his audience reflects something of Dreiser's own relation to his fictions and his readers.

From the start of the novel one of the most striking things about Cowperwood is his apparent autonomy. Unlike Carrie, Laura, and other actress figures in realist texts, Cowperwood seems to have no trouble differentiating between "himself" and the various roles he plays. With many voices, many faces, he adapts quickly and easily to changing conditions. Manipulating, appropriating, and creating, Cowperwood's "self" does not seem to need the support of its surroundings.

Yet Dreiser's narrative voice repeatedly suggests that "our" self is more deeply colored by what it makes, wears, and owns than may appear. "We think we are individual, separate, above houses and material objects generally," says the narrator, describing Cowperwood's growing interest in the architectural plan and the interior furnishings of his new house:

> But there is a subtle connection which makes them reflect us quite as much as we reflect them. They lend dignity, subtlety, force, each to the other, and what beauty, or lack of it, there is, is shot back and forth from one to the other as a shuttle in a loom, weaving, weaving. Cut the thread, separate a man from that which is rightfully his own, characteristic of him, and you have a peculiar figure, half success, half failure, much as a spider without its web, which will never be its whole self again until all its dignities and emoluments are restored. (98)

Joining author, narrator, Cowperwood, and reader in the inclusive "we" of its opening sentence, this passage implies a symbiotic relationship between the self and the things that represent it, not only to others but also to itself.[45] Ultimately *The Financier* suggests that the creative activities of both Cowperwood and Dreiser implicate them in a relation of dependency like that of a spider to its web.

According to this passage, considerable danger results from "cutt[ing] the thread [that connects] a man [to] that which is rightfully his own, characteristic of him." Indeed, Dreiser's work is full of characters who do not survive the separation. When George Hurstwood, having crossed the border into Canada with Carrie, uses a fictitious surname to sign the hotel registry, he realizes that this "was the largest concession to necessity he felt like making. His initials he could not spare."[46] After Roberta's death in *An American Tragedy*, Clyde Griffiths too finds he cannot "spare" his initials when choosing an alias, although his inability to "cut the thread," so to speak, only hastens his destruction. Even Cowperwood draws considerable support from his own name. On one occasion his full name complete with middle initial, becomes a source of stability and reassurance.[47]

Many of Dreiser's "editorial" passages suggest that Frank A. Cowperwood is less autonomous than he believes—more implicated in and dependent on the things that reflect him back to himself as himself. But if Cowperwood's "self" is implicit in and reflected by numerous artifacts, possessions, and signs (from the house built by his architect[48] to his own middle initial), how much more so is a writer implicated in his or her text. The analogy between Cowperwood and his creator is only reinforced by Dreiser's choice of spider and web and the figure of weaving to illustrate the point. Drawing attention to the "subtle connection which makes [the things we own] reflect us quite as much as we reflect them," the trope of spinning and weaving introduces the question of art, or at least craft, into the discourse.[49]

Traditionally, both spiders and weavers have long been associated with storytelling. The spider image reflects Dreiser's relationship to his work in several ways. Most prominently, it reveals Dreiser's uncertainty about just how separate from his text, or how well concealed within it, he really is. But the analogy between insect and novelist raises further questions about how the reader and the act of reading are imagined. A writer's work, like a spider's, is created to interest others. But does a writer trap victims as a spider does a fly? In the course of *The Financier*, images drawn from the world of nature repeatedly point to both the aggression and the deceptions implicit in the idea of author-text-reader relations.

One of the best-known scenes in *The Financier* is the struggle between lobster and squid in a fish market window, an ongoing "drama" (8) that mesmerizes the young Cowperwood and "clear[s] things up considerably" (7) for him.[50]

Conceived as Darwinian parable, this battle demonstrates to Cowperwood how life is "organized" (8). As Walter Benn Michaels puts it, the "moral of this story [for] Cowperwood . . . is the irrelevance of anything but strength in a world 'organized' so that the strong feed on the weak."[51]

Yet the fish tank "drama," this "tragedy" (7)—cast in theatrical language from the start—also teaches the young Cowperwood the value of illusion as a source of strength and an aid to survival. Although the lobster in the tank does not appear to be watching its enemy ("You could not tell in which way his beady, black . . . eyes were looking [7]), its "eyes are never off the body of the squid" (7). It is not far-fetched to see the lobster as a model for Cowperwood himself. Cowperwood's own "cold, fishy eye[s]" are "inscrutable" (203, 25), "you could tell nothing by his eyes" (25).[52] As Donald Pizer notes, "'subtlety'—the ability to mask one's true nature and intentions . . . is the key to Cowperwood's success in *The Financier*."[53]

But if the lobster is linked to Cowperwood, it is also linked to Dreiser, whose own capacity for "illusion-making" belongs to another medium. In an early article, "The Aquarium," Dreiser draws a direct analogy between the strategies of sea creatures and the "daily career" of human beings.[54] In spite of Dreiser's own claims to "truth" and to an utter lack of "subterfuge," these deceptive sea creatures (like the spider) become figures for the novelist. In this context the voracious lobster also becomes a figure for the reader.

The fish market "drama" bears a fanciful but compelling relation to the potential dangers of authorship. The squid in the tank—"the rightful prey" of the lobster (7)—is slowly consumed by the predator. The lobster's beady black inscrutable eyes seem to see nothing, but in fact see everything. The lobster's opponent has no weapon of defense at his disposal—only ink. With the benefit of this resource he hides himself from the eyes of the lobster and tries to escape, disappearing in "a cloud of ink" (8). But eventually his ink bag is depleted—"emptier than ever" (8). As a figure for the writer, insufficiently protected from the devouring eyes of readers, the squid is trapped in a public place beneath a cloud of ink that only partially conceals him.

For the squid, the cloud of ink is on the one hand a protective cover, on the other hand life's blood. From this point of view, the squid's situation highlights certain advantages inherent in the writer's position. A writer is, unlike a squid, separate from his ink, his text, his projected illusion—and his watchful readers, especially at the moment of consumption. Still, like Wharton's veteran fiction writer Mrs. Dale, who imagines that she literally has ink in her veins,[55] Dreiser's figure of the squid restates some of the questions already raised by his spider image—questions of separation, of the tangled interconnections between a creature, what it creates, for whom, and to what end.[56] Dreiser's rendering of the life-and-death struggle between squid and lobster, blurring the boundaries between self, ink, and other, reflects a fantasy about writing, and especially about the dangers of being read, that is highly charged, intensely personal, and culturally characteristic.

At the end of *The Financier,* Dreiser describes another sea creature that "gets his living" through an astounding capacity for camouflage (441). The black grouper, with its various names and dazzling color changes, is a source of wonder and envy to the narrator, who contemplates the fish with rapt attention, particularly impressed by its "almost unbelievable power of simulation":

> In electrical mechanics we pride ourselves on our ability to make over one brilliant scene into another in the twinkling of an eye, and flash before the gaze of an onlooker picture after picture, which appear and disappear as we look. The directive control of Mycteroperca [the black grouper] over its appearance is much more significant. You cannot look at it long, without feeling that you are witnessing something spectral and unnatural, so brilliant is its power to deceive. (447)

The novelist's own capacity to produce "brilliant scene[s]" and "picture after picture" necessarily pales by comparison with the power of this "implement of illusion[,] . . . [this] living lie, [this] creature whose business it is to appear what it is not" (447).

Insofar as the "business" of Dreiser's sea creatures reflect aspects of his own profession, the highly defensive function of their "simulations," and the aggressive posture of those who watch, deserve additional attention. Throughout *The Financier,* the "authorial" narrator is variously envious and contemptuous of creatures who thrive as a result of the illusions they project. Remaining hidden, making it one's "business . . . to appear what [one] is not," is the ground of both power and beauty in this text; conversely, the failure of illusion has devastating consequences. For the squid (as for the black grouper), to be left, so to speak, with an empty ink bag, unable to manipulate appearances, means death. In the final image of the book, Cowperwood himself is said to be as "bereft of illusion as a windless moon" (448).

When Aileen Butler tells Cowperwood that she means to visit him in prison, he instructs her to disguise herself. But like George Hurstwood and Clyde Griffiths clinging to their initials, so Aileen with her flamboyant clothes: she cannot spare them. In a rare comic moment in Dreiser's work, Aileen appears at the prison, "her face . . . concealed by a thick green veil" (411) but otherwise conspicuously dressed as usual. Cowperwood's prison "overseer," Bonhag, is immediately "struck by the evident youth of Aileen, even though he could not see her face. This now was something in accordance with what he had expected of Cowperwood. A man who could steal five hundred thousand dollars and set a whole city by the ears must have wonderful adventures of all kinds and Aileen looked like a true adventure" (412). More like Lily Bart than Cowperwood, Aileen can only represent herself (both her own deepest needs and her cultural situation) even when she thinks she is disguised. This is Dreiser's worry too. From his early evocation of the shame Carrie feels when she becomes "conscious of being gazed upon and understood for what she was,"[57] through *An American Tragedy*, where he explores the question of imposture and exposure more elaborately than ever before (and with no "editorial" intrusions),[58] Dreiser's work is pervaded by his own uncomfortable sense of being all too visible beneath his "cloud of ink," exposed to readers who might see more about his way of working, his cultural status, or his own personality than he had intended.

At one point in *The Financier*, Cowperwood is represented as a consummate game player, like "one of those . . . famous and historic chess-players, who could sit with their backs to a group of rivals playing fourteen men at once, calling out all the moves in turn, remembering all the positions of all the men on all the boards, and winning" (99).[59] As a novelist, Dreiser often imagined himself in an analogous position of concealment, with his readers as potential rivals. The idea of the invisible author as something of a game player is a harbinger of modernism. While working on *The Financier*, Dreiser often referred to writing as a game;[60] yet playfulness was never one of his specialties. Even late in his career, the issue of imposture and exposure was still too urgent, the suspicion of being visible in one's own text was too strong, for Dreiser to joke about these things.

By the second decade of the twentieth century, many writers had come to feel quite comfortable with the sense of being absent from or invisible within their own writing, "refined out of existence," as James Joyce put it in 1916.[61] Twenty-three years earlier Henry James had seized on Flaubert's notion that the writer "must be present in his work like God in Creation, invisible and almighty, everywhere felt but nowhere seen."[62] Joyce's subsequent version of this formula represents the author rather less majestically: still "like the God of the creation," but one who is "paring his fingernails" (221). This change of register was only one sign that authors would soon be occupying increasingly comic and skeptical positions vis-à-vis both text and reader. Edith Wharton's *Age of Innocence* is a good example of a borderline text that still affirms the principles of the realist enterprise while playing an elaborate, sometimes comic game of authorial hide-and-seek with the reader.

Excavating Granny: Locating the Author in *The Age of Innocence*

Like many of the other writers we have considered, Edith Wharton advocated a neutral, objectified mode of narration, condemning "the old-fashioned intrusion of the author"[63] into the text. *The Age of Innocence* is a novel that directly thematizes "the superiority of implication and analogy over direct action, and of silence over rash words"[64]—or, one might say, any words. Within the represented world of the novel, the inhabitants of Old New York, epitomized by May

Welland, regularly convey pointed messages through silence. Alternatively, they say one thing and mean another. Those familiar with the code have no trouble reading the real import of seemingly innocuous gestures and statements. Newland Archer comes to despise this "hieroglyphic world" (41) full of "mute message[s]" (224); but he learns to respect its power.

The effectiveness of silent manipulation and words that mean what they do not say is nowhere more impressively demonstrated (to both Archer and the reader) than in the final banquet that sets the seal on Ellen Olenska's removal from Old New York. Early in the novel, when Archer dines with Sillerton Jackson, he has the feeling that the old man "would probably finish his meal on Ellen Olenska" (36). But the cannibalistic destruction of Ellen takes place only later, at the farewell dinner—or so Archer comes to believe, as he sits at the festive table, "his glance travell[ing] from one placid well-fed face to another" (279). This episode, a tour de force of narration, is entirely focalized through Archer, who both observes and interprets the scene. It would be hard to find, even in the work of James or Cather, a scene more fully purged of the authorial persona. Experiencing himself as disembodied ("float[ing] somewhere between chandelier and ceiling" [279]), Archer nonetheless arrives at a radical perception. Seeing himself and Ellen as victims of a destructive conspiracy, he suddenly understands that they have been both unmasked and misread. "And then it came over him, in a vast flash made up of many broken gleams, that to all of [the other guests] . . . he and Mme. Olenska were lovers, lovers in the extreme sense peculiar to 'foreign' vocabularies" (279).

In one sense the climactic dinner scene demonstrates Wharton's own disembodiment in the text, her disappearance into discourse;[65] but it also implies a link between being disembodied or dislocated (floating "somewhere between chandelier and ceiling") and being powerless, nullified. Wharton's own perspective on the events and characters of *The Age of Innocence,* her judgment of the represented world as a whole, is effectively obscured throughout the novel. It is not so easy to read the irony of this narrative voice; unlike the double messages of the characters, Wharton's irony is irresolvably ambiguous. Few of her novels have evoked so much disagreement. The question whether *Age of Innocence* is a devastating indictment or a nostalgic evocation of patriarchal (or matriarchal) Old New York continues to be debated by readers of the book.[66]

The Age of Innocence is clearly informed by Wharton's awareness of the debate over whether or not authorial personality should pervade a work of fiction, even though the question of what would constitute such personality remains unresolved.[67] As Judith Fryer, Elizabeth Ammons, and others have shown, aspects of Wharton's own experience and attitudes are projected through all the central characters of *Age.*[68] Identified with Old New York like May, ambivalent about it like Archer, living in Paris like Ellen, Wharton herself is everywhere and nowhere in the novel. It is precisely her position as disembodied, invisible presence that repays further attention.

In principle, Wharton was increasingly committed to professionalism and narrative masking. The narrative voice in *Age of Innocence*, unlike that of *House of Mirth* (and unlike Dreiser's), never takes a pontificating, "authorial" tone with regard to either aesthetic or moral issues. Yet despite the irony and other distancing strategies that inform the narration, the novel reveals considerable conflict about whether novelists are (or should be) hidden or accessible within their own work. It is worth noting in this context that among the many theatrical motifs in the text is a recurrent allusion to Boucicault's comic drama *The Shaughraun*—a play in which, as we have already seen, the author himself often appeared onstage in the title role.[69] Wharton knew as well as Henry James that Boucicault's success as "the Shaughran" was an element of the play's popularity. She probably assumed that at least some of her readers would know this as well. But if recurrent passing references to *The Shaughraun* in *Age of Innocence* constitute a sly reminder of a possible authorial presence in the work, the repeated reenactment of *The Shaughraun*'s parting scene (the one that Archer "always . . . went to see" [98]) foregrounds the motif of invisibility itself. The renunciation scene in all its forms depends for its meaning on the kiss and/or the lover's presence going unnoticed, or at least unremarked.

In *Age of Innocence*, as in *House of Mirth*, being seen is a recurrent thematic focus and a trigger for major plot developments. Like Lily coming out of Selden's bachelor apartments or leaving Trenor's house at midnight, Ellen (and Archer) have a talent for being seen in the wrong place at the wrong time. Yet *not* being seen—being absent or invisible—becomes a more prominent motif in the later novel. Many of Wharton's texts are pervaded by a tension between visible and invisible, absent and present women in particular. Virtually every woman character in *Age of Innocence* provides a variant of the set of problems surrounding authorial positioning. If Ellen, like her own thin shoulders, is too exposed from the first moment of her appearance in the Wellands' opera box,[70] May is the perfect example of a masked figure, unobtrusively measuring and plotting every move, up to and including her own deathbed speeches. (Before she dies, she tells her son Dallas that "once, when she asked [Archer] to, [he'd] given up the thing [he] most wanted." But as Archer says, "She never asked me" [297].)[71]

From the first, May manages to make her absent presence felt in every encounter between Ellen and Archer: Ellen realizes that Archer is to "take care of" her, by May's request, while May is in Florida (112); May tells Archer that he "must be sure to go and see Ellen" when he lies to her about his reason for going to Washington (223). Working quietly behind the scenes, May engineers Archer's exclusion from the family councils, and finally Ellen's expulsion from

Old New York itself. Like James's Maggie Verver in *The Golden Bowl*, May acts decisively, even masterfully, but she is never seen to be doing so.

As a silent presence, working carefully offstage, May is a good candidate for an authorial figure (as is Ellen, destroyed in part by her own high profile). Yet Old Granny Mingott is a still more evocative one, and one who is comically framed as such, with specific emphasis on the issue of reemergence. The portrait of May raises questions about the function of masking and silence and their relation to hidden intentions or realities. But the portrait of Granny also foregrounds the expectation and possibility that the absent figure will reappear. In addition, many other signs point to a connection between Granny Mingott and Edith Wharton as woman, person, and author.

With her "characteristic independence" (27) and social propriety, her "moral courage" (15) and her flair for innovative, functional interior design,[72] Granny (as Martin Scorsese implied in his 1993 film adaptation) reflects aspects of Wharton's own character and experience.[73] Moreover, as the generally unseen mover behind the scenes of Old New York, the "Matriarch of the line" (14) shares certain qualities with the professional fiction writer. Plotting the entrances, exits, and costumes in the Mingott opera box and drawing rooms, "Granny's orders" (17) leave their indelible mark on society; yet Granny herself never appears there in the flesh.[74]

The wedding scene epitomizes the governing paradox with comic force. This official ceremony, which takes place right in the middle of the novel, celebrates a veiled figure and the removal of her veil in a representation of consummated desire. But Wharton's rendering of the wedding also raises questions about a number of desires less fully endorsed by the community of Old New York. The wedding scene centers not only on several veiled, unknown, and unseen women, but also on several modes of public exposure. "A stormy discussion as to whether the wedding presents should be 'shown' had darkened the last hours before the wedding . . . and . . . the matter [had been] . . . decided (in the negative) by Mrs. Welland's saying, with indignant tears: 'I should as soon turn the reporters loose in my house'" (153).

As Archer awaits May's arrival, his consuming preoccupation is not his bride but rather the absent Ellen Olenska, specifically the question whether or not Ellen will make an unexpected appearance in church. Yet the suspense-filled hush with which the wedding episode begins is also due to uncertainty over the whereabouts of another missing woman: a persistent topic of discussion throughout the wedding preparations had been whether or not Granny Mingott would decide to subject the assembled company to the "monstrous exposure of her person" in church (154).

Granny's immobile "person" with its layers of fat is a vivid image in the novel. With considerable panache, Wharton repeatedly draws attention not only to the defensive armor of Granny's flesh but also to "the traces of a small face [that] survived as if awaiting excavation" (27). Granny's habit of making provocative statements and unexpected decisions adds spice to the debate about whether her retired person will or will not emerge into public space at her granddaughter's wedding. "Wild rumours had been abroad the day before to the effect that Mrs. Manson Mingott, in spite of her physical disabilities, had resolved on being present at the ceremony; and the idea was so much in keeping with her sporting character that bets ran high at the clubs as to her being able to walk up the nave and squeeze into a seat" (154). So fervent is Granny's determination to overcome the logistical obstacles to her desire that she consults her carpenter about making changes in the structure of the front pew, and "her relations . . . could have covered with gold the ingenious person who suddenly discovered that [Mrs. Mingott's enormous bath chair] was too wide to pass between the iron uprights of the awning which extended from the church door to the curbstone" (154).

By the time the ceremony begins, the question of Granny's appearance in church seems to have been settled in the negative. But at a crucial moment, a blurring of syntactic reference creates a climactic disruption both of the discourse and of Archer's inner equilibrium, underscoring the ambiguity that still surrounds the question of precisely which women will remain invisible. When the best man catches his first glimpse of the bride, his sudden exclamation, "I say: *she's here!*" (156), recalls the conviction of the "sporting minority" that Granny might after all make an appearance in church at the very last moment (155). From both Archer's and the reader's point of view, however, the ambiguity of the best man's exclamation also reopens the possibility that Ellen Olenska will suddenly turn up behind Medora Manson's "fantastic figure" at the end of the wedding procession (156).

The veil of ambiguous reference and the very profusion of "anonymous spectators" and "unknown" ladies (157) in this scene imply that an additional figure hovers behind and around the absent and present women of Old New York. Given the text's emphasis on reading through the unsaid, it is not far-fetched to link Granny's wish to appear in church with Edith Wharton's ambivalent position in relation to her represented world. Here and elsewhere the absent/present matriarch of the tribe, whose audacity is always threatening to violate hallowed conventions, becomes a figure for Wharton herself, hidden by her text but threatening to appear, perhaps "awaiting," even inviting "excavation." Granny, we are told, had "philosophically" accepted her "submergence" in "the immense accretion of flesh which had descended on her in middle life" (27). Yet, as we have seen, Granny herself reopens the shocking and tantalizing possibility of her bodily "exposure" in public; her doing so provides a fine focus on Wharton's mixed feelings about the pleasures and pitfalls of authorial "visibility in fiction."[75]

Unlike Norris's jongleur or Curtis Jadwin, and unlike Dreiser's Cowperwood—symbiotically attached to and ultimately threatened by their own public performances—Wharton's Mrs. Manson Mingott grows out of a comic impulse which suggests that perhaps not every narrative crux is a life-and-death issue after all. Once authorial positioning becomes a game and a source of comedy, we can be sure that authorial invisibility has been firmly established as a narrative convention and in some sense defused as a source of fear and trembling.

Reconstituting the Authorial Person

By the 1920s the invisible author and the freestanding text were widely familiar principles of narration. Still, the difficulty of imagining a text without an author remained. In an early passage of *The Financier*, Cowperwood is said to appreciate art because it is life interpreted through "a personality" (60).[76] As we have seen, the association of fiction with the individuality of the writer was a firmly rooted interpretive practice until well after the turn of the century. Despite the realist emphasis on authorial self-effacement, the idea that a book expressed the personality of its author was encouraged by much popular fiction and many discussions of books and reading.[77] We have seen that even writers such as James, Cather, and Norris, who adopted authorial invisibility as an aesthetic principle, not only were susceptible to the notion of authorial presence when they read the work of others, but also could still imagine the fading pleasures of being read that way themselves.

Dreiser was well aware that the presence of an author's personality within a text was a projected "illusion,"[78] but he was also convinced that a central pleasure of reading for many people was the sense of personal connection that certain kinds of texts allowed. As an editor, Dreiser capitalized on this understanding. Unlike his published statements about his own fiction, Dreiser's letters to those who wrote for him, or held the purse strings of the magazines he managed, reveal the considerable thought he devoted to both reading habits and narrative strategies. In 1907, when Dreiser had been editor of *The Delineator* for six months, H. L. Mencken was adapting a series of baby-care articles by a Baltimore doctor for Dreiser to print. Dreiser recommended some changes in the rhetorical strategy of the piece, with particular emphasis on the advantage of direct address. "Now, in regard to 'When the Baby Has Diptheria,'" Dreiser wrote,

> I want to say that this is a fine article. I like this man and his ideas . . . [but] instead of talking at the mother, [he] talks *about* diptheria; it ought to be a direct statement. . . . Instead of saying ["there still lingers in the United States a superstitious dread of antitoxin",] it ought to be about as follows: "You probably know a great deal about doctoring your children and some one has told you that

antitoxin is a deadly poison or a filthy drug. It is nothing of the sort; if you are a wise mother you will listen closely to the wonderful facts in connection with this discovery." (*Letters,* 85)

Dreiser took it for granted that readers assumed the presence of a person at the other end of a text—even a conglomerate text such as a magazine—and he believed that this assumption, this desire or need in the reader, could be cultivated. Early in his term at *The Delineator,* he proposed the establishment of a correspondence department to handle the influx of thousands of readers' letters which he had successfully elicited.[79] Writing to the president of the Butterick Publishing Company, Dreiser suggested that a correspondence department could provide "serious personal consideration" of all the letters received by the magazine. Dreiser notes:

> The average person who writes to *The Delineator* does not for one minute suppose that he is writing to an organization which receives his letter and passes it around more or less perfunctorily from place to place. He thinks he is writing to a magazine which has a single effective personality at the head of it, and that this personality will see his or her letter, understand his or her needs and answer in accordance with the same. It is this sense of personal contact which makes so many of the readers of the *Ladies' Home Journal* think that paper is their particular paper. They can get a personal reply every time they write. (*Letters,* 83)

Dreiser's analysis is informed by a keen sense of the practical advantages to the magazine of promoting an illusion of personal responsiveness to readers. In this Dreiser shares the attitude of many other ambitious turn-of-century editors, whose practices Christopher Wilson has described.[80] Dreiser's conviction that readers read "for the author"—for a "sense of personal contact"—is here pressed into the service of promotional goals. He proposes to use his insight into people's reading habits for the benefit of the magazine by setting up a department that will represent the responsive personality which he believes all readers seek. Like the wizard in *The Wizard of Oz* (1900), he will create the fiction of a strong personality behind the disembodied voice.

But to say that Dreiser knew how to manipulate the illusion of the "man behind the pen" is neither to discount the force of his perception about reading habits nor to show that Dreiser was above reading for the author himself. By the end of the century, editors, advertisers, and interviewers were increasingly aware of the advantages to be gained by using the printed word to manipulate personality. Dreiser saw how to capitalize on his conviction that magazine readers turned to the printed page for a "sense of personal contact." But at the same time, he often relished "the flavor of [an author's] personality" when he himself was reading. "I like this man," Dreiser wrote to Mencken after reading the doctor's baby-care article. Like many other readers of the period, Dreiser himself often read "through" printed matter to some perception of an originating author. "*With the Procession* is as clear to me today as the day I read it," Dreiser wrote to Henry Blake Fuller in 1911, "and the flavor of your personality stays with it, of course" (*Letters*, 126). Despite Dreiser's readiness to profit from illusions of personal presence that he could manipulate, he himself read Fuller—as Cather read Du Maurier, as James read H. G. Wells, as Norris read Bullen[81]—with considerable pleasure at the sense of entering into "relations" with "a new acquaintance." Although realist writers were well aware at one level that the sense of personality in a text was created by means of a rhetorical strategy, such knowledge did not dispel the "flavor" of an author's "personality" when they themselves were readers.[82]

The most sophisticated turn-of-century novelists knew that in some sense they could control the relation between themselves and their own fictions only up to a point. In personal letters, Norris often joked about his literary persona and his "immortal worruk." "Don't this look like the kind of letter a real live literary man would write," he quipped, "the kind they reproduce in the autobiographies?"[83] Yet for Norris, as for others, the authorial masquerade was always uncertain, even treacherous. Norris's comic habit of signing his letters "Owgooste" (Trina's pants-wetting brother in *McTeague*) only reasserts the characteristic authorial concern with potential self-exposure. So too, Wharton generates a comic game of peekaboo with Granny, but as late as 1935 she spoke of having put her "soul" into her novels.[84] Authorial personality was a construct made of words, to be manipulated for effect; but at the same time it was often felt to be deeply identified with what Hawthorne called the writer's "inmost me"—something dangerously far from a fiction.

Afterword

**All civilization comes through literature now, especially in
our country.**

William Dean Howells, *The Rise of Silas Lapham* (1885)

Among writers such as Howells, James, and Wharton, Theodore Dreiser was
an outsider. He was a first-generation American from a poor family in the
Midwest. He had little education, not to speak of "culture." When he published *Sister Carrie,* his work elicited outrage on grounds that ranged from the
moral to the grammatical. Until well into the 1940s, scholars who were interested in Dreiser had to explain themselves.[1] In 1950, in an influential essay
titled "Reality in America," Lionel Trilling attacked Dreiser for his aesthetic
limitations and his lack of moral consciousness.[2] Dreiser's work survived the as-
sault, but it remained an anomaly throughout the era of the New Criticism,
when aesthetic harmony, structural complexity, and linguistic subtlety were the
criteria for "literature."

Despite the low standing that Dreiser's work had for so long, Dreiser participated in a cultural elite from the moment he began to write fiction. When
he began his first novel, he chose to write in a mode that had a specific cultural
meaning. He himself clearly distinguished between his fiction and his other
"literary" work. As a novelist, he moved "up" to a cultural position higher than
the one he had occupied as a journalist or as an editor of women's magazines,
and higher too than the position occupied by his successful songwriter brother.
As a young novelist, Dreiser did not make more money than his brother Paul
(whose "On the Banks of the Wabash" became the official state song of Indiana), but he gained an imaginative foothold on a higher cultural plane.[3]

I want to end this book by suggesting that the realist enterprise participated
in the consolidation of a "high culture" of letters toward the end of the nineteenth century. By conceiving of the text as a window that would open onto reality without the mediation of an authorial "personality," the realist aesthetic
shared a conception of discourse and of audience with other emergent "high"

cultural modes of the period. The ideal of depersonalized narration embraced by the realists has its analogues not only in the "objective" reporting that came to distinguish the *New York Times* from popular tabloids, but also in the impersonality that began to characterize legal and medical discourse, and in the "disinterestedness" that became the sign of serious scholarship.[4] By the same token, the distance between author and reader prescribed by realist theory has a parallel in the separation of the audience from the stage which became conventional in American theaters and opera houses toward the end of the nineteenth century. Like the rhetoric of realism, the emerging norms for "civilized" behavior in the theater and the opera constructed the audience as silent observers, not active participants in the aesthetic performance presented to view.[5]

As Lawrence Levine, Richard Brodhead, and others have suggested, the emerging "high culture" that took shape at the end of the century was a reality intensely experienced both by the many people who sought to get in and by those who struggled to keep the upstarts out. But it is important to note that American high culture was a fluid and porous idea, not a well-defined space with policeable borders. Conventions, whether literary or social, gain meaning and force in a particular context. In the 1880s and 1890s, realism was affirmed as a superior mode of fiction by many writers and reviewers who looked down on sentimental or historical romance. There was considerable cultural capital in writing (and reading) realism. But, as we have seen, many contemporary readers resisted what they experienced as the passive reader role inscribed in the realist text,[6] and realist authors themselves were not always consistent in their reading habits or their criteria for literary value. The most widely agreed upon conventions cannot constrain the behavior of everyone in a particular social or cultural formation. Conventions of reading are even more protean than most. There are many ways to enforce the norm of silence in a theatrical audience (or public school or library). But within the limits of what is published and available, readers in a democracy can choose to read texts that their teachers and peers might reject; and readers can read the same texts in different ways.

The realists and those who endorsed them looked down their noses at the idea of reading as "a kind of conversation" with an author. Writers who went on encouraging this practice at the turn of the century were inferior by the prevailing standards of literary sophistication. But while the idea of an engaged human author receded as a value in some quarters, it reemerged as a value in others. The point is not merely that, as we have seen, the stubborn habit of identifying a book with an author persisted, even among many writers and readers who believed they should have known better. The point is also that the very conventions denigrated in one area of literary culture regained new vitality in another.

We have seen that just when the realists were consolidating their position in the pantheon of the "serious" by eliminating dedications, forewords, afterwords, narrative interventions, and the personal voice, many best-sellers were reaffirming these same devices. At the same time, moreover, the personal voice and the rhetoric of direct address were also adapted to new uses by writers engaged in other modes of discourse, especially writers who were intent on crossing cultural boundaries.

In his preface to *The Souls of Black Folk* (1903), W. E. B. Du Bois begins: "Herein lie buried many things which if read with patience may show the strange meaning of being black here at the dawning of the Twentieth Century. This meaning is not without interest to you, Gentle Reader; for the problem of the Twentieth Century is the problem of the color line. . . . Need I add," Du Bois notes, by way of concluding his prefatory remarks, "that I who speak here am bone of the bone and flesh of the flesh of them that live within the Veil [separating white from black]?"[7]

When Du Bois addresses the "Gentle Reader," he does not, like many of the popular novelists we have considered, define his readers as his friends and draw them into an exclusive circle of the like-minded. On the contrary, he invokes the "Gentle Reader" in his "Forethought," and again in the "After-Thought" that ends the book, to emphasize his own distance and difference from his audience. One might say that he uses the rhetorical strategy rejected by the realists to achieve some of their own goals. He seeks to represent a social reality with accuracy and indeed objectivity. But for his particular purposes it is indispensable to draw expressly on personal experience and to identify himself, the author, as a black man: "I who speak here am bone of the bone and flesh of the flesh of them that live within the Veil."

In one of the most frequently cited passages of *The Souls of Black Folk,* Du Bois projects an image of himself as a reader which becomes an image of himself as a full-fledged member of American society. "I sit with Shakespeare and he winces not," Du Bois writes. "Across the color line I move arm in arm with Balzac and Dumas. . . . I summon Aristotle, Aurelius, and what soul I will, and they come all graciously with no scorn nor condescension" (87). We have seen that the common practice of imagining a book as a person had become a sign of naïveté or nostalgia for many writers at the turn of the century. But by drawing on the familiar idea of reading as intercourse with an author, Du Bois adapts the trope of books as people to new rhetorical and social ends.

Du Bois's image of himself as a reader serves his purposes in several ways. First and foremost, of course, the authors he mentions are white. To read them is to cross the "color line" and indeed to seize the initiative there: to "summon." Second, Du Bois specifies writers who in one sense or another had come to be thought of as "classics" by the turn of the century.[8] To assert his familiarity with these authors was to claim a place not only in America but in the recently sacralized American high culture of letters.[9]

Du Bois mentions no American writers in this passage. Perhaps by omitting

Americans from the list of authors with whom he imagined himself walking "arm in arm," he made his point more palatable to some of the "Gentle Readers" he addressed.[10] But in 1903 American writers were still a small minority in most discussions of recommended "great books." When James Russell Lowell designated "The Five Indispensable Authors" in 1894, he named Homer, Dante, Cervantes, Goethe, and Shakespeare. For Lowell, as for many writers of his day, the authors one read, like the rhetoric one used, pointed directly to where one stood in a social and cultural hierarchy. As a long-standing member of a cultural elite, Lowell could unabashedly argue that by "putting a library within the power of every one," the "invention of printing" threatened to "level . . . the ancient aristocracy of thought."[11] The question for Lowell—as for Du Bois—was not only what American "culture" was but also who would have access to it. The issue of access was of vital concern both to those within and those without.

"Dover Street was never really my residence," Mary Antin wrote in *The Promised Land* (1911). Describing her first years in America as a Russian Jewish immigrant girl in the 1890s, Antin insists that Dover Street "happened to be the nook where my bed was made, but I inhabited the city of Boston." She continues:

> I was empress of all I surveyed from the roof of the tenement house. . . . Off towards the northwest . . . was one of my favorite palaces. . . . It was my habit to go very slowly up the low, broad steps to the palace entrance, pleasing my eyes with the majestic lines of the building and lingering to read again the carved inscriptions: *Public Library—Built by the People—Free to All.*
> Did I not say it was my palace? Mine, because I was a citizen; mine, though I was born an alien; mine, though I lived on Dover Street. My palace—mine![12]

The extravagant imagery of an empress and her "majestic" palace here displaces the more pragmatic question of precisely which doors could actually be opened by books (see figure 10). When Du Bois wrote of sitting with Shakespeare, walking with Balzac and Dumas, summoning Aristotle and Aurelius, his language too was lofty. Like Antin, Du Bois associated reading with the possibility of attaining the heights: "So, wed with Truth, I dwell above the Veil," Du Bois wrote by way of concluding the famous passage. "Is this the life you grudge us, O knightly America? . . . Are you so afraid lest peering from this high Pisgah, between Philistine and Amalekite, we sight the Promised Land?" (87). In *The Souls of Black Folks* literature is seen to open vistas. Through reading, Du Bois can soar "above the Veil" and take imaginative possession of "knightly America." But this "Promised Land"—like Mary Antin's—remains abstract: Mount Nebo, like empresses and palaces, is far removed from the reality of contemporary America.

FIGURE 10. "The Famous Study, That Was Fit to Have Been Preserved as a Shrine." The study belonged to Edward Everett Hale, Antin's mentor and patron. From *The Promised Land* (New York: Houghton Mifflin, 1912).

Cultural levels in America were finely differentiated according to a variety of measures at the turn of the century, just as they are today. One such measure was an awareness of the writers generally acknowledged to be "great," and a sense of what might and might not qualify as "literature." Another measure was (and is) the cultural standing of particular vocabularies and narrative strategies. When Mary Antin began her introduction to the autobiographical *Promised Land,* she emphasized that she was now so different from the young girl whose life she was setting out to represent that she could "speak in the third person and not feel like I was masquerading" (xi). By beginning her book in this way, Antin signaled her awareness that the third-person pronoun, and a posture of objectivity in general, had become a sign of value in literary discourse. At the same time, she insisted on her right to speak in her own voice in "the honest first person" (126).[13]

Conventions of reading and writing have specific cultural meanings, and some of these combine with peculiar force at certain historical junctures. Nonetheless, interpretive conventions and their cultural significance are continually in flux. At the end of the nineteenth century, commentators such as Lowell sought to restrict the canon of "great books" as radically as possible, as if to keep literature "refined" was to ensure the "refinement" of society itself.

But just when Lowell was limiting the number of "indispensable" authors to five classics, largely from the distant past, handbooks to "the best reading" were flooding the literary marketplace in a great variety of shapes and sizes. George Palmer Putnam's essay in a popular collection of *Hints for Home Reading* included fifty titles to make up the "core" of a library, and three additional lists of up to a thousand volumes, "comprising . . . the titles of books which are considered, on the whole, the most essential and desirable for the family library and for the use of the student of general literature."[14]

I began this "Afterword" by saying that the realist project participated in the consolidation of American high culture. For many arbiters of taste at the turn of the century, however, realist works seemed far from "high" or cultured. Novels (not to speak of realist novels) constituted a small minority of recommended titles even in popular handbooks.[15] Nonetheless, Du Bois included Balzac and Dumas on his own eclectic "short" list. And Mary Antin, who dreamed of becoming a "great poet" (292) and could translate the *Aeneid* at the kitchen table for the benefit of her less-educated sister (338–39), was proud to proclaim her love of "boys' [adventure] books." "I could put myself in the place of any one of these heroes and delight in their delights," she wrote (322).

Having been brought up "almost without a book," Mary Antin felt that being "set down [at the library] in the midst of all the books that ever were written" was nothing short of a "miracle" (342). The meanings she attached to sitting in a library, like those Du Bois attached to walking "arm in arm" with Aristotle or Balzac, were shaped not only by personal experience within a substratum of American culture, but also by a wider contemporary reality, which included the most sweeping promises of American ideology. Neither for Antin nor for Du Bois could reading or writing transform social reality or the cultural situation of the thousands that they both claimed to represent.[16] Yet for both Du Bois and Antin, as for Dreiser, the ongoing interplay of cultural imperatives and individual needs did make it possible to reshape well-worn reading conventions, bringing "literature" to life for ends that were at once intensely private and socially significant.

NOTES

Introduction

1. Gerald Stanley Lee, *The Lost Art of Reading* (New York: G. P. Putnam's Sons, 1902), 26.

2. Frank Norris, "Weekly Letter," *Chicago American*, July 13, 1901, reprinted in *The Literary Criticism of Frank Norris*, ed. Donald Pizer (New York: Russell & Russell, 1976), 55. Throughout this book I use the term "realism" to refer to the self-consciously "serious" late nineteenth-century novelists who agreed in principle to write "with as little of the author apparent as possible" (William Dean Howells, "My Favorite Novelist and His Best Book," *Munsey's Magazine* [April 1897], reprinted in *European and American Masters*, ed. Clara Marburg Kirk and Rudolf Kirk [New York: Collier Books, 1963], 30). Generally speaking, with anomalies for certain definitions of "realism," these are also the writers who have constituted the academic canon for the fiction of this period: William Dean Howells, Henry James, Edith Wharton, Frank Norris, Stephen Crane, Kate Chopin, Jack London, Theodore Dreiser, and Willa Cather. I have left Mark Twain out of consideration because both his frequent use of first-person narrators and his dramatically foregrounded authorial persona make him an exception in the present context.

3. Hans Robert Jauss takes generic "change[s] in direction" as a starting point for historicizing the evolution of literary forms by contextualizing them within the "lived-world" of a particular historical moment (*Toward an Aesthetic of Reception*, trans. Timothy Bahti [Minneapolis: University of Minnesota Press, 1982], 90–91).

4. See Nina Baym, *Novels, Readers, and Reviewers: Responses to Fiction in Antebellum America* (Ithaca: Cornell University Press, 1984), chap. 12. See also James L. Machor, "Fiction and Informed Reading in Early Nineteenth-Century America," *Nineteenth-Century Literature* 47.3 (1992): 331. The assumption that an author is somehow immanent in his or her written discourse involved a departure from the neoclassical model in which ideas were expected to speak for themselves. As Michael Warner has shown, the "negation of persons" was a "condition of legitimation" for public discourse in eighteenth-century America. Warner's "principle of negativity" makes the absence of a personal author "a ground rule of argument in a public discourse that defines its norms as abstract and universal." Warner approaches early American novels as part of "the republican public sphere" as well. See his *Letters of the Republic: Publication and the Public Sphere in Eighteenth-Century America* (Cambridge, Mass.: Harvard University Press, 1990), 42, 151–76.

5. On some of the tensions that inform the relation between the self and its representations in this period, see Michael Fried, *Realism, Writing, Disfiguration: On Thomas Eakins and Stephen*

Crane (Chicago: University of Chicago Press, 1987); Walter Benn Michaels, *The Gold Standard and the Logic of Naturalism: American Literature at the Turn of the Century* (Berkeley: University of California Press, 1987); and Mark Seltzer, *Bodies and Machines* (London: Routledge, 1992). The end-of-century debate about the "right to privacy" raises additional questions about what constitutes "inviolable personality" and its expression in words and images. For the landmark decision of this debate, see Samuel D. Warren and Louis D. Brandeis, "The Right to Privacy," *Harvard Law Review* 4.5 (1890), reprinted in *The Philosophical Dimensions of Privacy*, ed. Ferdinand D. Schoeman (New York: Cambridge University Press, 1984).

6. See Robert H. Wiebe, *The Search for Order: 1877–1920* (New York: Hill and Wang, 1967), esp. chap. 1. "As the network of relations affecting men's lives each year became more tangled and more distended, Americans in a basic sense no longer knew who or where they were" Wiebe writes (42–43). In *No Place of Grace: Antimodernism and the Transformation of American Culture (1880–1920)* (New York: Pantheon Books, 1981), T. J. Jackson Lears makes a related point, citing the sociologist Edward A. Ross. "How many of my vital interests must I entrust to others!" Ross wrote in 1905. "Nowadays the water main is my well, the trolly car my carriage, the banker's safe my old stocking, the policeman's billy my fist" (34).

7. Henry James, *The Portrait of a Lady* (New York: Norton, 1975), 175.

8. See Warren I. Susman, "'Personality' and the Making of Twentieth-Century Culture," in *Culture as History: The Transformation of American Society in the Twentieth Century* (New York: Pantheon Books, 1984). Susman has suggested that after the 1880s, the nineteenth-century "culture of character," in which "the highest development of self ended in a version of self-control or self-mastery," was gradually replaced by a "new culture of personality" in which "the social role demanded of all . . . was that of a performer" (280 and passim). Amy Kaplan has employed this distinction to emphasize that the realism of William Dean Howells depended on his own commitment to the notion of "character" (*The Social Construction of American Realism* [Chicago: University of Chicago Press, 1988], 23–42). Yet Joan Shelley Rubin draws attention to "the difficulty of sorting out the [connotations of] . . . the two terms" (*The Making of Middlebrow Culture* [Chapel Hill: University of North Carolina Press, 1992], 24). As we shall see, reviewers at midcentury already used the notion of authorial "personality" to conceptualize a valuable feature of literary works. Moreover, the idea of personality was often associated with some essential quality of the "person" even after the turn of the century. The terms are neither as sharply opposed nor as easy to classify by period as they seem.

9. Noah Porter, *Books and Reading: What Books Shall I Read and How Shall I Read Them?* (New York: Charles Scribners, 1871; reprint 1882), 51.

10. See Jauss, *Toward an Aesthetic of Reception*, on the idea of a "horizon of expectations" which in its variations, extensions, and transformations ultimately defines the boundaries of a genre (23–34, 79, 88–89, 94, 108, 171–72). Although Jauss's "horizon of expectations" is inferred from textual changes, not from the responses of particular readers, his "horizon" often presumes just the kind of interplay between text and context that is at issue in the present discussion of reading conventions.

11. Robyn R. Warhol has suggested that by the middle of the nineteenth century, narrative "interventions" in fiction (especially when "earnest" rather than comic or ironic) had come to be considered a feminine and therefore inferior rhetorical strategy. Yet as we shall see, such intrusions (whether "engaging" or what Warhol calls "distancing") retained considerable popularity among writers, reviewers, and other readers until the end of the century, and even beyond. See her *Gendered Interventions: Narrative Discourse in the Victorian Novel* (New Brunswick: Rutgers University Press, 1989), esp. chaps. 2 and 8.

12. For a comprehensive discussion of how realism has been debated in the twentieth century, see Kaplan, introduction to *Social Construction*.

13. "Tradition and the Individual Talent," in *Selected Prose of T. S. Eliot*, ed. Frank Kermode (New York: Harcourt Brace and Jovanovich, 1975), 42–43.

14. Henry Dwight Sedgwick, "The Novels of Mrs. Wharton," *Atlantic* 98 (August 1906): 219. See also Samuel McCord Crothers, "The Gentle Reader," *Atlantic* 86 (November 1900): 656.

15. The phrase is from Daniel H. Borus, *Writing Realism: Howells, James, and Norris in the Mass Market* (Chapel Hill: University of North Carolina Press, 1989), 101. Over twenty-five years ago, Erving Goffman noted the possible effects of "spectatorship" on passivity: "On-the-spot TV news coverage now offers up the world, including its battles, as . . . performances," Goffman wrote, "this incidentally inclining the citizenry to accept the role of audience in connection with any and all events" ("The Theatrical Frame," in *Frame Analysis: An Essay on the Organization of Experience* [New York: Harper and Row, 1974]). The issue of passive spectatorship inculcated by literary realism has been much discussed. June Howard (*Form and History in American Literary Naturalism* [Chapel Hill: University of North Carolina Press, 1985]) takes the spectatorship of naturalist writers as a distancing strategy (see esp. chap. 4). Realism has been seen "either as a way of staging a 'series of acts of exhibition' for public consumption, or as a means of engaging in one of the most common activities of modern urban life: 'just looking'" (Kaplan, *Social Construction*, 7). Christopher P. Wilson has argued that the "engineered 'realism'" of new popular magazines in the American 1890s "threatened to deepen the passivity of the reader [by encouraging] . . . the idea that 'real life' was beyond the pale of the reader's existence . . . [as if] *others* experienced the real [whereas] . . . the reader . . . was an outsider looking in. . . . Instead of promoting participation, the magazines elevated 'seeing'" ("The Rhetoric of Consumption: Mass-Market Magazines and the Demise of the Gentle Reader," in *The Culture of Consumption: Critical Essays in American History 1880–1980*, ed. Richard W. Fox and T. J. Jackson Lears [New York: Pantheon, 1983], 61).

16. Walter J. Ong, "The Writer's Audience Is Always a Fiction," *PMLA* 90.1 (January 1975): 9, 12, and passim.

17. Wolfgang Iser, *The Act of Reading: A Theory of Aesthetic Response* (London: Routledge and Kegan Paul, 1978), 34, 37. Wai Chee Dimock, among others, has challenged the "a-historical" nature of Iser's model; see "Feminism, New Historicism, and the Reader," in *Readers in History: Nineteenth-Century American Literature and the Contexts of Response*, ed. James L. Machor (Baltimore: Johns Hopkins University Press, 1993), 85–106. Up to a point, however, Iser does acknowledge the import of cultural and historical norms in the development of reading conventions. See, for example, chap. 1 of Iser's study *The Act of Reading*. For a balanced account of "the historical gap in reader-oriented criticism," see James Machor's introduction to *Readers in History* (xi).

18. Feminist criticism has devoted considerable attention to the question of readers who resist their fictionalized roles. See, for example, Judith Fetterley, *The Resisting Reader: A Feminist Approach to American Fiction* (Bloomington: Indiana University Press, 1978); Elizabeth A. Flynn and Patrocinio P. Schweickart, eds., *Gender and Reading: Essays on Readers, Texts, and Contexts* (Baltimore: Johns Hopkins University Press, 1986). The work of Roger Chartier, Carlo Ginzburg, Janice Radway, and others has emphasized a reader's freedom to create or appropriate meanings rather than passively absorb them. See Roger Chartier, "Texts, Printings, Readings," in *The New Cultural History*, ed. Lynn Hunt (Berkeley: University of California Press, 1989); Carlo Ginzburg, *The Cheese and the Worms: The Cosmos of a Sixteenth-Century Miller*, trans. John and Anne Tedeschi (Baltimore: Johns Hopkins University Press, 1980); Janice Radway, *Reading the Romance: Women, Patriarchy, and Popular Culture* (Chapel Hill: University of North Carolina Press, 1984).

19. For Iser, the disappearance of an authoritative narrator contributed to a kind of "indeterminacy" in fiction that gave modern readers a more active role in making meaning. Indeterminacy, Iser claims, "is the fundamental precondition for reader participation" ("Indeterminacy and

the Reader's Response in Prose Fiction," in *Aspects of Narrative: Selected Papers from the English Institute,* ed. J. Hillis Miller [New York: Columbia University Press, 1971], 14). Yet this "fundamental precondition" is partially shaped by reading conventions that are culturally particular. For many nineteenth-century readers, as I will argue, the disappearance of the "intrusive" narrator seemed to diminish the sense of reading as intercourse, thereby making it feel like a more passive process because less of an imagined transaction or human exchange.

20. Sarah Orne Jewitt to Thomas Bailey Aldrich, 1890. Cited by Melissa J. Homestead, "'Links of Similitude': The Narrator of *The Country of the Pointed Firs* and Author-Reader Relations at the End of the Nineteenth Century," in *Jewett and Her Contemporaries: Reshaping the Canon,* ed. Karen L. Kilcup and Thomas S. Edwards (Gainesville: University Press of Florida, 1999), 76.

21. Robert Darnton, "First Steps Toward a History of Reading," in *The Kiss of Lamourette: Reflections in Cultural History* (New York: W. W. Norton and Co., 1989), 182.

22. Robert Darnton, "Readers Respond to Rousseau: The Fabrication of Romantic Sensitivity," in *The Great Cat Massacre and Other Episodes of French Cultural History* (New York: Basic Books, 1984), 215–56.

23. Roger Chartier stresses the importance of "bring[ing] together two perspectives that are often disjoined: on the one hand, the study of the way in which texts . . . organize the prescribed reading, and on the other, the collection of actual readings tracked down in individual confessions or reconstructed on the level of communities of readers—those 'interpretive communities' whose members share the same reading styles and the same strategies of interpretation" ("Texts, Printings," 157–58). On "interpretive communities," see Stanley Fish, *Is There a Text in This Class? The Authority of Interpretive Communities* (Cambridge, Mass.: Harvard University Press, 1980), 167–73.

24. The commonplace books, letters, and diaries of nineteenth-century readers, however, are full of scattered remarks about books that were loved or hated. The work of Ronald J. Zboray and Mary Saracino Zboray offers a reconstruction of reading habits based on a large sample of letters and diaries written by both women and men in antebellum New England. See, for example, "'Have You Read . . . ?': Real Readers and Their Responses in Antebellum Boston and Its Region," *Nineteenth-Century Literature* 52 (September 1997); "Reading and Everyday Life in Antebellum Boston: The Diary of Daniel F. and Mary D. Child," *Libraries and Culture* 32.3 (Summer 1997). On the use of diaries by young business clerks in nineteenth-century New York, see Thomas Augst, "The Business of Reading in Nineteenth-Century America": The New York Mercantile Library," *American Quarterly* 50.2 (June 1998). On scrapbooks, see Ellen Gruber Garvey, *The Adman in the Parlor: Magazines and the Gendering of Consumer Culture, 1880s to 1910s* (New York: Oxford University Press, 1996). On letters and commonplace books as evidence of reading practices among nineteenth-century women, see the work of Mary Kelley and Barbara Sicherman. Following Jonathan Rose, I define the "common" or nonprofessional reader as "any reader who did not read books for a living" ("Rereading the English Common Reader: A Preface to a History of Audiences," *Journal of the History of Ideas* 53 [1992]: 51).

25. James L. Machor, Respondent's Comments, "Historical Readers: Reconstructive Strategies," Modern Language Association Convention, Toronto, December 1997.

26. Ginzburg, *The Cheese and the Worms;* Barbara Sicherman, "Sense and Sensibility: A Case Study of Women's Reading in Late-Victorian-America," in *Reading in America: Literature and Social History,* ed. Cathy N. Davidson (Baltimore: Johns Hopkins University Press, 1989); Barbara Sicherman, "Reading and Ambition: M. Carey Thomas and Female Heroism," *American Quarterly* 45.1 (March 1993); Mary Kelley, "Reading Women/Women Reading: The Making of Learned Women in Antebellum America," *Journal of American History* 83 (September 1996).

27. Cathy N. Davidson, *Revolution and the Word: The Rise of the Novel in America* (New York: Oxford University Press, 1986), 5.

28. Janice Radway, "Reading Is Not Eating": Mass-Produced Literature and the Theoretical, Methodological, and Political Consequences of a Metaphor," *Book Research Quarterly* 2 (Fall 1986): 12. In a more recent discussion, Radway herself has reexamined the distinction between "trained" and "ordinary" readers, partly by focusing on her own reading practices. See "Introduction," in *A Feeling for Books: The Book of the Month Club, Literary Taste, and Middle-Class Desire* (Chapel Hill: University of North Carolina Press, 1997). For another challenge to the notion that "professional readings . . . are appropriate paradigms for *the* experience of reading narrative," see Peter Rabinowitz, *Before Reading: Narrative Conventions and the Politics of Interpretation* (Ithaca: Cornell University Press, 1987), 12.

29. On the separation of cultures and the emergence of a "high" culture of letters, see Burton Bledstein, *The Culture of Professionalism: The Middle Class and the Development of Higher Education in America* (New York: Norton, 1976); Richard Brodhead, *Cultures of Letters: Scenes of Reading and Writing in Nineteenth-Century America* (Chicago: University of Chicago Press, 1993); Lawrence W. Levine, *Highbrow/Lowbrow: The Emergence of Cultural Hierarchy in America* (Cambridge, Mass.: Harvard University Press, 1988).

30. Edith Wharton, *A Backward Glance* (New York: Scribner's Sons, 1985) 180–81.

31. Frank Norris often signed letters "the boy Zola," a nickname that stuck. On Norris's predilection for *Trilby,* see Jesse S. Crisler, "Norris's 'Library,'" *Frank Norris Studies* 5 (Spring 1988), and David A. Zimmerman "The Mesmeric Sources of Frank Norris's *The Pit,*" *Frank Norris Studies* 26 (Autumn 1998): 2–4. On Willa Cather's fortunes in the canon, see Sharon O'Brien, "Becoming Noncanonical: The Case against Willa Cather," *American Quarterly* 40 (March 1988): 110–26; and Joan Acocella, "Willa Cather and the Academy," *New Yorker,* November 27, 1995. On Cather's appreciation of *Trilby,* see chapters 2 and 4. On Jack London's relation to *Rebecca of Sunnybrook Farm* see Paul Sorrentino, "A Biographical Connection between Jack London and Kate Douglas Wiggin," *American Literary Realism* 32.1 (Fall, 1999) 83.

32. Henry James, "The Art of Fiction," in *Theory of Fiction: Henry James,* ed. James E. Miller (Lincoln: University of Nebraska Press, 1972), 30.

33. On "the desire for an author" as a persistent factor in the experience of reading, see John Carlos Rowe, *The Theoretical Dimensions of Henry James* (Madison: University of Wisconsin Press, 1984), 234 and chap. 7 passim. See also Radway's discussion of romance readers who "can be said to read *authors* rather than books" ("Reading Is Not Eating," 22). Publishers often employ the living person of the author to promote reading (or at least purchase) of the book. Book signings ("Meet the Author") may imply that reading a text does not in itself provide imaginative access to the writer of the book, or, on the contrary, that having "met" the author, a reader is invited to pursue the acquaintance. Either way, contemporary marketing techniques continue to emphasize the relation of a book to a concretely imagined and individuated human author.

34. Gustave Flaubert, cited by Henry James, "Gustave Flaubert," in Miller, *Theory of Fiction,* 178.

35. Lee, "The Lost Art of Reading," 25.

36. Percy Lubbock, *The Craft of Fiction* (1921, reprinted New York: Peter Smith, 1947), 35. Lubbock praises Tolstoy, for example, for steering away "from the mere telling of the story on his own authority; at high moments he knew better than to tell it himself" (38). In 1925 Edith Wharton criticized the "old-fashioned intrusion of the author among his puppets" (*The Writing of Fiction* [New York: Charles Scribner's Sons, 1925], 91). By the 1950s both literary criticism and handbooks for writing employed the distinction between "showing" and "telling" to describe and reinforce a

hierarchy of values in narrative modes. Literary history was seen as a progression, and modernist techniques became the natural culmination of an ongoing development. Wayne Booth was the most influential critic to challenge the sharp distinction between "artful showing and inartistic, merely rhetorical telling." Nonetheless, the dichotomy retained its force in practical criticism long after Booth's discussion had qualified it in principle. See *The Rhetoric of Fiction* (1961, reprinted Chicago: University of Chicago Press, 1967), 27 and passim.

37. The October 1996 issue of *PMLA* opened with a "guest column" on this development in literary studies; see "Four Views of the Place of the Personal in Scholarship," *PMLA* 111.5 (October 1996): 1063–79. Marjorie Perloff has raised questions about the "loss" of the first-person plural in critical discourse, taking "the loss of this *we* [as] a sign that there is no longer a generic intellectual class to which 'you' or 'I' or 'one' might belong." Perloff herself uses the first-person pronoun throughout her discussion ("Forum: The Intellectual, the Artist, and the Reader," *PMLA* 112.5 [October 1997]: 1129). See also David Bleich and Deborah Holstein, eds., *Personal Effects in Scholarly Writing* (New York: MLA, forthcoming).

1. Reading for the Author

1. Jack London, *The Sea-Wolf and Other Stories* (London: Penguin, 1989), 167. *The Sea-Wolf* was first published in 1904.

2. London corresponded with Cloudsley Johns for years after responding to a fan letter in February 1899. Two months later, London described Johns as an "ideal chum," even while acknowledging that "personality, as reflected by pen and paper, and personality face to face, are very different things" (April 17, 1899). See *Letters from Jack London,* ed. King Hendricks and Irving Shepard (London: Macgibbon and Kee, 1966), 29. Johns was not the only friend London made in this way. On the "community of writers" which London and his friends generated through letters, see also Jonathan Auerbach, *Male Call: Becoming Jack London* (Durham: Duke University Press, 1996), 13–14.

3. Crothers, "The Gentle Reader," 655.

4. Henry James, "Ivan Turgenieff," in Miller, *Theory of Fiction,* 174–75.

5. On the differentiation of "cultures" in this period, see Bledstein, *The Culture of Professionalism;* Brodhead, *Cultures of Letters;* Levine, *Highbrow/Lowbrow.*

6. The formulation is from Nancy Glazener, *Reading for Realism: The History of a U.S. Literary Institution* (Durham: Duke University Press, 1997), 125. Glazener notes that this "truism of classical rhetoric" was promoted by such widely used textbooks as Hugh Blair's *Lectures on Rhetoric and Belles Lettres* (see Glazener, 308; notes 107 and 108). Thomas Augst stresses the role of "physical and emotional evidence of conviction" in his discussion of popular elocution manuals, "The Fate of Eloquence and the Popular Science of Rhetoric in Nineteenth-Century America," delivered at the American Studies Association, Washington, D.C., 1997.

7. Jay Fliegelman has explored the paradox of dramatized signs of "sincerity" in eighteenth-century public discourse. He emphasizes that "for all the insistence that eloquence was an act of magnifying feelings actually experienced and not of deceptively fabricating feeling, to teach the code of voice and gesture . . . was to equip all men to deceive, to act a role." See *Declaring Independence: Jefferson, Natural Language, and the Culture of Performance* (Stanford: Stanford University Press, 1993), 80.

8. A. Potter, *A Handbook for Readers* (New York: Harper and Bros., 1843); George Philes, *How to Read a Book* (New York, 1873); Porter, *Books and Reading.* An entire chapter of Porter's book focuses on "The Relations of the Reader to His Author," in the words of the chapter title. Charles Richardson put it this way: "Behind the book stands the author; if the reader chooses the book or the chapter as he ought, he shares the author's best self and best hours. . . . [N]o reader, whoever

he may be . . . can consider the book without an estimate of the author" (*The Choice of Books* [New York: American Book Exchange, 1881], 47).

9. In "The Fate of Eloquence," Augst suggests that "impersonate" was the "most common single direction" given for reading in elocution manuals of the period (10). As one manual on practical elocution remarks, "How little of the spirit can go along with the letter—how little of the inspiration which the true teacher should impart, can accompany the monotonous lines of the printed page." J. W. Shoemaker, *Best Things from Best Authors: Humor, Pathos, and Eloquence Designed for Public and Social Entertainment and for Use in Schools and Colleges* (Philadelphia, 1882), ix. In a chapter titled "Reading Aloud, Reading Clubs," Charles Richardson notes, "No study and no teaching is so delightful as that which is full of the element of personality" (*The Choice of Books,* 71).

10. Review of "The Life and Correspondence of Robert Southey," *North American Review* 73 (July 1851): 11.

11. Philes, *How to Read a Book,* 12. Alcott is cited in James Baldwin, *The Booklover: A Guide to the Best Reading* (1894, reprinted Chicago: McClurg & Co., 1898). "We seek [books] in our need of counsel or amusement," Alcott writes, "without impertinence or apology, sure of having our claims allowed. . . . What were days without such fellowship? We were alone in the world without it" (15). Variations on the theme of reading as "a kind of conversation" with the author of the book are legion until well after the turn of the century (the phrase is from Crothers, "The Gentle Reader," 655). In *The Aims of Literary Study* (New York: Macmillan & Co., 1894), Hiram Corson emphasizes the value of coming "into relationship with [an author's] absolute personality" as "the highest result of the study of his works" (57). Cf. the notion of being in "pleasant company" through reading ("Culture of the Old School," *Atlantic* 55 [January 1885]: 118); the idea of a "bond between writer and reader" (J. Rogers Rees, *The Diversions of a Book Worm* [New York: George J. Coombes, 1887], 65); and the assertion that "in literature, as in life, one has a right to choose one's own friends" (Martha Dunn, "A Plea for the Shiftless Reader," *Atlantic* 85 [January 1900]: 136). Looking back at the elaborate decorations and ceremonial uses of medieval books, Edith Wharton and Ogden Codman Jr. note that "it remained for the Italian printers and binders of the sixteenth century and for their French imitators, to adapt the form of the book to its purpose, changing as it were a jewelled idol to a human companion" (*The Decoration of Houses* [1902, reprinted New York: W. W. Norton, 1978], 146).

12. "The man behind the pen," asked Frank Norris, "—what has the public to do with him?" ("Weekly Letter," 55).

13. "The Life and Poetry of Wordsworth," *North American Review* 73 (1851): 487.

14. In antebellum reviewing, women were a significant exception to this rule. See Baym, *Novels, Readers, and Reviewers,* chap. 12. For a cogent exploration of the contested boundaries between women's private and public selves, see Katherine Henry, "Angelina Grimké's Rhetoric of Exposure," *American Quarterly* 49.2 (June 1997).

15. Although narrating personas have been central to fiction at least since Cervantes, the discourse of authorial presence, companionship, even love, is pervasive in discussions of books and reading during much of the nineteenth century. Nineteenth-century reading conventions presumed wholeness and continuity in character, just as in our own time we have come to assume fragmentation.

16. Arguing for the education of black women, Anna Julia Cooper evokes the potential comfort of communing with the work of "the best [authors] the world has known." She not only projects the idea of books as a welcome part of the "charmed circle . . . of friendship" but also graphically represents the experience of reading an active interchange between author and reader. The black woman who turns to books for comfort, Cooper suggests, "can commune with Socrates about the *daimon* he knew and to which she too can bear witness. . . . She can listen to the pulsing

heart throbs of passionate Sappho's encaged soul . . . and the fires of her own soul cry back as she listens. 'Yes; Sappho, I know it all; I know it all.' Here, at last, can be communion without suspicion; friendship without misunderstanding, love without jealousy." (*A Voice from the South* [1892, reprinted New York: Oxford University Press, 1990], 69). The trope of reading as social exchange or communion here gains additional resonance as an image of crossing the color line. On class, race, and reading, see also my Afterword.

17. Kelley, "Reading Women/Women Reading."

18. This excerpt, cited by Kelley in an early version of the published paper, can be found in *The Diary of Elizabeth Sandwith Drinker,* ed. Elaine Forman Crane (Boston: Northeastern University Press, 1991), entry dated 7 March 1800.

19. "I found her alone," Elizabeth Drinker recorded in her diary after coming upon a friend, "if a person with a [book in hand] may be called so" (*Diary,* entry of 22 June 1801). "'Come then my Books,' Mary Eliza Sweet of Savannah, Georgia, wrote in her Commonplace Book, 'companions safe / Soothers of pain, and antidote to care'" (cited in Kelley, "Reading Women/Women Reading," 412). Kentuckian John Price put the idea this way in a letter to his ten-year-old daughter: "Books are the best company you can have—they never tell tales upon you and you always have them at command" (also cited in Kelley, 424). The idea of books as company that is always available but can be dismissed at will recurred frequently in letters and essays throughout the nineteenth century.

20. Cited in Zboray and Zboray, "'Have You Read . . . ?'" 144. "'I am sorry you do not like my friend, Mrs. C. E. Tonna,' Elizabeth Pierce wrote to her sister Mary in 1843, 'as you think it is evident she has some vanity, but who is faultless?'" (ibid., 160). As Thomas August points out, "the popular values of nineteenth-century literary culture remained committed to the *idea* if not always the fact of an author personally addressing a crowd that extended only so far as the average person's hearing and vision" ("Composing the Moral Senses: Emerson and the Politics of Character in Nineteenth-Century America," *Political Theory* 27.1 [February 1999]: 108). In the perspective of nineteenth-century values, August suggests, "moral authority [was] always finally embodied in persons" (109).

21. Always assuming that a good plot was also present. On plot as an indispensable feature of the novel form for antebellum reviewers, see Baym, *Novels, Readers, and Reviewers,* esp. 24 and chap. 4.

22. *North American Review* 71 (1850): 136. Further references are cited in the text. The rhetoric of friendship also pervades Hawthorne's preface itself.

23. From chap. 5 of *Hawthorne* (1879), cited in *The Portable James,* ed. Morton Dauwen Zabel (New York: Viking, 1958), 443. Jane Tompkins notes the popularity of the preface and points out that the public furor surrounding Hawthorne's dismissal from the Custom House made for "advance publicity" that contributed to the success of *The Scarlet Letter* (*Sensational Designs: The Cultural Work of American Fiction, 1790–1860* [New York: Oxford University Press, 1985], 24).

24. Edwin Whipple, *Lectures on Subjects Connected with Literature and Life,* 2nd ed. (Boston: Ticknor and Fields, 1850), 14–15. Whipple contributed essays and reviews to the *Atlantic Monthly, Harper's, North American Review,* and other journals.

25. Whipple himself discourages the impulse to look beyond the text itself to the author's private life: "Every prudent man would wish to avoid" such issues as "the relation of authors to domestic life, their glory or shame as lovers and husbands" (ibid., 30). Recent work on nonprofessional readers suggests, however, that knowledge of an author's private life did indeed color response. Elizabeth Drinker grew ambivalent about the work of Mary Wollstonecraft when she read about her affair with Gilbert Imlay, noting that she "should be charmed by some of [Wollstonecraft's] pieces if I had never heard her Character" (6 March 1799). The Zborays suggest that "readers sometimes emphasized authors' personalities over the texts they produced" ("'Have you Read . . . ?'" 157).

26. Emily Dickinson to Thomas Wenthworth Higginson, July 1862, cited in *The Norton Anthology of American Literature,* shorter 4th ed. (New York: Norton, 1995), 1152.

27. Not surprisingly, when this review was reprinted in one twentieth-century collection of criticism, these lines were omitted, along with the reviewer's extended emphasis on Hawthorne as a man. See J. Donald Crowley, ed., *Hawthorne: The Critical Heritage* (London: Routledge, 1970), 164–67. The omissions are themselves the result of changes in interpretive conventions.

28. Chartier examines reading as a "creative practice" through which readers often "invent . . . singular meanings and significations" ("Texts, Printings, Reading," 156). See also Radway's argument for how readers appropriate meanings to suit their own needs (*Reading the Romance,* 16–17, 90–93, 97, 100, and passim). In *The Cheese and the Worms,* a reconstruction of "the cosmos of a sixteenth-century miller," Ginzburg exemplifies a process of active meaning creation by stressing two aspects of reading that are particularly relevant here: noting "the gulf between the texts read by [the miller] Menocchio and the way in which he understood them" (xxii), Ginzburg shows not only that Menocchio read many texts which the authorities in his own day (and historians in ours) did not expect him to read, but also that, like the women readers discussed by Barbara Sicherman and Mary Kelley, he appropriated meanings that were not meant for him. Menocchio appropriated these meanings so completely that they became his own—as if they "came out of *his* head," as he put it to the inquisitors (33). The "aggressive originality" of Menocchio's reading (33) enabled him to make unconventional and subversive interpretations of his world and his own place in it. His reading shaped his personality as his personality shaped his reading; the books he read impelled him to stand up defiantly before his inquisitors. In the context of nineteenth-century America, one need only recall the strenuous prohibition on literacy for slaves in order to see what widespread amorphous and transgressive powers were attributed to reading.

29. David Leverenz, *Manhood and the American Renaissance* (Ithaca: Cornell University Press, 1989), 232.

30. Later in the century, as we shall see, the practice of reading "through" the text in this manner became widespread. One particularly clear example is Anna Julia Cooper's reading of Maurice Thompson's "Voodoo Prophecy." "In penning this portrait of the Negro," Cooper writes, Thompson "has unconsciously, it may be, laid bare his own soul—its secret dread and horrible fear" (*A Voice from the South,* 216–17). Such reading practices impelled many authors to efface themselves as assiduously as possible. See chapter 2.

31. Herman Melville, "Hawthorne and His Mosses," in *Norton Anthology of American Literature,* 1041. According to an editorial note, "The manuscript shows that the pseudonymous 'Virginian Spending July in Vermont' was an afterthought." In the editors' view, the change was "designed to account for the emotional outpouring that Melville had written in his own voice" (1032, note 1). References to this edition will be cited in the text.

32. See Susan S. Williams, "Widening the World: Susan Warner, Her Readers, and the Assumption of Authorship," *American Quarterly* 42.4 (December 1990): 572–73.

33. See Barbara Sicherman, "Reading *Little Women:* The Many Lives of a Text," in *U.S. History as Women's History: New Feminist Essays,* ed. Linda K. Kerber, Alice Kessler-Harris, and Kathryn Kish Sklar (Chapel Hill: University of North Carolina Press, 1995), 253.

34. "The orchard of the Old Manse seems the visible type of the fine mind that has described it," writes Melville. "Such touches as are in this piece cannot proceed from any common heart. . . . Still more. Such touches . . . furnish clews, whereby we enter a little way into the intricate, profound heart where they originated" (1033–34). Melville draws numerous inferences about Hawthorne's character and experience—his melancholy, the probable suffering in his past, his "humor" and capacity for "love," the "great beauty" and "strength" of "such a mind." Moreover, noting that "the world is mistaken in this harmless Hawthorne," Melville speculates about the "hither side of Hawthorne's soul" and wonders "whether there really lurks in him, perhaps unknown to

himself, a touch of Puritan gloom" (1035). Collapsing the distinction between author and text altogether, Melville asserts that a "black conceit pervades him through and through" (1035).

35. According to Scott E. Casper, representing the "inner man" was a prime goal of antebellum autobiography; see "Defining the National Pantheon: The Making of Houghton Mifflin's Biographical Series, 1880–1900," in *Reading Books: Essays on the Material Text and Literature in America*, ed. Michele Moylan and Lane Stiles (Amherst: University of Massachusetts Press, 1996), 183–84.

36. A note in the Norton edition points out that, "contrary to the assertion within the essay, Melville wrote the review after meeting Hawthorne during a literary outing in the Berkshires on August 5, 1850" (1033, note 1).

37. On the common practice of reading aloud and books as a ground of relations to others, near and far, see Ronald J. Zboray and Mary Saracino Zboray, "Books, Reading, and the World of Goods in Antebellum New England," *American Quarterly* 48.4 (December 1996): 588, 590–91, 596–97, 600; "'Have You Read . . . ?'" 168–70; and "Reading and Everyday Life in Antebellum Boston," 288, 290–93. The term "imagined community" is from Benedict Anderson, *Imagined Communities: Reflections on the Origins and Spread of Nationalism* (London: Verso, 1991).

38. Sicherman, "Reading and Ambition," 79.

39. On women's reading as "collective practice," see Kelley, "Reading Women," 403, 419–24.

40. Melville claims in the review that Hawthorne's "Mosses" was given him "the other day" by "a cousin." As note 3 points out, that was not the case (1033).

41. Michael T. Gilmore, *American Romanticism and the Marketplace* (Chicago: University of Chicago Press, 1985), 61–62. Further references are cited in the text. I am indebted to Gilmore's discussion of Melville and Thoreau. My own intention here, however, is to suggest that both of these writers participated in widely shared reading practices that were also at a crucial point of transition.

42. On the rhetoric of reading as eating, see Steven Mailloux, "The Rhetorical Use and Abuse of Fiction: Eating Books in Late Nineteenth-Century America," *Boundary 2* 17.1 (1990): 133–57. Among challenges to the metaphor because of its association with passivity, see Radway, "Reading Is Not Eating"; Radway's introduction to *Reading the Romance;* and Glazener's chapter "Addictive Reading and Professional Authorship" in *Reading for Realism*. Norman N. Holland engages the psychological underpinnings of the connection between reading and eating in *The Dynamics of Literary Response* (New York: W. W. Norton, 1975), 75–77.

43. Glazener discusses some of the class implications of a notion like "discriminating palate," stressing the "difference between a 'draught' or 'dram' and a 'vintage' whose 'aroma' is savored." Such distinctions, Glazener argues, contributed to the association of realism with connoisseurship (*Reading for Realism*, 97). In *A Feeling for Books*, Janice Radway traces how books that could be "consumed" (i.e., used up and discarded) were identified as "inferior" and situated at a lower level of "culture" at the turn of the century. See especially chap. 4, "The Struggle over the Book."

44. Cited in Mary Kelley, *Private Woman, Public Stage: Literary Domesticity in Nineteenth-Century America* (New York: Oxford University Press, 1985), 112.

45. Georges Poulet, "The Self and Other in Critical Consciousness," *Diacritics* 2 (Spring 1972): 46–50, and "Criticism and the Experience of Interiority," in *Reader-Response Criticism: From Formalism to Post-Structuralism*, ed. Jane P. Tompkins (Baltimore: Johns Hopkins University Press, 1980), 41–49.

46. Michael Steig, *Stories of Reading: Subjectivity and Literary Understanding* (Baltimore: Johns Hopkins University Press, 1989), 11. Steig notes that there is a "phenomenologically sound use for a term like interaction or transaction" to describe the reading process. "For even if the text does not really 'act,' reading often feels like interaction simply because as one's perceptions change, the text itself seems to change. In all such processes the text is perceived as an 'other,' no matter how strongly one may be committed to the principle of meaning-in-the-reader" (11). Steig posits

an "unavoidable duality of self and other in the process of reading" and suggests that the text is perceived as both "other" and "self" (16). Louise Rosenblatt proposes another way of conceptualizing the reader's relation to a text as a kind of "transaction" ("On the Aesthetic as the Basic Model of the Reading Process," *Bucknell Review* 26.1 [1981]: 17–32).

47. The notion that fiction reading in particular might stimulate "unreasonable" fantasies of advancement through identification was the cause of much disapproval of fiction among educators and moralists from the eighteenth century onward. Taking Richardson as his target, one satirist made a characteristic case against the novel:

> Thus Harriet reads, and reading really
> Believes herself a young *Pamela*,
> The high-wrought whim, the tender strain
> Elate her mind and turn her brain:
> Before her glass, with smiling grace,
> She views the wonders of her face;
> There stands in admiration moveless,
> And hopes a Grandison, or Lovelace.

Cited in Borus, *Writing Realism,* 29. For a concise and useful analysis of the anti-fiction prejudice in eighteenth-century Britain, see Paul J. Hunter, "The Loneliness of the Long-Distance Reader," *Genre* 10 (Winter 1977). On the disapproval of novel reading in nineteenth-century Britain, see Patrick Brantlinger, *The Reading Lesson: The Threat of Mass Literacy in Nineteenth-Century British Fiction* (Bloomington: Indiana University Press, 1998). Davidson analyzes hostility to novel reading in the early American republic in *Revolution and the Word,* 39–44 and chap. 3 passim. To some degree, charges against novel reading continued right down to the turn of the century. For one contemporary discussion of the passivity and even dissipation supposedly encouraged by fiction reading, see George Clarke, "The Novel-Reading Habit," *The Arena* 19 (May 1898): 670–79.

48. Casper suggests that the Houghton Mifflin "American Men of Letters" series, following its British predecessor, "English Men of Letters," made "authors' lives . . . [the] models of the bourgeois success ethic, thus validating their works" ("Defining the National Pantheon," 184). On the British series, see John L. Kijinsky, "John Morley's 'English Men of Letters' Series and the Politics of Reading," *Victorian Studies* 34.1 (1990).

49. Henry David Thoreau, *Walden, or Life in the Woods,* in *Walden and Other Writings of Henry David Thoreau* (New York: Random House, 1950), 97. Further references are cited in the text.

50. The exclusionary implications of this emphasis may account for the removal of both Melville's review and the "On Reading" section of *Walden* from the "shorter fifth edition" of the *Norton Anthology of American Literature.*

51. See John Higham, *Strangers in the Land: Patterns of American Nativism, 1860–1925* (New York: Atheneum, 1975), esp. chap. 3, "Crisis in the Eighties." Higham stresses the role of economic difficulties in triggering incipient nativism: "During the first half of the [1880s,] . . . [w]herever an optimistic indifference toward social problems prevailed, the tradition persisted of the immigrant as an economic blessing easily assimilated into America's mixed nationality" (38). But later in the decade, according to Higham, social critics discovered "an immigration *problem*" and "raised the question of assimilation in a broadly significant way by connecting it with the central issues of the day. They gave intellectual respectability to anti-immigrant feelings" (38–39). In 1890, in what Higham describes as "the first scholarly book on the subject," Richmond May-Smith asked whether immigration was "endangering America's free, self-reliant, orderly culture, the unique economic well-being of its working people, and the prestige of industrial pursuits? His answer, though measured and good-tempered, was emphatically yes" (41).

52. "There are . . . as many different publics as there are separate authors. There is really no such entity as *the* public." Brander Matthews, "On Pleasing the Taste of the Public," in *Aspects of Fiction and Other Ventures in Criticism* (New York: Charles Scribner's Sons, 1902), 61, 72. "At times realists regarded their audience almost as a foreign entity, an undifferentiated conglomerate," Borus writes (*Writing Realism,* 117). See also Kaplan, *Social Construction,* 11, 20–21, and chaps. 2 and 4.

53. Owen Wister, "The Evolution of the Cow-Puncher," cited in Marcus Klein, *Easterns, Westerns, and Private Eyes: American Matters, 1870–1900* (Madison: University of Wisconsin Press, 1994), 124.

54. The last twenty years of the nineteenth century revolutionized the conditions within which fiction was written, published, sold, and read, turning the novel into big business. For discussions of relevant changes in the publishing industry and reading public, see Borus, *Writing Realism,* esp. chap. 5; Kaplan, *Social Construction,* esp. intro. and chap. 1; Christopher Wilson, *The Labor of Words: Literary Professionalism in the Progressive Era* (Athens: University of Georgia Press, 1985), esp. intro. and chap. 3; Alan Trachtenberg, *The Incorporation of America: Culture and Society in the Gilded Age* (New York: Hill and Wang, 1982), 122–23. For a discussion of related issues earlier in the century, see Gilmore, *American Romanticism,* esp. chap. 1.

55. John Albee, "The Spectral Publisher," *The Dial* (May 1, 1895): 261; "Men, Women, and Books," *The Critic,* February 15, 1896, 105.

56. William Dean Howells, "Novel-Writing and Novel-Reading: An Impersonal Explanation" (1899), a lecture first published in the *Bulletin of the New York Public Library* 62 (January–February 1958): 18, 22.

57. See Brodhead, *Cultures of Letters,* 66–67.

58. Borus emphasizes the shift of focus in the *kind* of publicity writers received after midcentury (*Writing Realism,* 118, 125–26). Cf. Wilson, *Labor of Words,* 2–3, 8, 76, 79–82.

59. See Sicherman, "Reading *Little Women,*" 248, 252–53. The identification of author and protagonist is reinforced by *Jo's Boys* (1886), with its fictionalized account of the writing of *Little Women.* See Brodhead, *Cultures of Letters,* 69–70. Of course, aspects of Alcott's life and work that did not serve the identification of Alcott and Jo March were simply elided in promotion and discussion of the book. For attention to those deleted elements, see Judith Fetterley, "Impersonating 'Little Women': The Radicalism of Alcott's *Behind a Mask,*" *Women's Studies* 10 (1983): 1–14; Elaine Showalter, "Introduction," in *Alternative Alcott,* ed. Elaine Showalter (New Brunswick, N.J.: Rutgers University Press, 1988).

60. Figure 2, the frontispiece of *Louisa May Alcott: The Children's Friend* (1888), represents Alcott reading to a large group of children.

61. Borus, *Writing Realism,* 124. Further references are cited in the text.

62. William Walsh, *Authors and Authorship* (New York: G. P. Putnam's Sons, 1882), iii.

63. Jeannette Gilder, *Authors at Home: Personal and Biographical Sketches of Well-Known American Writers* (New York: Cassell Publishing Co., 1888), editor's note and 327.

64. Ibid., 199. As Casper has suggested, the publishing history of the Houghton Mifflin "American Men of Letters" series reflects an analogous uncertainty about whether writers could be best "known" via their lives or their works ("Defining the National Pantheon," 180, 196, 209, 215).

65. Hippolyte A. Taine, *History of English Literature,* vol. 4, trans. H. Van Laun (1883, reprinted New York: Frederick Ungar, 1965), 117.

66. On the growing attention to word counts, see Borus, *Writing Realism,* 71–72; Fried, *Realism, Writing, Disfiguration,* 137; Seltzer, *Bodies and Machines,* 16. The literary agent, a new phenomenon in the 1890s, gained popularity after the international copyright agreement of 1891, generating a heated debate among writers, critics, and publishers. Discussions of literary agents,

authors' guilds, and so on also served to turn the author into businessman, worker, unionizer—everything but friend and peer.

67. "Men, Women, and Books," 106.

68. "Author, Agent, and Publisher," *The Critic,* December 23, 1895, 447.

69. Charles Dudley Warner, *Fashions in Literature and Other Literary and Social Essays and Addresses* (New York: Dodd, Mead, and Co., 1902), 286.

70. Addressing the first public meeting of the National Institute of Arts and Letters in 1900, Warner affirmed copyright legislation by comparing the writer's "talent" to a mine from which a limited "vein of valuable ore" is extracted (ibid., 272). But he also drew attention to the reading public's anxieties about the ceaseless production of books: "The public expresses its fear . . . in the phrase it has invented," Warner comments; the presses "must be kept running . . . the maw of the press must be fed" (286). Frank Norris used similar imagery with a slightly different emphasis. The "American public is ready . . . to devour anything," Norris wrote. "And the great presses of the country are for the most part merely sublimated sausage machines that go dashing along in a mess of paper and printer's ink turning out the meat for the monster" ("The American Public and 'Popular' Fiction," February 2, 1903, reprinted in Pizer, *Literary Criticism,* 126).

71. Milton's words were inscribed over the portal of the main reading room when the New York Public Library opened in 1911. The inscription is part of a passage from Milton's *Areopagitica,* a protest against censorship. It is still visible today. See Henry Hope Reed, *The New York Public Library: Its Architecture and Decoration* (New York: W. W. Norton and Co., 1986), 146; see also 29–30, 144, and the plate between 18 and 19. "Uncut," *Atlantic* 98 (April 1906): 576.

72. For relevant discussions of copyright, see Mark Rose, *Authors and Owners: The Invention of Copyright* (Cambridge, Mass.: Harvard University Press, 1993); Alice D. Shreyer, "Copyright and Books in Nineteenth-Century America," in *Getting the Books Out: Papers of the Chicago Conference on the Book in Nineteenth-Century America,* ed. Michael Hackenberg (Washington, D.C.: Center for the Book, Library of Congress, 1987); Meredith McGill, "The Matter of the Text: Commerce, Print Culture, and the Authority of the State in American Copyright Law," *American Literary History* 9.1 (Spring 1997): 21–59.

73. Howells, "Novel-Writing and Novel-Reading," 22.

74. W. R. Thayer, "The New Story-Tellers and the Doom of Realism," *Forum* 18 (1894): 476. The idea of the "transparent" text is still taken as a defining feature of realism, but now the idea, when invoked, is colored by postmodernist skepticism about the very possibility of "mimetic" representation. "The classical canons of novelistic realism . . . convey the illusion that they are literal transcriptions of reality, forms in which, as it were reality writes itself." Tony Bennett, *Formalism and Marxism* (London: Methuen, 1979), 24. As Walter Kendrick puts it in *The Novel Machine* (Baltimore: Johns Hopkins University Press, 1980), "The art of the mid-Victorian realistic novel flourished in innocence of theory" (1). But "the realistic novel, far from being the transparent transcription of life, is a metarhetorical trick . . . a thoroughly rhetorical not representational work of art" (7). Cf. Howard, *Form and History in American Literary Naturalism,* 14, 17.

75. Porter, *Books and Reading,* 51.

76. Brook Thomas, *American Literary Realism and the Failed Promise of Contract* (Berkeley: University of California Press, 1997), 77. Thomas emphasizes the problematics of separating the right to privacy from that of property: "[The] entire point of a right to privacy is to protect aspects of the personality from circulation in the marketplace. Privacy, therefore, had to be related to an inalienable part of one's personality" (60). At stake here is precisely the question of how to conceptualize what Warren and Brandeis called an "inviolate self."

77. William James, *Psychology: Briefer Course* (New York: Collier, 1962), 191.

78. Georg Simmel, "Female Culture," in *On Women, Sexuality, and Love,* trans. Guy Oakes (1911, reprinted New Haven: Yale University Press, 1984), 100. Quoting Hugo, Richardson strikes

a similar note in *The Choice of Books* while assuming a closer "fit" between author and work: "There is truth and wisdom in the aged Victor Hugo's curious and Frenchy, but grave and deep-felt preface to the recently made edition of his complete works: 'Every man who writes a book; that book is himself. Whether he knows it or not, whether he wishes it or not, it is so. From every work, whatever it may be, mean or illustrious, there is shaped a figure, that of the writer. It is his punishment if he be small; it is his recompense if he be great'" (*The Choice of Books*, 47). Hugo's terms, to be sure ("small" and "great") may well be intended to refer primarily to literary reputation, to the place of the author in the canon of the West—and yet, not only so. For just as Richardson, when quoting Hugo, does not hesitate to assess Hugo's "sincerity" (his "grave and deep-felt" if "Frenchy" sentiments), so for many other readers as well, "reading for the author" meant assuming that the character of the person who wrote the book could be inferred from the text.

79. Stephen Crane, *Maggie: A Girl of the Streets* (New York: W. W. Norton and Co., 1979), 132.

80. As Hamilton W. Mabie remarked in an essay titled "The Feeling for Literature" (1895), art is an expression of "personality"; it expresses "what is deepest and most significant" in the human being (*The Bookman* 1 [June 1895]: 326). In "Literature in Schools: An Address and Two Essays," in *Methods of Teaching* (New York: Houghton Mifflin & Co., 1888), Horace Scudder advocates the pedagogical value of linking works to men as he promotes the idea of teaching American books in their entirety: "We are not so much concerned to discriminate the work of the older Americans as we are ready to accept the men themselves, with their well-recognized personality. The process of sifting goes on silently, but however it may come to set the mark of approbation on this or that particular production, it is not likely that the group of men will be much enlarged or diminished" (53). He goes on: "With American literature for the great body of reading in our common schools, there would be the further advantage that just when the boy or girl was beginning to appreciate the personal element in books, to associate the author with what the author said, the teacher would be able to satisfy and stimulate an honorable curiosity. The increasing attention paid to authors' birthdays illustrates the instinctive demand from the schools that authors thus commemorated should be part and parcel of the school life" (56). This formulation also testifies to the growing interest in authors outside or apart from the text itself.

2. The Erosion of "Friendly" Reading

1. Porter, *Books and Reading*, 48, 53; cf. 228–29.

2. Henry James, "The Private Life," in *"The Figure in the Carpet" and Other Stories* (London: Penguin, 1986), 212, 219.

3. That Blanche herself is an actress is very much to the point: she is well aware of what makes for self-revelation or self-concealment in performance. The motif of the actress and its relevance to the realist project is discussed later on. See especially chapter 4.

4. Howells, "Novel-Writing and Novel-Reading," 22. Further references are cited in the text.

5. Winston Churchill's popular novel *The Celebrity: An Episode* (1897) makes an author's decision to travel incognito a sign of moral turpitude. On how popular fiction of the period defied the realist agenda, see chapter 3.

6. Porter, *Books and Reading*, 53.

7. Walsh, *Authors and Authorship*, iv.

8. "Congress of Authors," *The Dial* 15 (July 1893): 29. Clearly my concern is not with the real increase in the size of the reading public, which I would not try to assess. My interest here is in the way the increase in readers and reading—whatever it was—was perceived in literary discourse and the impact such perceptions had on fiction itself. On the size of the reading public, see Borus, *Writing Realism*, and Ronald Zboray, *A Fictive People: Antebellum Economic Development and the American Reading Public* (New York: Oxford University Press, 1993).

9. Addressing the "Congress of Authors" in 1893, Walter Besant noted: "A writer of importance in our language may address an audience drawn from a hundred millions of English-speaking people ... [;] never before in the history of the world has there been such an audience.... [Soon] the popular writer ... will command ... so vast an audience ... as he has never yet even conceived as possible" ("Congress of Authors," 29). "The preponderance of fiction in the literature of the closing decades of this century is the most salient feature in the literary history of our times," wrote George Clarke in 1898 in "The Novel-Reading Habit," 670. James strikes a similar note in "Future of the Novel" (1899), in Miller, *Theory of Fiction,* 336.

10. As Joan Shelley Rubin notes, "the most famous predecessor" of the "middlebrow" institutions that flourished after World War I (book clubs, "great books" groups, radio programs, etc.) was Charles W. Eliot's "Five-Foot Shelf of Books," designed to "furnish a liberal education to anyone willing to devote fifteen minutes per day to reading them" (*The Making of Middlebrow Culture,* 27–28). But this notion of making culture available in time-efficient, bite-sized pieces is already apparent in the 1880s and 1890s. "The quantity of reading that may be done in a year by the employment of even small portions of time is surprising to those who have not observed the matter," according to an article ("The Reading Habit") published in *Harper's* and partially reprinted in *The Critic,* July 30, 1892, 60. Affirming the benefits to be gained by investing even small amounts of reading time, the article sings the praises of "a lady whom we know ... the head of a large family, entertaining much company and doing a great deal of benevolent work" (60). Although this "lady" has little spare time, her "reading-habit" stands her in good stead. She has "several books on hand at once" and so need never sit "idly through even those moments of waiting [e.g., "intervals between 'fittings' in the sewing room"] which are inevitable in every large family" (60). With books on different subjects stationed in various rooms (and "books of short stories to be read in carriages or horse cars"), the lady in question becomes a great asset to her family—chatting knowledgeably to her children and "irrigating" the "arid" mind of her tired husband after he has returned from a day engaged in business (60). While this description may veer toward parody, it points to the disciplined, "purposive" reading which was promoted by many educators and publishers but which was anathema to Wharton and others.

11. In the last twenty years of the century, a number of new journals appeared, specifically devoted to literature and the arts. The commentators who discussed books and reading in these periodicals formed an interpretive community of limited influence; yet their words reflected changing assumptions about reading that were characteristic of the culture at large. *The Dial* was founded in 1880 (Chicago); *The Critic* in 1881 (New York); *The Arena* in 1889 (Boston). "*The Critic* is read by people who love books," a small box announced. "It is the first *literary* journal in America" (November 19, 1895, vi). *The Bookman's* American edition first appeared in 1895.

12. See Kaplan, *Social Construction,* esp. 19–35, 89–91, 101–2.

13. Edith Wharton, "The Vice of Reading," *North American Review* 177 (1903): 514, 516.

14. Crothers, "The Gentle Reader," 655.

15. Ibid., 654, 658.

16. William Dean Howells, *The Rise of Silas Lapham* (New York: W. W. Norton, 1982), chap. 9.

17. The phrase is Wharton's ("Vice," 516).

18. Edith Wharton, "Xingu," in *The Muse's Tragedy and Other Stories* (New York: New American Library, 1990), 378.

19. Frank Norris, "Dying Fires," in *The Complete Edition of Frank Norris,* vol. 4 (New York: Doubleday Doran and Co., 1928). Presley, Norris's poet figure in *The Octopus* (1901), suggests another version of this scenario. Late in the novel, "taken up" by the culturally pretentious railroad magnate's wife, the "poor dear poet ... thin as a ghost" hovers uncomfortably at the margins of a dinner party, where he imagines the other participants as cannibals "tearing human flesh."

Although his work is misunderstood, Presley himself is flattered and appropriated on the one hand, threatened with "consumption" on the other. Frank Norris, *The Octopus* (New York: New American Library, 1964), 415, 428.

20. James, *"The Figure in the Carpet" and Other Stories*, 370. A word about gender: In the stories I have cited, the "author" is often male, the adulating readers generally female. Yet the revered writer in "Xingu" is a woman; and many of James's benighted readers are male. Since the widespread assumption was that novels were mainly read by women, many writers of realism were directly concerned with appropriating the novel for "serious" (i.e., male) readers. Yet, as Ronald Zboray has shown, more nineteenth-century men read novels than many people believed (see chap. 11, "Gender and Boundlessness in Reading Patterns," in *A Fictive People*; cf. Borus, *Writing Realism*, 111–14).

21. This view of reading, already implicit in *Walden*, is explicit in a text such as Porter's *Books and Reading*. Porter insists that a "healthy diet" of "effective" reading is increasingly urgent in the face of the growing numbers of available books. His emphasis on reading purposively, for "nutriment" as well as "succulence," anticipates the drive for self-improvement through the reading habit that would provide a virtual ocean of "helpful hints for home reading" as the century went on. Thus Porter's work itself displays a characteristic tension in late nineteenth-century conceptions of books and reading: the idea of reading for use and profit competes with the idea of reading for attraction and pleasure. Baldwin's *The Booklover* reflects the same tension. Ample citations, mainly from writers of the past, stress the notion of books as friends (10, 15, 24); yet this emphasis coexists with a sense of the need for rigor, for reading with "a purpose" (34). Like Porter, Baldwin castigates "desultory and profitless reading" (37), noting the troubles created by the superfluity of printed matter ("I cannot but think the very infinity of opportunities is robbing us of the actual power of using them" [35]).

22. On impersonality as part of the "culture of professionalism," see Bledstein, *The Culture of Professionalism*, 55, 76–79, 85–99. Morton Horwitz discusses the factors that contributed to the "shift toward formal and objective rules" in legal theory, especially after 1850, in *The Transformation of American Law, 1780–1860* (Cambridge, Mass.: Harvard University Press, 1977), 263 and chap. 8.

23. Ong, "The Writer's Audience Is Always a Fiction," 9, 12, and passim. See also Iser's idea that "the real reader is always offered a particular role to play" (*The Act of Reading*, 34).

24. With the "return of the reader" into theoretical discussions of fiction in the 1970s, numerous terms have been generated to conceptualize "ideal," "implied," and other readers and to place them in a variety of relations to the text itself. I invoke Erwin Wolff's "intended reader" here because it relates the image of the reader inscribed in the fictional text to features of the contemporary reading public. See Erwin Wolff, "Der Intendirte Leser," *Poetica* 4 (1971). Because Wolff's "intended reader" is explicitly derived from the author's social context, it constitutes a potential key to the author's conception of real readers. Iser takes Wolff's idea of the intended reader as an index to "the public which the author *wished* to address" (*Act of Reading*, 33; my emphasis); but insofar as the intended reader is grounded in contemporary norms, the image is also likely to reflect an author's misgivings about contemporary readers and reading habits. Such "intended" readers would point not only to the "public the author wished to address" but also, in Stephen Railton's terms, to "the author's ambitions and anxieties about performing for a particular group" ("The Address of the Scarlet Letter," in Machor, *Readers in History*, 139). For an overview of reader theory, see Elizabeth Freund, *The Return of the Reader: Reader-Response Criticism* (London: Methuen, 1987).

25. Michael Newbury has discussed the "profession of authorship" in antebellum America with emphasis on the way publicity for public figures contributed to the association of author and slave via the trope of bodily consumption. Although Newbury is not concerned with how the reading

process itself was imagined, I suggest that for many writers at the end of the century, the threat of "consumption" was most vividly experienced as an imagined consequence of being read. See Michael Newbury, "Eaten Alive: Slavery and Celebrity in Antebellum America," *ELH* 61 (Spring 1994): 159–87.

26. Norris, "Weekly Letter," 55.

27. James, "Ivan Turgenieff," 174–75.

28. Once, Crothers reflects, books were dedicated to the reader, with "long rambling prefaces" and intermissions in "the very middle of the story," where "the writer would stop with a word of apology or explanation" ("The Gentle Reader," 654). From Crothers's point of view, turn-of-century readers were too busy, skeptical, or scientific to linger and dally for an "interchange of thought" (655) with the reader. Whether or not we accept this assessment, it is undeniable that by 1900 many works of fiction no longer acknowledged the reader at all. Yet, as we shall see, some of the most popular turn-of-century authors retained this rhetorical strategy. See chapter 3.

29. "The Life and Poetry of Wordsworth," 487.

30. See Borus, *Writing Realism*, 118, 123–25; Wilson, *Labor of Words*, 82.

31. Edith Wharton, "Copy: A Dialogue," in *Crucial Instances* (1901, reprinted New York: AMS, 1969), 113. Further references are cited in the text.

32. Robert Darnton's French bourgeois would seem to have been guided by similar reading conventions when he read the work of "*l'Ami* Jean-Jacques" ("Readers Respond to Rousseau," 222).

33. Review of *Representative Men, North American Review* 70 (1850): 520. Here as elsewhere the terms "personality" and "individuality" seem to be loosely synonymous and to signify something more than a public persona ("who and what Mr. Emerson is"). Compare the previously cited reviewer on Hawthorne's "rare . . . individuality." See also chapters 4 and 5. Modern theory rejects the association of written text and "originating author" on many grounds. On the "author" as a defensive construct that limits the proliferation of meaning in a text, see Michel Foucault, "What Is an Author?" in *Language, Counter—Memory, Practice: Selected Essays and Interviews*, ed. Donald F. Bouchard, trans. Donald F. Bouchard and Sherry Simon (Ithaca: Cornell University Press, 1977). On the author as a formal aesthetic effect that allows for a sense of harmony and totality, see Rowe, *The Theoretical Dimensions of Henry James*, chap. 7. See also Roland Barthes's classic "The Death of the Author," in *Image-Music-Text*, trans. Stephen Heath (New York: Hill and Wang, 1977), 143–48. Roger Chartier contextualizes the idea of the author historically in *The Order of Books*, trans. Lydia G. Cochrane (Stanford: Stanford University Press, 1994). Chap. 2, "Figures of the Author."

34. See Ong, "The Writer's Audience." Paul J. Hunter says of invocations to the "dear reader" in early first-person narratives, "It is as if they were trying to reestablish the communality which narrative necessarily left behind when it turned to the printed page" ("The Loneliness of the Long-Distance Reader," 472). Peter Brooks also emphasizes how certain rhetorical strategies serve to counteract the impersonality of print culture ("The Tale vs. the Novel," *Novel* 21.1 (1988): 285–92).

35. See Warhol, *Gendered Interventions*, esp. chap. 2.

36. Even today, after deconstruction and the "decentering of the subject," the first-person pronoun tends to be associated with an individual, even personal, speaker. That is exactly why, as Warhol suggests, it elicits "embarrassment" from readers of criticism in an age of scholarly "professionalism." More recently however, the rise of autobiographical, even confessional, criticism has given the wheel another spin.

37. Part of this quote is cited in F. O. Matthiessen, *American Renaissance: Art and Expression in the Age of Emerson and Whitman* (New York: Oxford University Press, 1968), 235; part is cited in Kendrick, *The Novel Machine*, 6.

38. Ibid., 7. Kendrick's main concern, however, is not the figure of the giant-author but the notion of the transparent text.

39. James, "The Art of Fiction," 30.

40. The best example from Eliot would be chap. 17 of *Adam Bede,* "In Which the Story Pauses a Little," but fleeting examples abound in her work as they do in that of Thackeray and Trollope.

41. The irony that Warhol calls "distancing" nonetheless serves as a ground of connection through humor, and the sense of privileged understanding that irony always implies.

42. Quoted in James D. Hart, *The Popular Book: A History of America's Literary Taste* (New York: Oxford University Press, 1950), 94–95. Fanny Fern's real name was Sara Payson Willis. According to Susan Barrera Fay, the practice of using pseudonyms began to play a significant role in American fiction from the 1840s ("A Modest Celebrity: Literary Reputation and the Marketplace in Antebellum America" [Ph.D. diss., George Washington University, 1992]).

43. Fay, "A Modest Celebrity," chap. 4.

44. On the shift from the editorial "we" to the seemingly more personal "I" in certain journals of the 1890s, see Wilson, "Rhetoric of Consumption," 40–64. Wilson's discussion of the new breed of editors at the turn of the century stresses their more aggressively purposive conception of a magazine and their active attempt to create the feel of a more personal relationship to readers. Part of this change in strategy was a rejection of the anonymous "we." But for many readers, even at the turn of the century, that "we" seemed inviting, if not inclusive and reassuringly familiar. Editors such as S. S. McClure, Edward Bok, and George Horace Lorimer may have seen the genteel "we" as cold or exclusionary, partly because as first-generation immigrants or midwesterners, they themselves were, as Wilson suggests, "outsiders" to literary "culture" (45). Wilson also shows that the personal "I" and "you" that these editors encouraged their authors to use were in fact self-conscious manipulations, radically dissociated from their own sense of self (63). Nonetheless, for many readers of the period, both the "I" of earlier writers and the "I" of popular fiction were still readily associated with a whole, often biographically concrete authorial figure. On popular fiction, see chapter 3. See also my discussion of Dreiser as writer and editor in chapter 5.

45. In his introduction to *Our Nig* (1859, reprinted New York: Vintage Books, 1983), Henry Louis Gates, Jr., draws attention to the interplay between the "non-fictional and fictional discourses" of the text" (xxxv), the "tensions between autobiography and fiction" (xxxvi), and the shifts from third- to first-person narration (xxxvii). For many readers, I suggest, such shifts and mergers reinforced the sense of a text's represented world as "real" and the experience of reading it as an active give-and-take with an authorial "person." See also chapter 3.

46. Sicherman, "Reading *Little Women,*" 248.

47. Henry James, preface to *The Golden Bowl,* in *The Art of the Novel* (New York: Charles Scribner's Sons, 1950), 328.

48. The term "narrative voice" itself displaces the idea of an author by implying a principle that exists exclusively in and through narration. The term was coined by Gérard Gennette in 1972, but it was anticipated by James. In the interim, the figure of the author recedes as a whole discourse of narrators emerges. In 1950 Walker Gibson writes: "It is now common in the classroom as well as in criticism to distinguish carefully between the *author* of a literary work . . . and the fictitious *speaker* within the work" ("Authors, Speakers, Readers, and Mock Readers," in *Reader Response Criticism,* 1). Nonetheless, Gérard Gennette could complain in 1972 that even professional readers persisted in "identify[ing] . . . the narrator with the author, and the recipient of the narrative with the reader of the work" (*Narrative Discourse,* trans. Jane E. Lewin [Ithaca: Cornell University Press, 1980], 213; first published 1972 as a portion of *Figures Three*). The distinction between author and narrating voice became increasingly absolute in literary studies, as structuralist poetics proliferated terms to differentiate ever more finely between authors, implied authors, implied readers, narratees, and so on. Yet many readers continued to read for the author nonetheless. As

Peter Rabinowitz wrote in 1987, "[Despite] the critical revolutions of the 1970s and 1980s . . . the initial question most commonly asked of a literary text in our culture [still] is, what is the author saying." Rabinowitz suggests that this reading practice prevails "even among the most jaded readers—academics" (*Before Reading*, 30). Outside the classroom, of course, reading for the author flourishes more abundantly. As Radway points out, for example, many romance readers "can be said to read *authors* rather than books" ("Reading Is Not Eating," 12, 22).

49. The vocabulary generated by structuralist poetics encouraged far greater precision in pinpointing the narrator's location with regard to both represented world and reader. See Shlomith Rimmon-Kenan's discussion of narrative levels in *Narrative Fiction: Contemporary Poetics* (London: Methuen, 1983), 94-96.

50. Norris, "Weekly Letter," 55.

51. Ibid.

52. Frank Norris, "Simplicity in Art" (1902), in Pizer, *Literary Criticism*, 63. James agreed: "We take for granted by the general law of fiction a primary author. Take him so much for granted that we forget him in proportion as he works upon us and that he works upon us most in fact by making us forget him" ("The New Novel," in Miller, *Theory of Fiction*, 253). Cf. Jack London: "PUT ALL THOSE THINGS WHICH ARE YOURS INTO THE STORIES . . . *ELIMINATING YOURSELF*. . . . Don't narrate—paint! draw! build!—CREATE . . . Put in life, and movement—and for God's sake no creaking. Damn you! Forget you! And then the world will remember you" (*Letters from Jack London*, 108).

53. Lee, *The Lost Art of Reading*, 20. The feeling of loss fueled an ongoing debate about reading habits in journals, lectures, and books about literature and reading. Further references to Lee are cited in the text.

54. Crothers, "The Gentle Reader," 655, 658.

55. Dunn, "A Plea for the Shiftless Reader," 132, 136.

56. Wharton, *The Writing of Fiction*, 91. Wharton attacks the "slovenly habit of some novelists of tumbling in and out of their characters' minds, and then suddenly drawing back to scrutinize them from the outside as the avowed Showman holding his puppets' strings" (89). Yet she also expresses her reservations about James's "rigorous . . . confining [of] every detail . . . to the range, and also to the capacity, of the eye fixed on it" (90). On Wharton's ambivalence about authorial invisibility, see also chapters 4 and 5.

57. The question of addressing one's public in one's own voice, so to speak, was often a focus of discussion and irony in the *Atlantic*. "In this corner we are privileged, I take it, to talk of personal experience and impression," writes a commentator in the magazine's "Contributors' Club" in 1906, "leaving formality and eloquence to our betters in the more public parts of the magazine" (*Atlantic* 98 [February 1906]: 283). Later, E. M. Forster apologizes, half seriously, for his use of the first-person pronoun and his "informal, indeed talkative" mode of address in a prefatory note to *Aspects of the Novel* (New York: Harcourt, Brace and Co., 1927). See also chapters 3 and 5.

58. Echoes of Thoreau are evident in this passage; see chapter 1.

59. Levine aptly illustrates this point in *Highbrow/Lowbrow*, 13-15.

60. Michaels explores some implications of "making a mark that is not only yours but you" (*The Gold Standard*, 11). See also Fried, *Realism, Writing, Disfiguration*, 147-48.

61. Levine clarifies the image of a classic as a dead thing in discussing the transformation of Shakespeare from a familiar source of pleasure to a cultural icon at the end of the nineteenth century. See *Highbrow/Lowbrow*, sec. 1, "William Shakespeare in America."

62. Jack London, *Martin Eden* (New York: Penguin, 1993), 114. Further references are cited in the text.

63. This section of *Martin Eden* is a fictionalized rewrite of London's "Getting into Print" (*The Editor* [March 1903]).

64. *The Letters of F. Scott Fitzgerald*, ed. Andrew Turnbull (New York: Charles Scribner's Sons, 1963), 158.

65. Charles Norris, *Frank Norris* (New York: Doubleday, 1914), 10.

66. Elaine Showalter speaks of the reference to Chopin as self-reflexive in "Tradition and the Female Talent: *The Awakening* as a Solitary Book," in *New Essays on "The Awakening,"* ed. Wendy Martin (New York: Cambridge University Press, 1988), 47.

67. Kaplan, *Social Construction*, 84; R. W. B. Lewis, *Edith Wharton: A Biography* (London: Constable, 1975), 67. Lewis also points out that Lily Bart bears Wharton's own nickname (26, 155).

68. Fried, *Realism, Writing, Disfiguration*, 147-48.

69. Willa Cather, "Death in the Desert," in *"The Troll Garden" and Selected Stories by Willa Cather* (New York: Bantam, 1990), 156.

70. The idea of fiction as an open invitation for social interaction recurs throughout the period. An article in the *Atlantic* suggests that the sense of affinity that prompts readers to write to authors might provide a better basis for friendship than many others ("The Hap-Hazard of Our Friendships," *Atlantic* 57 [June 1886]: 857-58). "What you say of the Altrurian greatly interests me," William Dean Howells wrote to a reader. "I wish I might talk with you of these matters. But . . . if we never meet, still I hope you will always think of me as your friend, and not read me as a personal stranger" (cited in Borus, *Writing Realism*, 107).

71. In an early essay James himself stresses mutuality in the dynamic and reciprocal "labor" of novel writing, whereby "the work is divided between the writer and the reader" ("The Novels of George Eliot," *Atlantic* 18 [October 1866]: 485). See chapter 4.

72. Corson, *The Aims of Literary Study*, 57. A professor of English at Cornell, Corson had written several discussions of English verse. For Corson, to "get at" an author is to experience what one discussion of his book calls "living in the company of great writers" (Review of Corson, *The Aims of Literary Study, The Bookman* 1 [February 1895]: 123-24). Still, the term itself has aggressive connotations. On Corson's "generalist" ideology, see Gerald Graff, *Professing Literature: An Institutional History* (Chicago: University of Chicago Press, 1987), 82-84. When Samuel Crothers writes that "appreciation of literature is the getting at an author" ("The Gentle Reader," 656), he would seem to intend the phrase as Corson does, to evoke the idea of reading as "a kind of conversation" (Crothers, 655).

73. James, *"The Figure in the Carpet" and Other Stories*, 358, 361. Further references are cited in the text. Cf. "The Death of the Lion," "The Private Life," "The Middle Years," among others. Wolfgang Iser has suggested that James's "Figure in the Carpet" constitutes an attack on a way of reading that sees meaning as "a thing" which is to be "extracted" from the work (546). In Iser's terms, James's story anticipates the subsequent demise of reading practices that drain the literary work of content while turning the text into an "empty shell," a mere husk to be discarded once its meaning is consumed (*The Act of Reading*, 4-5). But James's story also represents a turning point in interpretive conventions with regard to the idea of the author in particular.

74. Like "Figure in the Carpet," *The Aspern Papers* is clearly marked as a "written" tale: the narrator asserts, for example, that he "shall not take up *space* with attempting to explain" a certain point." See Henry James, *The Aspern Papers*, in *The Aspern Papers and The Turn of the Screw* (London: Penguin, 1986), 48; my emphasis. Further references are cited in the text. Like Juliana Bordereau, who refuses to give the narrator "so much as a morsel of paper with her name on it" (72), the narrator never commits his name to paper. Jonathan Auerbach suggests that the "absolutely crucial insistence on anonymity for his first-person commentators enables James to protect his own impersonality in the face of the form's terrible fluidity of self-revelation" (*The Romance of Failure: First-Person Fictions of Poe, Hawthorne, and James* [New York: Oxford University Press, 1989]), 130.

75. "A Word for Silent Partners," *Atlantic* 61 (January 1888): 137-38.

76. See Wilson, *Labor of Words*, 44. Discussing "The Literary Remains" of Henry James, Sr., for example, the *Atlantic* reviewer characteristically insists that the use of James's notebooks "invade[s] no privacy" ("Henry James," *Atlantic* 55 [May 1885]: 702). In 1885, when Henry James, Jr., reviews a new edition of Pepys's *Diary*, he notes the qualities in the *Diary* that allow the reader to "escape . . . the guilty consciousness of evesdropping" ("A Word for Pepys," *Atlantic* 55 [February 1885]: 273). Yet recurrent attention to "the man behind the pen," however discreet, could not but upset the balance by which the work in itself had once seemed to constitute the person with whom a reader could engage.

77. See, for example, Catherine Golden, "The Writing of 'The Yellow Wallpaper': A Double Palimpsest," *Studies in American Fiction* 17.2 (1989): 193–201.

78. On the shift from writing to reading within the story, see Annette Kolodny, "A Map for ReReading: Or, Gender and the Interpretation of Literary Texts," in *The Captive Imagination: A Casebook on "The Yellow Wallpaper*," ed. Catherine Golden (New York: Feminist Press, 1992), 156–57; and Richard Feldstein, "Reader, Text, Referentiality," in *Feminism and Psychoanalysis*, ed. Richard Feldstein and Judith Roof (Ithaca: Cornell University Press, 1989), 276–79.

79. Charlotte Perkins Gilman, "The Yellow Wallpaper" (New York: Feminist Press, 1973), 19, 27. Further references are cited in the text.

80. The issue of text and "subtext" is a recurrent focus in feminist readings of the story. See Judith Fetterley, "Reading about Reading: 'A Jury of Her Peers,' 'The Murders in the Rue Morgue,' and 'The Yellow Wallpaper,'" in Flynn and Schweickart, *Gender and Reading*, and Golden, "Palimpsest."

81. In another sense, the merging of the narrator with the woman in the wallpaper can be seen as a version of that blend of self and other that certain theorists argue is an inevitable (and positive) element in every act of reading. See, for example, Poulet, "Criticism and the Experience of Interiority." I would suggest that it is Gilman's intention to force her own reader to read the story in a way that is quite different from the protagonist's mode of reading.

82. Theodore Dreiser, *The Financier* (New York: New American Library, 1981), 7–8. See chapter 5.

83. Baldwin, *The Booklover*, 36; Corson, *The Aims of Literary Study*, 57; Mabie, "The Feeling for Literature," 324–26.

3. Refusing Authorial Self-Effacement

1. Throughout this chapter I use the term "popular" to refer to fictional works that achieved best-seller status by the criteria of James Hart (*The Popular Book*) or Frank Luther Mott (*Golden Multitudes: The Story of Best Sellers in the United States* [New York: Macmillan, 1947]). Although some realist novels (e.g., *The House of Mirth* and *The Pit*) also achieved this status, the popular works of the present chapter are novels that not only fit the best-seller category but also share two other features: they employ a mode of narration resistant to realist imperatives, and they were excluded from the academic canon for most if not all of the twentieth century.

2. Bourdieu speaks of the "positions" open to participants in a literary "field" and notes that "a position-taking changes, even when the position remains identical, whenever there is a change in the universe of options that are simultaneously offered for producers and consumers to choose from. The meaning of a work (artistic, literary, philosophical, etc.) changes automatically with each change in the field within which it is situated for the spectator or reader." Pierre Bourdieu, *The Field of Cultural Production: Essays on Art and Literature*, ed. Randal Johnson (Cambridge: Polity Press, 1993), 30–31.

3. To take just one example: "We will draw a veil over the scene that occurred after Rebecca's return from school," Wiggin writes. "You who read this may be well advanced in years, you may

be gifted in rhetoric, ingenious in argument; but even you might quail at the thought of explaining [Rebecca's] tortuous mental processes." Kate Douglas Wiggin, *Rebecca of Sunnybrook Farm* (Boston: Houghton Mifflin and Co., 1904), 129. Further references are cited in the text. The "personal" element in narration receives further support from a passage in which the narrator comments on Rebecca's rhetorical practices, explicitly affirming "personality" as an indispensable aid to discourse. Rebecca, we are told, "had her own way of recombining and applying" things she had heard so that they had a curious effect of belonging to her. The words of some people might generally be written with a minus sign after them, the minus meaning that the personality of the speaker subtracted from, rather than added to, their weight; but Rebecca's words might always have borne the plus sign (189).

4. Nancy Glazener notes that the idea of "a storyteller" was central to what she calls the "romantic revival" of this period (mainly Kipling and Stevenson). Although Glazener does not focus on the narrating postures of realism, or on the realists' ambivalence about their own professional "impartiality," she touches on questions related to the ones that concern me here when she notes that "the storyteller model . . . [was a] critical departure from the realists' construction of authorship as professionalism" and suggests that "the model of storytelling guarded writers against charges of manipulation and commercialism" (*Reading for Realism*, 163).

5. Willa Cather, "Du Maurier's *Trilby*," *Nebraska Journal*, December 23, 1894, reprinted in *The Kingdom of Art: Willa Cather's First Principles and Critical Statements, 1893–96*, ed. Bernice Slote (Lincoln: University of Nebraska Press, 1966), 363–64. In the passage that precedes the cited one, it is still more evident that the "wise, gentle, sympathetic man" in question is imagined as the author. "A young man could not have written *Trilby*," Cather notes. "It is the work of a man whose heart is still young and tender, but whose blood has lost the mad impetuosity of youth. . . . The man treats [Trilby] . . . as an old man might treat a foolish child for whom he cared" (363).

6. Cited in Hart, *The Popular Book*, 188. Ouida (Louise de la Ramée) was a popular writer of romance.

7. For Kaplan "the major work of the realistic narrative is to construct a homogeneous and coherent social reality by conquering the fictional qualities of middle-class life and by controlling the specter of class conflict which threatens to puncture this vision of a unified social totality" (*Social Construction*, 21).

8. See Howard, *Form and History*, chap. 4; Trachtenberg, *Incorporation*, chap. 6. For Glazener, realism not only "reproduc[ed], justif[ied], and obscur[ed] class hierarchy" but also "helped to reinforce racial hierarchy" (*Reading for Realism*, 120). She suggests that in magazines such as the *Atlantic*, realism was presented as an "object of connoisseurship" partly by constructing certain social groups as "inferior" (95, 98–99). Generally speaking, the "other" populations of realism are immigrants, Jews, working-class figures, and "outcasts" such as thieves and prostitutes. African Americans tend to be conspicuous by their absence from both realist texts and the popular novels that concern me here. The racist trilogy of Thomas Dixon is one salient exception to the invisibility of black figures in turn-of-century texts by white authors. Kenneth W. Warren explores the ways in which "concerns about 'race' may structure our American texts, even when those texts are not 'about' race in any substantive way." See *Black and White Strangers: Race and American Literary Realism* (Chicago: University of Chicago Press, 1993), 10.

9. Owen Wister, *The Virginian: A Horseman of the Plains* (1902, reprinted New York: Macmillan, 1967), 54. Further references are cited in the text.

10. Walter Benn Michaels, *Our America: Nativism, Modernism, and Pluralism* (Durham: Duke University Press, 1995), 10.

11. Higham, *Strangers in the Land*, 64.

12. Earlier, Molly's good friend Mrs. Taylor expresses her impatience with Molly's failure to appreciate the Virginian. "Kind!" she exclaims. "There's a word you shouldn't use, my dear. No

doubt you can spell it. But more than its spelling I guess you don't know. The children can learn what it means from some of the rest of us folks that don't spell so correct, maybe. . . . Since the roughness looks bigger to you than the diamond, you had better go back to Vermont. I expect you'll find better grammar there, deary" (278).

13. Lee Clark Mitchell, "'When You Call Me That . . .': Tall Talk and Male Hegemony in *The Virginian,*" *PMLA* 102.1 (1987): 71; Klein, *Easterns, Westerns, and Private Eyes,* 128.

14. Mitchell notes the "ready concession [Wister made] . . . to his acerbic mother when she complained (in a judgment since widely shared) that 'the heroine is a failure'" ("'When You Call Me That,'" 73). James's comment is cited in Mitchell (76).

15. Klein explores the novel's consistent emphasis on "status and privilege"—and "blood" (*Easterns, Westerns, and Private Eyes,* 127).

16. In Frances Hodgson Burnett's *Little Lord Fauntleroy,* another highly popular novel of the period, the little "lord's" American mother and his "nature" are the main factors that enable him to lay claim to his "aristocratic" position (inherited, technically speaking, from his British father). According to Hart, *Little Lord Fauntleroy* began as a serial in the juvenile magazine *St. Nicholas,* moving "into adult circles as a book published in 1886 and as a play, which ran on Broadway for four years and toured the nation with road companies almost as numerous as those that produced *Uncle Tom's Cabin* or *Ben Hur.*" Books that we now think of as children's books but that in their own time were "read by young and old alike" (Hart, *The Popular Book,* 187) constitute a phenomenon that deserves further study. From *Little Women* through *Rebecca of Sunnybrook Farm* and the work of Frances Hodgson Burnett, there were many such books in the latter half of the nineteenth century, most of them written by women.

17. "Edducation [*sic*] is going to be the making of me," Rebecca says early on (48).

18. See chapter 2.

19. Cited in Klein, *Easterns, Westerns, and Private Eyes,* 125.

20. See chapter 2.

21. Gérard Gennette emphasizes the "shifting but sacred frontier between two worlds, the world in which one tells, and the world of which one tells" (*Narrative Discourse,* 236). For an overview of how narrative poetics theorizes the problem of "narrative levels" (the narrator's relation to the represented reality of the text on the one hand and to the implied reader on the other), see Rimmon-Kenan, *Narrative Fiction,* esp. 94–96.

22. The dust jacket of a 1967 reprint of *The Virginian* (New York: Macmillan) stresses Wister's firm place in "good" society as well: "Two famous actresses—the great Mrs. Siddons and Fanny Kemble—as well as four generations of writers, were among Owen Wister's ancestors." After noting Wister's study at Harvard (he graduated with "highest honors"), the ill health that prompted his first trip West, and his success as an author ("editors and the reading public [began] . . . to clamor for his work"), the copy concludes: "Among his many distinguished friends was President Theodore Roosevelt, who never ceased to encourage him to present in his books the true ideals of America. He died in 1938, honored both here and abroad as a distinguished man of letters."

23. Shirley Samuels traces the importance of "blood" for the idea of both family and nation in the early republic (*Romances of the Republic: Women, the Family, and Violence in the Literature of the Early American Nation* [New York: Oxford University Press, 1996]). Amy Kaplan explores the link between the discourse of nation and that of family in the antebellum period ("Manifest Domesticity," *American Literature* 70.3 [September 1998]). On the shifting relations between the idea of family and nation in the discourse of the Progressive era, see Michaels, *Our America.*

24. Wister's preface did not appear until *The Virginian* was first published in book form. Readers had presumably written to him in response to "some chapters of this book which were published separately at the close of the nineteenth century" (ix).

25. "Recent Novels," review of *The Virginian*, *Nation* 23 (October 1902): 331. A poem by S. Weir Mitchell, "Books and the Man," which was "read to the Charaka Club of New York March 4, 1905," elaborates the identification of a book with its author at some length. It includes the following lines:

> When the years gather round us like stern foes
> That give no quarter and the ranks of love
> Break here and there, untouched there still abide
> Friends whom no adverse fate can wound or move.
>
> . . . .
>
> Some ghostly presence haunts the lucid phrase
> Where Bacon pondered o'er the words we scan.
> Here grave Montaigne with cynic wisdom played
> And lo, the book becomes for us a man!

(New York Public Library, Astor, Lenox, and Tilden Foundations, 1905).

26. Klein has pointed to the irony "in the fact that Wister felt his proper audience was not those tremendous numbers who bought the book, but an elite" (*Easterns, Westerns, and Private Eyes*, 111–12).

27. Winston Churchill, *Richard Carvel* (1899, reprinted London: Macmillan, 1900), 16. Further references are cited in the text.

28. As James Hart points out, with patriotic and ancestral societies proliferating at the end of the century, money sometimes could in fact buy "an improved version of one's grandfather" or (through marriage) "somebody else's noble ancestry for the children" (*The Popular Book*, 181).

29. On readers who use texts to make meanings different from those that have been legislated by literary critics or other "professionals," see Ginzburg, *The Cheese and the Worms*; Radway, *Reading the Romance*; Sicherman, "Reading and Ambition." For a theoretical perspective on the issue, see Chartier, "Texts, Printings, Readings."

30. The practice of addressing the reader as a member of the family, while assuming "that strangers too . . . will be interested in what [one] says," goes back, in America, at least to Benjamin Franklin's *Autobiography*, which begins "Dear Son." See Kenneth Dauber, *The Idea of Authorship in America: Democratic Poetics from Franklin to Melville* (Madison: University of Wisconsin Press, 1990), xvi and chap. 1.

31. Even the coward-villain who has intended to "betray" Carvel repents at last and parts from the hero saying, "I believe I am better at this hour than I have been since I last knelt at my mother's knee" (528).

32. By contrast, Churchill's novel *The Celebrity* makes a comic butt of an author who disguises himself for no good reason and does not even stand by the moral truths espoused in his own writing. He is, however, juxtaposed with (and bested by) the reliable integrity of an exemplary, if innocent, first-person narrator.

33. S. Weir Mitchell was another popular writer whose work reflects his attention to narration. In *Hugh Wynne: Free Quaker* (1896), for example, the preface ("Introductory") explicitly proposes to account for the novel's narrative method. Addressing the difficulties created by the "constant need to use the first person in a narrative of adventure and incidents which chiefly concern the writer," Mitchell declares his professional concern with narrative method. He finds a consistent (if cumbersome) solution to the problem by citing a "diary," written by his hero's boyhood friend, whenever an "outside" view of the narrator is required. S. Weir Mitchell, *Hugh Wynne* (New York: The Century Co., 1905), 1, 2–3.

34. *A Roman Singer* was not the most popular of Crawford's novels, but it constitutes a particularly good example of narration that at once acknowledges and defies realist criteria, creating a

bond between writer and reader which also reinforces the thematic concern with the threat of "outsiders."

35. Francis Marion Crawford, *A Roman Singer* (Leipzig: Bernhard Tauchnitz, 1884), 31. Further references are cited in the text. For other examples of the narrator defending his sources of information, see 112, 248, 277.

36. For analogous digressions, see 53–54, 106, 283.

37. "But you want to hear of Nino . . . without hearing . . . my reflections and small-talk about goodness, and success, and the like," the narrator notes (17). And again: "I must satisfy your curiosity before anything else, and not dwell too long on the details" (53–54); and "you object that I am not proceeding with my task and telling you more facts" (283).

38. Irene Kacandes, "Are You in the Text?: The 'Literary Performative' in Postmodernist Fiction," *Text and Performance Quarterly* 13 (1993): 139–42. Kacandes's discussion of the French linguist Emile Benveniste, especially his contention that "the appearance of 'you' implies an 'I/you' pair and concomitantly relationship and communication," is especially relevant to the present context (140). The narrator of *A Roman Singer* repeatedly foregrounds his ongoing relationship with the reader of the text ("I am writing this story to tell you . . ." [14]; "I would like you to admire my boy's audacity" [74]; and so on).

39. Other popular novels informed by this theme include Mitchell's *Hugh Wynne* and Crawford's own *Marietta: A Maid of Venice* (New York: Macmillan, 1901). With more Americans moving and traveling than ever before, the theme of sustaining human connections across distances must have had a particular appeal of its own.

40. In Crawford's *Marietta: A Maid of Venice,* for example, expulsion is the fate of a violent Greek sailor and a slave girl, even though they play a crucial role in saving Zorzi, the hero. Zorzi himself is a kind of outsider too, a "Dalmatian waif" of a lower "caste" than Marietta and her family. But (like Nino and the Virginian) Zorzi proves to have not only the ambition and the independent spirit but also all the "natural" moral qualities required for entry into the inner circle. As a superior glassblower, moreover, Zorzi is a match for Italians of the highest "caste." (Zorzi's professionalism would in itself have been an asset to a turn-of-century hero.)

41. Hedwig's Italian (unlike her father's) is presumably fluent. And she is prepared to adapt her own goals to her lover's: "So long as one of us can be a great musician it is enough," she declares; "and I am just as great as though I did it all myself" (316).

42. The theme of education combines with that of natural superiority to justify Nino's marriage with Hedwig despite his peasant origins: "Do you think it is for nothing that you have taught me the language of Dante, of Petrarca, of Silvio Pellico?" Nino asks the narrator; "Do you think it is for nothing that Heaven has given me my voice?" (29). Others consistently recognize Nino as a "great genius" (167, 327).

43. According to Hart, *Trilby* was more popular in America than in England (*The Popular Book,* 194–95). L. Edward Purcell notes that sales of *Trilby* only became brisk in England after the book's impressive success in America ("*Trilby* and *Trilby*-Mania: The Beginning of the Bestseller System," *Journal of Popular Culture* 11 [Summer 1977]: 64). On the *Trilby* phenomenon, see also Emily Jenkins, "*Trilby:* Fads, Photographers, and 'Over-Perfect' Feet," *Book History* 1 (1998): 221–67. Jenkins analyzes several forms of "*Trilby* mania" and the commercial mechanisms that supported them. Although I agree with Jenkins that "it is impossible to pinpoint precisely the cause of *Trilby*'s unprecedented popularity" (258), I propose a relation between the novel's popularity and its indirect way of addressing widely shared cultural concerns—in part through the confident voice of its friendly authorial narrator.

44. George Du Maurier, *Trilby* (London: Osgood, McIlvaine & Co., 1895), 151. Further references are cited in the text.

45. Jenkins, "*Trilby,*" 229.

46. Svengali's

vicious imaginations . . . which look so tame in English print, sounded much more ghastly
in French, pronounced with a Hebrew-German accent, and uttered in his hoarse, rasping,
nasal, throaty rook's caw, his big yellow teeth baring themselves in a mongrel, canine snarl,
his heavy upper eyelids dropping over his insolent black eyes. . . .

Trilby felt . . . cold all over.

He seemed to her a dread powerful demon, who . . . oppressed and weighed on her like
an incubus. (131–32)

47. For other examples, see 133, 134, 218–19.

48. Even when Trilby is dying, Mrs. Bagot's position ("facts are facts and the world is the world
and we've got to live in it" [186]) is restated and affirmed by the narrator: "Poor Mrs. Bagot felt
herself turn hot red all over, and humbled herself to the very dust, and almost forgot that she
had been in the right, after all, and that 'la grande Trilby' was certainly no fit match for her son"
(398).

49. See Jenkins, "*Trilby,*" 228.

50. In *The Literary History of the United States,* ed. Robert E. Spiller, Willard Thorp, Thomas
H. Johnson, and Henry Seidel Canby (New York: Macmillan, 1955), this comment by Henry
Miles Alden is cited to account for the popularity of *Trilby* partly in terms of the "emancipation"
of women in America (957). *Trilby* also figures in *The Literary History* in a chapter on "the discovery of Bohemia," where the success of the novel is seen partly as a result of its "picturesque and
sentimental conception of the artist's life" (1066).

51. The narrator's authorial prerogatives in *Trilby* range from deciding "that it is high time to
cut this part of [the story] short" (201), to considering the option of killing off a rich uncle for the
benefit of his second hero, Taffy: "It is a great temptation, when you have duly slain your first hero,
to enrich hero number two beyond the dreams of avarice and provide him with a title and a
castle and park, as well as a handsome wife and a nice family!" (427).

52. For analogous moments, see 256, 284.

53. To a brief description of the Luxembourg Gardens the following solitary footnote is ap-
pended: "1. *Glossary*—Pioupiou (*alias* pousse-caillou, *alias* tourlourou)—a private soldier of the
line. Zouzou—a Zouave. Nounou—a wet-nurse with a pretty ribboned cap. . . . Toutou—a non-
descript French lapdog, of no breed known to Englishmen (a regular little beast!) Loulou—a
Pomeranian dog—not much better" (297).

54. In *Somatic Fictions: Imagining Illness in Victorian Culture* (Stanford: Stanford University
Press, 1995), Athena Vrettos takes the image of Trilby onstage as a model of relations between performer and public; but by focusing on the role of Svengali's "mesmerizing gaze" and on the novel's
"discourses of suggestibility," Vrettos claims that the novel offers the reader two choices: "either
to become a voyeur who participate in Svengali's scopic manipulations of Trilby . . . or to overi-
dentify with the heroine and become femininized, indeed hypnotized, by her performance into a
state of emotional collapse" (103). Vrettos gives no attention to the way the narrating voice implies another relation to the public altogether. Garrett Stewart's analysis of *Trilby* in *Dear Reader:
The Conscripted Audience in Nineteenth-Century British Fiction* (Baltimore: Johns Hopkins University Press, 1996) focuses more directly on the novel's narrative rhetoric, but Stewart too centers
his discussion on Svengali's relation to Trilby: "Not only does du Maurier's explicit thematics of
mesmerism make an extrapolation to the transferential magic of reading . . . [hard] to avoid . . . ,
it does so across a flash point of minimal second-person interpolation which sutures your attention into line with the heroine's own" (353).

55. The phrase is taken from Kelley's *Private Woman, Public Stage.*

56. S. Weir Mitchell uses these terms when he considers the difference between face-to-face
counseling and writing for readers "without the aid of personal presence" in *Doctor and Patient*

(Philadelphia: J. B. Lippincott, 1887), 8. Mitchell, like many others, was committed to the idea of reading as an active, reciprocal enterprise: "The best readers are in a measure cooperative authors" (12).

4. The Return of the Author

1. Theodore Dreiser, *A Book about Myself* (New York: Boni and Liveright, 1922), 211.

2. Thayer, "The New Storytellers," 476.

3. Frank Norris, "A Problem in Fiction: Truth vs. Accuracy," *Boston Evening Transcript*, November 6, 1901, reprinted in Pizer, *Literary Criticism*, 57. Norris repeatedly affirmed authorial self-effacement in fiction, but he also praised works that offered "the flavor of an author's personality" to the reader. See chapter 5.

4. Howells, "Novel-Writing and Novel-Reading," 26.

5. Henry James, "Guy de Maupassant" (1888), in Miller, *Theory of Fiction*, 177–78.

6. Wharton, "Copy," 113.

7. Howells, "Novel-Writing and Novel-Reading," 22. Although Howells says in this lecture that "the chasm which parts authors and readers" (22) will "never be bridged" (18), he also speaks of the admiring letters from readers that "made it sweet to be a novelist" (23) and for the sake of which he "would willingly disown all the books that Mr. James ever wrote" (23). This emphasis on being "loved" by one's readers creates a certain tension with Howells's subtitle: "An Impersonal Explanation."

8. See chapter 3.

9. As John Berger puts it, "Men act and women appear" (*Ways of Seeing* [Harmondsworth: Penguin, 1972], 47). For a theoretical discussion of the social construction of gender with particular emphasis on the designation of women, see Judith Butler, *Gender Trouble: Feminism and the Subversion of Identity* (New York: Routledge, 1990), esp. 8–13. Also revealing in this context is Martha Banta's encyclopedic guide to the representation of American women by sculptors, painters, illustrators, advertisers, and others in late nineteenth- and early twentieth-century America (*Imaging American Women: Idea and Ideals in Cultural History* [New York: Columbia University Press, 1987]). On how the modern newspaper continues to juxtapose visual images of "emphatic [women's] bodies" with the "disembodied male voice," see Elaine Scarry, *The Body in Pain: The Making and Unmaking of the World* (New York: Oxford University Press, 1985), 359–60.

10. For cultural perspectives on the problem of actresses, see Jonas A. Barish, *The Antitheatrical Prejudice* (Berkeley: University of California Press, 1981); Julie Carlson, "Impositions of Form: Romantic Anti-Theatricalism and the Case against Particular Women," *ELH* 60 (1993); Juliet Blair, "Private Parts in Public Places: The Case of Actresses," in *Women and Space: Ground Rules and Social Maps*, ed. Shirley Ardener (New York: St. Martin's, 1981), 205–29.

11. Carroll Smith-Rosenberg explores the forces that made the "New Woman" "a condensed symbol of disorder and rebellion" in the second half of the nineteenth century (*Disorderly Conduct: Visions of Gender in Victorian America* [New York: Oxford University Press, 1985], 247; see also 197–216, 245–96). On the situation of nineteenth-century women who spoke in public, see Robyn Warhol, "The Victorian Place of Enunciation: Gender and the Chance to Speak," in *Gendered Interventions*, 159–91; and Henry, "Angelina Grimké's Rhetoric of Exposure." In an essay on Wharton's *House of Mirth*, Lori Merish notes that feminine fashions of the period intensified the conspicuousness of women's bodies and underscored the conflicting values of self-display and self-concealment, "the giving and withholding of self" increasingly associated with femininity at the turn of the century. Merish suggests that "the flirtatious foregrounding of the private, 'unattainable self'" was accentuated by the growing popularity of veils and other filmy garments in the burgeoning consumer culture of the period ("Engendering Naturalism: Narrative Form

and Commodity Spectacle in U.S. Naturalist Fiction," *Novel* 29.3 [1996]: 331, 330). As I have been suggesting, "the giving and withholding of self" are the very issues at stake in the theory and practice of narration at the turn of the century. A cogent contemporary source in this context is Georg Simmel, "Flirtation," in *On Women, Sexuality, and Love*, 133–52. Describing the "semi-concealment" of "the flirt," Simmel writes that "presentation of the self is suspended by partial concealment or refusal of the self, in such a way that the whole is fantasized all the more vividly and the desire for the totality of reality is excited all the more vividly . . . as a result of the tension between this form and the reality as incompletely disclosed" (136). Simmel's rendering of this dynamic could be aptly applied to the relation between spectators and the woman onstage in many realist texts. Another influential contemporary discussion of women's visibility is Thorstein Veblen, *The Theory of the Leisure Class: An Economic Study of Institutions* (1899, reprinted New York: Penguin, 1981), 68–101.

12. See Kelley, *Private Woman, Public Stage*, 130. Sedgwick's ambivalence about publication is richly reflected in her story "Cacoethes Scribendi," in *Tales and Sketches* (Philadelphia: Carey, Lea, and Blanchard, 1835).

13. Brodhead, *Cultures of Letters*, 55. Further references are cited in the text.

14. With the success of *Uncle Tom's Cabin*, Brodhead notes, Stowe "recapitulated the [tour of the celebrated singer Jenny Lind]. . . . Stowe drew her own dockside crowds, had her travel plans publicly announced, packed her own halls, appeared before audience after audience as her celebrated self" (ibid., 53).

15. Walsh, *Authors and Authorship*, 164–65.

16. Wharton, *A Backward Glance*, 109. Further references are cited in the text. The young Willa Cather noted the "hypnotic" effect of her own first appearance in print. See Acocella, "Willa Cather and the Academy," 60.

17. Edith Wharton, *The House of Mirth*, in *Novels* (New York: Library of America, 1985), 236. Further references are cited in the text.

18. Clarke, "The Novel-Reading Habit," 673.

19. Some writers seemed to draw the analogy between novel and stage with benign implications in mind. See, for example, Francis Marion Crawford, *The Novel: What It Is* (1893, reprinted New York: Macmillan, 1908), 27, 49–50, 57. But the recurrent association of writer with public performer became increasingly negative in the course of the 1890s. "Just as the vulgar music hall singer may earn a larger income than the profoundest statesman," one critic declared, "so may the tawdry tale-teller drive the thinker and artist out of the market" ("Men, Women, and Books," 106). At the end of the century the increasing popularity of spectacular entertainments left novelists both envious and contemptuous. Many critics attacked what Charles Dudley Warner called the "disease . . . [of] Barnumism . . . the striving to be sensational in poetry, in the novel, to shock, to advertise the performance" ("Congress of Authors," 30). In a similar vein, an article in *The Dial* castigated what it called "the star system in literature" (*The Dial*, May 16, 1900, 389–91). "What the actor was to the past generation, the author is to the present," another discussion began. ("Author, Agent, and Publisher," 446).

20. Crane, *Maggie: A Girl of the Streets*, 38. In an essay on Thomas Hardy, Julie Grossman provides an illuminating parallel to this aspect of my argument. She argues persuasively that "Hardy's attitude toward female power" is intertwined with "his desire both to be *and* not become a public image." Grossman focuses on the way Hardy's images for Tess "set up an alliance between Tess and the novelist as victimized objects of a public gaze" ("Hardy's *Tess* and 'The Photograph': Images to Die For," *Criticism* 35.4 [1993]: 610).

21. Fitzgerald, *Letters*, 307.

22. Norris, "Weekly Letter," 55.

23. Kaplan, *Social Construction*, 83.

24. Although Selden and Gerty take Lily's performance as a revelation of her best "self," other observers see it differently. The "experienced connoisseur Mr. Ned Van Alstyne" notes that "there isn't a break in the lines anywhere, and I suppose she wanted us to know it" (142). Trenor says, "It's not her fault if everybody don't know it now," and adds that *he* calls it "damned bad taste" (146). Jack Stepney asserts that while he himself is "no prude," he draws the line "when it comes to a girl standing there as if she was up at auction" (166). Lily's appearance continues to elicit reactions long after the performance is over. "Town Talk" is "full of her" in the morning (166). "My God," Rosedale exclaims, "if . . . Paul Morpeth [would] . . . paint her like that, the picture'd appreciate a hundred per cent in ten years" (167).

25. Wharton, "The Vice of Reading," 516, 513.

26. On the difficulty of separating the "real" Lily from her projected image, see Judith Fryer, *Felicitous Space: The Imaginative Structures of Edith Wharton and Willa Cather* (Chapel Hill: University of North Carolina Press, 1986), 75–82; Elaine Showalter, "The Death of the Lady (Novelist): Wharton's *House of Mirth*," in *Edith Wharton*, ed. Harold Bloom (New York: Chelsea House, 1986), 146–47. William E. Moddelmog explores Wharton's sense of the boundaries of personality in "Disowning 'Personality': Privacy and Subjectivity in *The House of Mirth*," *American Literature* 70.2 (1998).

27. William James's idea that we are all, in one degree or another, "haunted by [the] sense of an ideal spectator" can help elucidate the function Selden serves for Lily (*Psychology: The Briefer Course,* 204). On Selden as the "most important of [Lily's] reflectors," see Fryer, *Felicitous Space,* 75; cf. Cynthia Griffin Wolff, *A Feast of Words: The Triumph of Edith Wharton* (Oxford: Oxford University Press, 1977), 122–23, 130. On the trope of the sympathetic spectator, see David Marshall, *The Figure of Theater* (New York: Columbia University Press, 1986), 209–11. On the problem of Lily's "premeditated" effects, see Michaels, *Gold Standard,* 228–29; Seltzer, *Bodies and Machines,* 104; Bruce Michelson, "Edith Wharton's 'House Divided,'" *Studies in American Fiction* 12.2 (1984): 210–14.

28. See Wai-chee Dimock, "Debasing Exchange: Edith Wharton's *The House of Mirth*," in Bloom, *Edith Wharton,* 133–35; Judith Fetterley, "'The Temptation to Be a Beautiful Object'": Double Standard and Double Bind in *The House of Mirth, Studies in American Fiction* 5.2 (1977): 209–10. Fryer, *Felicitous Space,* 93; Michelson, "Edith Wharton's 'House Divided,'" 202, 212.

29. Although most of Lily's actions are scripted performances, contrived to create "opportunities" for her, the profit motive never fully accounts for Lily's impulse to be seen. Her desire for a receptive audience antedates her will to profit from one. It is a basic component of her sense of being as such. Fryer reflects on Lily in terms of the "gender-specific" aspect of women's being watched both by others and by themselves (*Felicitous Space,* 97–98; cf. 105). Cf. Blair, "Private Parts," 219. On other implications of watching in realist texts, see Seltzer, *Bodies and Machines,* 52, 95–100, 103–4; Howard, *Form and History,* chap. 4; Kaplan, *Social Construction,* 88–103. The act of reading itself of course depends on looking and seeing as well. The thematics of spectatorship and the emphasis on eyes become pointers to the concern with reading throughout texts of the period. "There's more in Vereker than [meets] the eye," says Corvick in James's "Figure in the Carpet"; and the narrator replies "that the eye seemed what the printed page had been expressly invented to meet" (371).

30. Lily's letter burning destroys the only evidence for refuting Bertha Dorset's incriminating version of Lily's story. Earlier, Gerty pleads with Lily to refute Bertha's report of their Mediterranean trip. "But what *is* your story, Lily?" Gerty insists. "I don't believe anyone knows it yet" (236). Cf. Showalter on the implications of Lily's "inability to speak for herself" ("Death of the Lady (Novelist)," 142, 145).

31. As R. W. B. Lewis points out, "Lily" was Wharton's own nickname (*Edith Wharton,* 26). For a discussion of the grounds of analogy between Wharton and her heroine, see my essay "*The Awakening* and *The House of Mirth*: Plotting Experience and Experiencing Plot," in *The*

Cambridge Companion to American Realism and Naturalism, ed. Donald Pizer (New York: Cambridge University Press, 1995). Michaels's discussion of the "risky activity" of writing in the context of *House of Mirth* is also relevant here. "If Lily herself and not the picture she impersonates is the object of interest [in tableaux vivants]," Michaels writes, "it may well be that Lily herself is only a stand-in for another person who is impersonating her, the person of the writer" (*Gold Standard,* 240–41). At the same time, Wharton's narrative voice in *House of Mirth* often distances the author from Lily, establishing a persona both morally and intellectually superior to the heroine, partly through what Kaplan calls Wharton's "intrusive narrative moralizing" (*Social Construction,* 97). But for many nineteenth-century readers, as we have seen, moral commentary fostered a desirable identification between the narrator and the author of the book. Thus Wharton's narrative "intrusions" may have helped make *House of Mirth* one of the few realist texts to achieve best-seller status. Nonetheless, some contemporary reviewers found Wharton's narration all too detached. In 1905 Alice Meynell, for example, criticized Wharton for "keeping her own counsel" too completely in *House of Mirth.* "In much of her writing," the reviewer notes, "we were admitted to . . . her noble mind; we are reluctant to forego [sic] an intimacy that we valued. . . . The author of *The House of Mirth* does not reveal herself " (*"The House of Mirth," Bookman* 29 [December 1905], reprinted in *Edith Wharton: The Contemporary Reviews,* ed. James W. Tuttleton, Kristin O. Lauer, and Margaret P. Murray [New York: Cambridge University Press, 1992], 125).

32. *The Letters of Edith Wharton,* ed. R. W. B. Lewis and Nancy Lewis (New York: Scribner's Sons, 1988), 95.

33. Wharton's mistrust of her audience is also clear in her later work. In *A Backward Glance,* Wharton notes with resentment "that the books into the making of which so much of one's soul has entered will be snatched at by readers curious only to discover which of the heroes and heroines of the 'society column' are to be found in it" (212). See also chapter 5, however.

34. In Wharton's essay "The Vice of Reading," the qualities she associates with "creative" reading bear a striking resemblance to many of the qualities Lily cannot "afford" in life: "the luxury of an impulse" (16) as well as other forms of "impulse and truancy" (60), spontaneous "intercourse" (71), and "mental vagrancy" (70). As I have noted, Lily is repeatedly accused of "premeditated effects"; it is partly her lack of spontaneity that bars her from Selden's "Republic of the Spirit." But in "Vice," "unpremeditated harmonies" make for entry into the "paysage choisi of the spirit" reached by reading and open to "The Happy Few." See also my essay "The Rewards of Representation: Edith Wharton, Lily Bart, and the Writer/Reader Interchange," *Novel* (Winter 1991): 153–54.

35. Cf., e.g., "The Touchstone," "Angel at the Grave."

36. Wharton, "The Vice of Reading," 513, 514. Further references are cited in the text. The notion of the writer-reader relationship as dynamic and reciprocal has its analogues in the work of critical theorists such as Wolfgang Iser and Georges Poulet. See, for example, Poulet's "Criticism and the Experience of Interiority," 44–47, and "The Self and the Other in Critical Consciousness," 46–47; cf. Peter Brooks on the "narrative exchange" in *Reading for the Plot: Design and Intention in Narrative* (New York: Knopf, 1985), chap. 8. Like many modern theorists Brooks insists that the reader's relations are with the text, not the writer. Yet the peculiarly vital illusion of contact with otherness as part of both the writer's and reader's experience is implicit in the work of theorists such as Poulet and Iser, as it is in the narratological approach of Dorrit Cohn. Cohn engages an aspect of the issue, for example, when she notes how "the special life-likeness of narrative fiction . . . depends on what writers and readers know least in life: how another mind thinks, another body feels" (*Transparent Minds: Narrative Modes for Presenting Consciousness in Fiction* [Princeton: Princeton University Press, 1978]), 5–6.

37. Sedgwick, "The Novels of Mrs. Wharton," 218. Further references are cited in the text. Sedgwick's essay discusses the question of Edith Wharton's "personality" (218–19) at some length

with characteristic but particularly explicit emphasis on the value of authorial "individuality" (219). For him, as for others, the two terms seem interchangeable. Sedgwick makes gender a crucial component of both: "The first rough and ready test as to whether the work has the flavor of personality is the determination of sex" (219).

38. *Letters of Edith Wharton,* 269. Perhaps one could say of the "person" of the writer what Michael Fried says of the "materiality of writing": that it is in a sense "simultaneously elicited and repressed" within the written work. (*Realism, Writing, Disfiguration,* xiv).

39. "In the case of describing a character it is doubtless more difficult to convey the impression of something that is not oneself (the constant effort, however delusive, . . . of the novelist) than in the case of describing some object more immediately visible." James, "Guy de Maupassant," 178.

40. On the question of actresses from this point of view, see Carlson, "Impositions of Form," esp. 160–63, and Laura Mulvey, "Visual Pleasure and Narrative Cinema," in *Feminism and Film Theory,* ed. Constance Penley (New York: Routledge, 1988). For a discussion that reverses the genders of watching and watched, see David Carroll, *The Matinee Idols* (New York: Galahad Books, 1972), 15–16. The problem of just what an actress represents pervades *The Tragic Muse.* Contemplating Miriam onstage, Nick Dormer "was so occupied in watching her face . . . that he was conscious only in a secondary degree of the story she illustrated." Henry James, *The Tragic Muse* (New York: Penguin, 1984), 283. "Sherringham more than once said to [Nash] . . . that he should really . . . attach more value to the stage or less to the interesting actress" (342). Nash, however, insists that Miriam's "greatest idea must always be to show herself; and fortunately she has a splendid self to show" (376). Miriam demurs: "Yes, we show [our person] for money, those of us who have anything to show, and some no doubt who haven't, which is the real scandal" (474). The terms "self" and "person" are porous and often interchangeable throughout the period. Further references to this novel are cited in the text.

41. Since the only "physical body" literally visible to a novel reader is the book itself—binding, cover, pages, print—the question of "physical body" versus representation has its analogue in the problem of the materiality of writing: the becoming visible of writing itself as marks on a page rather than as meaning. In order to make sense of a text, a reader must "forget" both his or her own immediate surroundings and the materiality of writing. On the materiality or physicality of writing, see Fried, *Realism, Writing, Disfiguration,* xiv, 100, 117–20; Michaels, *Gold Standard,* 3–28; and Seltzer, *Bodies and Machines,* 9–20, 78–80, 107–12. All three have suggested in different but related ways that the status of material objects (books, artifacts, the human body) is a source of uncertainty in late nineteenth-century texts. Such uncertainty is directly relevant to the present exploration of authors and readers.

42. Henry James, "Some Notes on the Theatre," *The Nation,* March 11, 1875; cited in *The American Theatre as Seen by Its Critics, 1752–1934,* ed. Montrose J. Moses and John Mason Brown (New York, 1934), 123. Wharton's use of Boucicault's *Shaughran* in *The Age of Innocence* reflects related issues. See chapter 5.

43. Michael Anesko has juxtaposed this humiliating moment with other images of James onstage, and with James's desire for what Edith Wharton called *gloire,* in *Friction with the Market* (Oxford: Oxford University Press, 1986), 21–24. For a detailed account of the episode, see Leon Edel, *The Life of Henry James,* 2 vols. (New York: Penguin, 1977), 2:145–52.

44. See chapter 2.

45. Henry James, "Anthony Trollope," in *The Art of Fiction and other Essays by Henry James* (New York: Oxford University Press, 1948), 59. Many of James's author figures are relevant in this context. "The Private Life" offers the sharpest (and funniest) version of the problem.

46. James, "Novels of George Eliot," 485. James's formulation has been much invoked by narrative theorists. See Booth, *Rhetoric of Fiction,* 49–50; Iser, *Act of Reading,* 36–37.

47. On friendly narrators, see chapter 3.

48. Henry James, *The Bostonians* (New York: Random House, 1956), 346, 408; cf. 149, 392. Further references are cited in the text.

49. See also Philip Page, "The Curious Narration of *The Bostonians,*" *American Literature* 46 (November 1974): 374–83.

50. On the "relationship" implied by the use of "I" and "you," see also Kacandes, "Are You in the Text?" Fried speaks of narrative ending as the moment of the "writer/reader's long-delayed removal from [the] representational 'space'" of the text (*Realism, Writing, Disfiguration,* 142). On resistance to the end, see Brooks, *Reading for the Plot,* 23, 95, 103–8. See also D. A. Miller, *Narrative and Its Discontents* (Princeton: Princeton University Press, 1981), 265–83.

51. "Reflector" is the Jamesian term, taken up by narratology as "focalizer."

52. Auerbach suggests that first-person narration makes it particularly difficult for an author "to maintain an identity apart from the voice he impersonates in the writing" (*Romance of Failure,* 12). Perhaps precisely for that reason, James gave most of his first-person narrators a blandly obtuse or morally dubious character, as if to discourage the reader from associating the narrator with the author. Nonetheless, as I have been arguing, readers often persisted in linking the two. It is because James's reflectors solved the problem of "inartistic telling" that the Jamesian "center of consciousness" became a virtue for Percy Lubbock and the many New Critics who followed his lead in the 1940s and 1950s. See also chapter 5.

53. The notion that fiction reading creates contact with or knowledge of an author is in some sense explained by theorists who claim that readers tend to associate "language with the idea of a person who originated it." See David Bleich, *Subjective Criticism* (Baltimore: Johns Hopkins University Press, 1981), 238 and chap. 9, "Conceptions and Documentation of the Author"; see also Steig, *Stories of Reading,* 15–16, 19–20, 68–70, 144–46. Georges Poulet calls this intimate effect of reading the "experience of interiority"—the "unheard-of license" to enter the consciousness of another, allowing that consciousness in turn to occupy one's own "innermost self" ("Criticism and the Experience of Interiority," 42).

54. James, *Portrait of a Lady,* 330.

55. See chapter 3.

56. Willa Cather, "Peter," in *Willa Cather: 24 Stories,* ed. Sharon O'Brien (New York: Penguin, 1993), 1. Further references are cited in the text.

57. Willa Cather, "Nanette: An Aside," ibid., 88. Further references are cited in the text.

58. Of the great singer in "Nanette" we are told: "Tradutorri holds back her suffering within herself; she suffers as the flesh and blood women of her century suffer. She is intense without being emotional. She takes this great anguish of hers and lays it in a tomb and rolls a stone before the door and walls it up. You wonder that one woman's heart can hold a grief so great. It is this stifled pain that wrings your heart when you hear her, that gives you the impression of horrible reality. It is this too, of which she is slowly dying now" (88).

59. Cather, "Du Maurier's *Trilby,*" 363, 365. The review was first published in the *Nebraska Journal* (December 23, 1894) when the novel came out in book form. Portions were reused in the unsigned piece "Death of George Du Maurier," *Home Monthly* (November 1896), reprinted in Slote, *Kingdom of Art,* 363.

60. Cather criticizes Mrs. Humphrey Ward, for example, for "appealing to one's intelligence rather than one's sympathies. . . . [She] writes admirable books rather than lovable ones" (*Nebraska Journal,* May 31, 1896, reprinted in Slote, *Kingdom of Art,* 376). "Art is temperament," Cather wrote, dismissing Hamlin Garland for "having no more temperament than a prairie dog" (*Nebraska Journal,* January 26, 1896, reprinted in Slote, *Kingdom of Art,* 331). By the same token Cather tempered her praise for James's "perfect" stories by noting that they "are sometimes a little hard, always calculating and dispassionate" (*Courier,* November 16, 1895, reprinted in Slote, *Kingdom of Art,* 361).

61. Slote, *Kingdom of Art*, 333.

62. Howells, "Novel-Writing and Novel-Reading," 18, 22.

63. Willa Cather, "Coming Aphrodite," in *Youth and the Bright Medusa* (New York: Alfred A. Knopf, 1920), 78. Further references are cited in the text.

64. Cather's concern with the relation between person and mask here is reemphasized in her hesitation with regard to the title of the story, changed from "Coming Eden Bower" to "Coming Aprodite." On the two versions and their differences, see Bernice Slote, "Introduction" to *"Uncle Valentine" and Other Stories: Willa Cather's Short Fiction, 1915–1929* (Lincoln: University of Nebraska Press, 1986), xvi–xviii and appendix.

65. In *The Writing of Fiction*, Edith Wharton notes "the perilous affinity between the art of fiction and the material it works in. . . . The attempt to give back any fragment of life in painting or sculpture or music presupposes transposition. . . . To re-present in words is far more difficult, because the relation is so close between model and artist. The novelist works in the very material out of which the object he is trying to render is made. He must use, to express soul, the signs which soul uses to express itself. It is relatively easy to separate the artistic vision of an object from its complex and tangled actuality if one has to re-see it in paint or marble or bronze; it is infinitely difficult to render a human mind when one is employing the very word-dust with which thought is formulated" (16–17).

66. Wharton, *A Backward Glance*, 197. Thirty years earlier, in *House of Mirth*, Wharton had already used this image to suggest incomplete illusion. See Wharton, *House of Mirth*, 290.

67. Fried's discussion of Thomas Eakins explores the tension between inviting a spectator into the represented space of a painting and, alternatively, drawing attention to the "worked artifact" as such (*Realism, Writing, Disfiguration*, 74). Borus raises the question of the worked artifact in a different sense, by stressing the conflict between an industrial and preindustrial conception of writing at work in realist theory. "The industrial conception," Borus writes, "took as natural the existence of a commodity divorced from . . . human action. . . . The preindustrial or artisanal mode stressed the individual human touches necessary to demonstrating that work had gone on" (*Writing Realism*, 67).

68. Seltzer, *Bodies and Machines*, 107.

69. "Pudding," one of James's recurrent (ironic) words for fiction, is also applied by Nash to one of Miriam's performances in *The Tragic Muse* (406; cf. 134, 153).

70. Theodore Dreiser, *Sister Carrie* (New York: Norton, 1970), 134. As I have argued elsewhere, Dreiser's representation of Carrie in *Under the Gaslight* makes Carrie a figure for the author in more ways than one. Carrie's experience as an amateur actress—learning her part, "buoyed up" by Drouet, and succeeding beyond her own expectations—constitutes a parallel to Dreiser's first effort as a novelist, his composition of *Sister Carrie* itself. See my essay "A Portrait of the Artist as a Young Actress: The Rewards of Representation in *Sister Carrie*," in *New Essays on "Sister Carrie,"* ed. Donald Pizer (New York: Cambridge University Press, 1991).

71. As Carrie, playing Laura, speaks for humility and devotion, Hurstwood begins "to feel a deep sympathy for her and for himself. He could almost feel that she was talking to him. He was . . . almost deluded by that quality of voice and manner which, like a pathetic strain of music, seems ever a personal and intimate thing. Pathos has this quality, that it seems ever addressed to one alone." Dreiser, *Sister Carrie*, 137; cf. 139.

72. Frank Norris, *The Pit* (New York: Grove Press, 1956), 312. See also chapter 5.

73. Wharton, "The Vice of Reading," 514.

74. James, preface to *The Golden Bowl*, 328.

75. *Nebraska Journal*, March 22, 1896, 9, reprinted in Slote, *Kingdom of Art*, 379.

76. Leon Edel, and Gordon N. Ray, eds., *Henry James and H. G. Wells: A Record of Their Friendship, Their Debate on the Art of Fiction, and Their Quarrel* (London: Rupert Hart-Davis, 1959), 75. Further references are cited in the text.

77. See chapters 1 and 2.

78. James himself often emphasized that the novelist's "very presence, his spiritual presence, in his work" was an inevitable effect of narration. Veil himself as he might, James wrote, "the nature of the [author] himself" is "the very complexion of the mirror in which the material is reflected" ("The Lesson of Balzac," in Miller, *Theory of Fiction*, 179); cf. preface to *The Portrait of a Lady*, 6–7.

79. "Those people who advocate the suppression of all traces of the creator in his creations are too ascetic, too marmorial, too super- or infra-human," Sedgwick insists ("Novels of Mrs. Wharton," 218). While other contributors to the same volume of the *Atlantic* support Sedgwick's approach, he acknowledges that reviewers who applaud authorial presence in fiction are in fact a dying breed. For affirmation of "personality" elsewhere in this volume of the *Atlantic* (98 [February 1906]), see "Books That Stay By," 283, and "Uncut," 575–76.

5. Getting at the Hidden Author

1. This hierarchy was reexamined and reaffirmed by the New Critics of the 1950s (Joseph Warren Beach, David Daiches, Leon Edel, F. R. Leavis, Mark Schorer, René Wellek, and others), many of whom not surprisingly use Henry James as a recurrent touchstone to literary value. The clear premium on "showing" and denigration of "telling" was significantly challenged only by Wayne Booth in *The Rhetoric of Fiction*. See especially Booth's opening chapter, "Telling and Showing." His descriptive bibliography is particularly useful in the present context.

2. See the prefatory note in Forster, *Aspects of the Novel*: "Words such as 'I,' 'you,' 'one,' 'we,' . . . will . . . occur on every page and will rightly distress the sensitive reader; but he is asked to remember that if these words were removed others, perhaps more distinguished, might escape through the orifices they left."

3. Wharton, *The Writing of Fiction*, 91.

4. Norris, "Weekly Letter," 55.

5. I have noted all along the criterion of a writer's "individuality" or "personality." For some easily accessible examples of the turn-of-century emphasis on a character's "reality," see the essays in Donald Pizer, ed., *Critical Essays on Theodore Dreiser* (Boston: G. K. Hall & Co., 1981), where William Marion Reedy ("A Strangely Strong Novel in a Queer Milieu") notes that Dreiser's Carrie is "a reality all through the book" (158); Joseph H. Coates ("Sister Carrie") speaks of Dreiser's "real people" (166); and H. L. Mencken ("Dreiser's Novel") notes that "Carrie Meeber is far more real than nine-tenths of the women you actually know" (230). In a letter to Dreiser, Mencken writes that Cowperwood is "as real as any man could be." See *The Letters of Theodore Dreiser: A Selection*, vol. 1, ed. Robert H. Elias (Philadelphia: University of Pennsylvania Press, 1959), 146. Further references to Dreiser's *Letters* are cited in the text. Radway shows that taking fictional characters as "real" remains a common practice (and a central reading pleasure) among "romance readers" (*Reading the Romance*, 200–203).

6. Lubbock amply attests to his own experience of novel reading as an experience of "knowing" both characters and authors: "After living for a time with people like Clarissa Harlowe or Anna Karenina or Emma Bovary, we have had a lasting experience, though the novels in which they figured may fall away into dimness and uncertainty" (*The Craft of Fiction*, 4). He adds, moreover, that "to have lived with their [i.e., the authors'] creations is to have lived with them as well; with so many hours of familiar intercourse behind us we have learnt to know them" (5). Although Lubbock takes such intercourse for granted as a prime pleasure of novel reading, his intention is to set new goals for criticism: "It is all undeniable, no doubt; from every side we make out that the criticism of a book—not the people in the book, not the character of the author but the book—is impossible"; that is, separating the elements out is impossible (11–12). Lubbock's focus thus becomes the "modest" question of how books "are made" (12).

7. Resisting the "scholarly" need for classification by period and subject, Forster writes: "We are to visualize the English novelists . . . as seated together in a room, a circular room, a sort of British Museum reading room—all writing their novels simultaneously. They do not, as they sit there, think I live under Queen Victoria, I under Anne, I carry on the tradition of Trollope. . . . The fact that their pens are in their hands is far more vivid to them. . . . [T]heir sorrows and joys are pouring out through their ink" (*Aspects of the Novel*, 21–22). Forster elaborates this image of English authors at some length (28ff.).

8. See also chapter 4.

9. See Bleich, *Subjective Criticism*, 238; Steig, *Stories of Reading*, 19–21. In a related formulation of the problem, narratologists suggest that every utterance presumes someone who has uttered (Rimmon-Kenan, *Narrative Fiction*, 88).

10. Norris, "Weekly Letter," 55, 54. Further references are cited in the text. As Richard Allan Davison noted in 1968, Frank T. Bullen's *Cruise of the "Cachalot" Round the World after Sperm Whale* (New York: Appleton, 1899) was one of "Norris's very favorite books." See Davison, "The Remaining Seven of Frank Norris' 'Weekly Letters,'" *American Literary Realism* 3 (Summer 1968): 60.

11. Norris often drew a distinction between "truth" and "accuracy" that is relevant here. "A thing that has actually happened . . . is not necessarily true when told as fiction . . . even when told with the most scrupulous adherence to fact, even when . . . pictured with the incontestable precision of the photograph" (Norris's "Weekly Letter," August 3, 1901, in Pizer, *Literary Criticism*, 73). Or again, "To be true is the all-important business. . . . Paint the horse pea-green, if it suits your purpose" ("A Problem in Fiction," 58).

12. Norris, "A Problem in Fiction," 57.

13. Frank Norris, "The Jongleur of Taillebois," in *The Complete Edition of Frank Norris*, vol. 10 (New York: Doubleday, Doran & Co., 1928), 14. See also my "Afterword," in *The Art of Frank Norris, Storyteller* (Columbia: University of Missouri Press, 1988).

14. On Norris's obsessive storytellers, see my *Art of Frank Norris, Storyteller*.

15. "Today is the day of the novel," Norris writes. "It is an instrument, a tool, a weapon, a vehicle. . . . Because it is so all-powerful to-day, the people turn to him who wields this instrument with every degree of confidence. . . . The unknown archer who grasps the bow of Ulysses may be expected by the multitude to send his shaft far and true. If he is not true nor strong he has no business with the bow." Frank Norris, "The Responsibilities of the Novelist," *Critic* 41 (December 1902), reprinted in Pizer, *Literary Criticism*, 95.

16. Norris, "The American Public and 'Popular' Fiction," 126. Further references are cited in the text.

17. Norris, "Weekly Letter," 55.

18. Norris, *Frank Norris*, 10. The passage reproduced on the title page of this biography is relevant here as well: "I have observed that a reader seldom peruses a book with pleasure till he knows whether the writer of it be a black or a fair man, of a mild or a choleric disposition, married or a bachelor, with other particulars of the like nature that conduce very much to the right understanding of the author.—*The Spectator*."

19. See my *Frank Norris, Storyteller*, 101–4. On Laura's role-playing, see Don Graham, *Frank Norris: The Aesthetic Context* (Columbia: University of Missouri Press, 1978), 137–43, 152–54; Joseph R. McElrath, *Frank Norris Revisited* (New York: Macmillan, 1992), 108–9. References to *The Pit* (New York: Grove Press, 1956) are cited in the text.

20. Norris's "Storytellers vs. Novelists" describes the evolution of a novelist in terms that stress the movement from dramatizing child to isolated figure (*World's Work* [March 1902]), reprinted in Pizer, *Literary Criticism*, 65–67.

21. One could easily conceptualize this difference along gender lines: many sociologists and

psychologists note how women have depended for a sense of self on seeing the role they play confirmed in the eyes of others (see chapter 4, note 9). Men, from this point of view, are often represented as more ready to specialize, split, and objectify. On the identification of "objective culture" with "male culture," see for example Simmel, "Female Culture," 67, 70, 72.

22. William Dean Howells's essay "The Man of Letters as a Man of Business" had made the link explicit on other grounds. But Norris (and Dreiser, as we shall see) made the financier a figure for the novelist with particular reference to the problems of narration and reading.

23. Howard Horwitz, "To Find the Value of X: *The Pit* as a Renunciation of Romance," in *American Realism*, ed. Eric J. Sundquist (Baltimore: Johns Hopkins University Press, 1982), 230.

24. Norris, "Weekly Letter," 55.

25. Norris, "Simplicity in Art," 63.

26. Wharton, "The Vice of Reading," 516. See also chapter 4.

27. Many of the scenes of reading in *The Pit* are part of Page's (and Laura's) effort to "educate" their men. As with Howells's evocation of Silas Lapham's library-building, there is irony here. We have seen that the determination to read for self-improvement was anathema to Edith Wharton and others (chapter 2). Lubbock too uses the term "creative reading," attributing it to Emerson (*The Craft of Fiction*, 16).

28. Frank Norris, "A Neglected Epic," in *World's Work* (December 1902), reprinted in Pizer, *Literary Criticism*, 120.

29. "The farm folk of Iceland to this very day treasure up and read to their little ones handwritten copies of the Grettla Saga chronicling the deeds and death of Grettir the Strong," Norris writes in "A Neglected Epic" (1902). "But the youth of the United States learn of their epic by paying a dollar to see the 'Wild West Show'" (Pizer, *Literary Criticism*, 120). The loss of oral and communal modes of storytelling became an increasingly prevalent theme in discussions of books and reading in the twentieth century. One of the most influential discussions of the issue in relation to fiction is Walter Benjamin's essay "The Storyteller" (in *Illuminations*, trans. Harry Zohn [New York: Schocken, 1969]). "The birthplace of the novel is the solitary individual," Benjamin claims (87). See also Brooks, "The Tale vs. the Novel." In a valuable essay, Elizabeth Long points to an "overprivileg[ing of] the moment of isolation" in our conception of reading. See "Textual Interpretation as Collective Action," in *The Ethnography of Reading*, ed. Jonathan Boyarin (Berkeley: University of California Press, 1993), 181.

30. Thayer, "The New Story-Tellers and the Doom of Realism," 476.

31. The "marvelous" lead soldier tales were created by Frank to entertain his brother Charles. "My earliest recollections," Charles Norris writes, "are of the endless and involved stories of love and chivalry woven about my lead soldiers to my never-failing enchantment and delight" (*Frank Norris*, 2). Later, that enchantment took the form of written narrative—written by Frank and sent to Charles when the family's departure from Paris disrupted the conditions of dining table invention and left Frank behind alone. The original game, played by two, was thus transformed into Frank's first work of fiction. "The story was written in the second person on closely ruled notepaper" (Joseph R. McElrath, Jr., "Frank Norris: Early Posthumous Responses," *American Literary Realism* 12 [1979]: 75). In other words, the form of this "story" was that of direct address, a narrative mode that in itself, as we have seen, often implies a sense of contact between writer and intended reader, and one that Norris soon rejected as a model.

32. The story of Laura and Page reflects many aspects of the relation between Charles and Frank. On other autobiographical elements of *The Pit*, see Edwin Haviland Miller, "Frank Norris's *The Pit* as Autobiography," *Hartford Studies in Literature* 17.3 (1985): 18–31.

33. Bruce Nicholson, "Frank Norris's 'Dedication' in *The Pit*," *Frank Norris Studies* 25 (Spring 1998): 1–2.

34. Ibid., 2.

35. Theodore Dreiser, *The Financier* (New York: New American Library, 1981), 94. Unless otherwise indicated, references to *The Financier* are from this edition and are cited in the text.

36. Dreiser's *Financier* was originally published in 1912 (New York: A. L. Burt). In 1927 it was reissued, radically cut. As noted above, unless otherwise indicated, the edition I will be citing is based on the 1927 version of the novel, which soon became the standard one. On Dreiser's writing and revision of *The Financier,* see Donald Pizer, *The Novels of Theodore Dreiser: A Critical Study* (Minneapolis: University of Minnesota Press, 1976), 164–66.

37. George J. Becker, ed., *Documents of Modern Literary Realism* (Princeton: Princeton University Press, 1967), 154, 155.

38. Kaplan stresses the centrality of "self-promotion" to Dreiser's conception of authorship throughout her chapter on Dreiser's literary apprenticeship in the world of mass-market newspapers and magazines (*Social Construction,* 139).

39. "Talks with Four Novelists: Mr. Dreiser," *New York Times Saturday Review of Books* (June 15, 1907), reprinted in *Theodore Dreiser: A Selection of Uncollected Prose,* ed. Donald Pizer (Detroit: Wayne State University Press, 1977), 164.

40. Stuart P. Sherman, "The Naturalism of Mr. Dreiser," in Becker, *Documents,* 458, 457. Early reviews of Dreiser's work often faulted his narrative intrusions—his "moralizing" and "philosophizing." See Pizer, *Critical Essays on Dreiser,* 160; cf. 164.

41. Still, the first edition of *The Financier* even includes at least one direct aside to the "dear reader" (467)! On the friendly narrative interpolations of popular fiction, see chapter 3.

42. For a classic account of Dreiser's cultural position, see Kazin's essay on Dreiser and Wharton, "Two Educations," in *On Native Grounds* (New York: Harcourt Brace and Co., 1942), 53–68.

43. See Kaplan, *Social Construction,* 108; cf. 110, 112.

44. See 11, 99, 120. In an early review of *The Financier,* Mencken notes the "over-development of the esthetic sense in Cowperwood." Mencken continues, "For the actual dollar . . . he has no liking at all, but only the toleration of an artist for his brushes and paint-pots" (Pizer, *Critical Essays on Dreiser,* 230). In an interview before publication of *The Financier,* Dreiser stressed that "there's to be a great deal about art in my book" ("Theodore Dreiser," in Pizer, *Selection of Uncollected Prose,* 192, reprinted from the *New York Times Review of Books,* June 23, 1912). Donald Pizer draws attention to the aesthetic component of Cowperwood's struggle for power and cites Stephanie's comment in *The Titan* that Cowperwood was "a very great artist in his realm" (*The Novels of Dreiser,* 169, 362). See also Michaels's exploration of Cowperwood's desire to acquire and "possess" art ("Dreiser's Financier: The Man of Business as a Man of Letters," in *Gold Standard,* 79).

45. This point is considerably elaborated and intensified in a passage that was cut from the first edition of *The Financier.* See 1912 edition (187–88). It ends with the following: "Be he ever so innately callous and brutal, the butcher or executioner, separated from his ax and the atmosphere of blood and grime surrounding him, loses much of his savage identity" (188).

46. Dreiser, *Sister Carrie,* 204. Kaplan notes that the pseudonyms Dreiser used when writing for *Ev'ry Month* retained the initials of members of his family (*Social Construction,* 120).

47. Waiting for the jury's verdict, Cowperwood "for the first time in his life . . . felt as though he were walking in his sleep. Was this the real Frank Cowperwood of two months before[?] . . . He looked around him at the court-room. How large and bare and cold it was! Still he was Frank A. Cowperwood. Why should he let such queer thoughts disturb him? His fight for freedom and privilege and restitution was not over yet" (326). The most significant challenge to Cowperwood's autonomy is his prison experience, when, stripped naked and deprived of all human and material supports, he experiences a "gone feeling" such as he has never known before (387). Here again his

own name becomes the marker of his unshaken identity: "After all," he tells himself, "he was Frank A. Cowperwood, and that was something, whatever he wore" (411).

48. "The sight of his new house going up made Cowperwood feel of more weight in the world" (98).

49. The spider motif recurs several times in the course of the novel; see 140, 291. The "Eastern District Penitentiary of Pennsylvania, [with its] . . . seven arms or corridors, ranged octopus-like around a central room or court," is structured like a web (381). In the prison episode, moreover, Cowperwood learns to cane chairs, a craft activity that gives him considerable satisfaction while implying another possible, if fanciful, link between the work of weaver, spider, and artist (406–9; see also 1912 edition, 408). An interesting parallel to Dreiser's image of artist as spider occurs in Cather's *Song of the Lark* (New York: Penguin, 1991). "Your work becomes your personal life," Thea says. "You are not much good until it does. It's like being woven into a big web. You can't pull away, because all your little tendrils are woven into the picture. It takes you up and uses you and spins you out" (380). Not surprisingly, Cather invokes the image of Oscar Wilde's *Picture of Dorian Gray* in a preface she wrote for a later edition of the novel.

50. Pizer calls this scene "perhaps the best known incident in all of Dreiser" (*Novels of Dreiser*, 166).

51. Michaels, *Gold Standard,* 76.

52. Cowperwood's "inscrutable" eyes are repeatedly noted (15, 25, 203, 291). "People . . . found it difficult to face Cowperwood's glazed stare. It was as though there were another pair of eyes behind those they saw, watching through thin, obscuring curtains. You could not tell what he was thinking" (123). In the first edition of the novel, Cowperwood is explicitly seen as a lobster in another context (378–79).

53. Pizer, *Novels of Dreiser,* 167. Pizer explores Dreiser's "imagery of deceit derived from animal life" in the context of Cowperwood's success (167). He is not concerned with the link between these modes of deception and those of the novelist, however.

54. Theodore Dreiser, "A Lesson from the Aquarium," *Tom Watson's Magazine* 3 (1906), reprinted in Pizer, *Dreiser: Uncollected Prose* (159). "Bless us, how closely these lesser creatures do imitate us in action—or how curiously we copy them!" Dreiser writes (162).

55. See Wharton's early story "Copy," 104. See also chapters 2 and 4.

56. Cowperwood's identification of himself with his assets is often implied. We learn that by the time of the Chicago fire, "Cowperwood had actually . . . spread himself out very thin" (142). "A student of finance once observed that nothing is so sensitive as money," the narrator notes, "and the financial mind partakes largely of the quality of the thing in which it deals" (347).

57. Dreiser, *Sister Carrie,* 13. That "what she was" is in this case "a wage-seeker" is not beside the point—but neither is it the only point. Carrie's responses to being watched range from shame to exhilaration. What often makes the difference for her, as for Dreiser, is the extent to which she feels she can control what is revealed to others.

58. On *An American Tragedy* in relation to questions of impersonation and exposure see Philip Fisher, *Hard Facts: Setting and Form in the American Novel* (New York: Oxford University Press, 1985); and Lee Mitchell, *Determined Fictions: American Literary Naturalism* (New York: Columbia University Press, 1989).

59. The figure of a powerful man with his back to his audience recurs in Dreiser's early interview with the lawyer Joseph Choate. See Kaplan, *Social Construction,* 130.

60. In letters of the period, Dreiser refers to "this book game," the "writing game," and so on. (*Letters,* III, 119; cf. 116).

61. James Joyce, *A Portrait of the Artist as Young Man,* in *The Essential James Joyce,* ed. Harry Levin (Harmondsworth: Penguin, 1967), 221. Further references are cited in the text. Joyce's

formulation became a recurrent touchstone for discussions of narration in the wake of the New Criticism. See, for example, Booth, *The Rhetoric of Fiction*, on the "impersonal narration" of *Portrait* (323–36).

62. Henry James, "Gustave Flaubert" (1893), in Miller, *Theory of Fiction*, 178.

63. Wharton, *Writing of Fiction*, 91.

64. Edith Wharton, *The Age of Innocence* (New York: Penguin, 1984), 280. Further references are cited in the text.

65. A narrative voice remains, referring to Archer in the third person. But this does not alter the fact that Archer's consciousness dominates the scene.

66. On the writing of *Age* as a "nostalgic act," see Wolff, *A Feast of Words*, 310. Wolff takes a positive view of Archer's "development" (324), and reads the novel as a successful *Bildungsroman* (314). On Old New York as a kind of matriarchy, though a problematic one, see Fryer, *Felicitous Space*, 139–40. Elizabeth Ammons, in *Edith Wharton's Argument with America* (Athens: University of Georgia Press, 1980), stresses Wharton's attack on the patriarchal coercion of society, in *Age* as elsewhere (see 127–28, 143–52).

67. As we have seen, in a review published in the *Atlantic* in 1906, Wharton herself was praised for imbuing her fiction with her own personality (Sedgwick, "The Novels of Mrs. Wharton"). Noting that in *A Backward Glance* Wharton claims to have discovered her "real" personality by writing stories, Kaplan underscores Wharton's "strategies for producing . . . a professional self" and argues that Wharton learned "to construct a separate 'personality' in the public eye . . . to externalize [her] name on a book" (*Social Construction*, 67). As I have been suggesting, however, personality was quite a fluid concept well into the twentieth century, loosely identified with notions of individuality, person, self, and even soul. Elaborating on the "real personality" that she acquired when her "first volume of short stories was published," Wharton writes: "*I* had written short stories that were thought worthy of preservation! Was it the same insignificant *I* that I had always known?" (*A Backward Glance*, 112, 113). I am suggesting that for many writers of the period the creation of a professional persona or projected personality only intensified the problem of which I/self/personality was the "real" one. In *A Backward Glance* Wharton identifies writing and publication not only with her "own . . . real personality" but with her "own soul" (112, 115, 119, 212).

68. See Fryer, *Felicitous Space*, 126–29; Ammons, *Wharton's Argument*, 145–47. Woolf stresses Wharton's use of biographical material throughout.

69. See chapter 4.

70. "The cause of the commotion . . . sat gracefully in her corner of the box, her eyes fixed on the stage, and revealing, as she leaned forward, a little more shoulder and bosom than New York was accustomed to seeing, at least in ladies who had reasons for wishing to pass unnoticed" (16).

71. The most striking example of May's plotting is the amazing orchestration of moves through which she first lies to Ellen about being pregnant, and then lets Archer see that she has lied, in order to make it clear to him (without ever saying so) both what she *knew* and what she *did* (286).

72. The unfashionable stone facade and and inconvenient location of her house is an example of her independence; putting the bedroom on the ground floor (as the French do) once she is too fat to go upstairs is an example of her creativity in interior design. Both Fryer (*Felicitous Space*, 75 and passim) and Kaplan (*Social Construction*, 78–79) note that for Wharton the idea of architecture had a particular relevance to fiction writing.

73. Scorsese surrounds the character of Granny with several dogs in the movie. Granny has no dogs in the novel, but Wharton was a great dog lover.

74. Directly facing [Newland Archer] was the box of old Mrs. Manson Mingott, whose monstrous obesity had long since made it impossible for her to attend the Opera, but who was always represented on fashionable nights by some of the younger members of the family" (9).

75. "Visibility in Fiction" is the title of an article Wharton published in the *Yale Review* (18 [March 1929]: 480–88). The "visibility" in question is not that of the author, however.

76. "One of his earliest and most genuine leanings was toward paintings. He admired nature, but somehow, without knowing why, he fancied one could best grasp it through the personality of some interpreter, just as we gain our ideas of law and politics through individuals" (60).

77. Dreiser himself was intermittently praised for his "compelling individuality" from the start of his career (Pizer, *Critical Essays*, 166).

78. Responding to a fan letter from a reader of *Sister Carrie*, Dreiser advises the writer to hope that he never comes to know Dreiser "personally": "remain illusioned if you can," Dreiser writes (*Letters*, 194).

79. After establishing a "Beauty Department" at *The Delineator*, Dreiser claimed that readers' letters averaged "from 300 to 400 a day, which would indicate a total of about 9,000 for the month." Charlotte C. West, the department's first head, corroborated Dreiser's claims. See *Letters*, 81.

80. Wilson, "The Rhetoric of Consumption," 49–50, 59–61.

81. See chapters 2 and 4.

82. Discussing experiments in Gestalt psychology in *Art and Illusion*, E. H. Gombrich writes, "Though we may be intellectually aware of the fact that any given experience *must* be an illusion, we cannot, strictly speaking, watch ourselves having an illusion" (cited in Iser, *Act of Reading*, 127).

83. See *Letters of Frank Norris*, ed. Franklin Walker (San Francisco: Book Club of California, 1956), 36, 41; letter to Frank Burgess 64–65.

84. Wharton, *A Backward Glance*, 115, 119, 212.

Afterword

1. "It is by now an established part of our folklore," Alfred Kazin wrote in 1942, "that Theodore Dreiser lacks everything except genius" (*On Native Grounds*, 89).

2. Lionel Trilling, *The Liberal Imagination* (New York: Viking Press, 1950). For an account of the immediate context and the far-reaching impact of this essay see Kaplan's introduction to *Social Construction*.

3. Donald Pizer notes that in the mid-1890s, when Dreiser wrote for some of the new ten-cent mass-circulation journals and spent two years editing his brother's magazine, *Ev'ry Month* ("The Woman's Magazine of Literature and Music"), he "devoted most of his writing outside of journalism to a sizable number of . . . high-minded poems" (*Novels of Theodore Dreiser*, 4). Poetry, of course, had been considered a "higher" genre than prose fiction for generations. Later, Dreiser often sought to differentiate between his own work and that of popular "sentimental" authors of the period. See Pizer, *Novels of Theodore Dreiser*, 37; Kaplan, *Social Construction*, 118–20.

4. Michael Schudson emphasizes the premium on objectivity in turn-of-century reporting and relates it to changes in the concept of science as well as shifting conceptions of law. See *The Origins of the Ideal of Objectivity in the Professions: American Journalism and American Law, 1830–1940* (New York: Garland Publishing, 1990), chaps. 1, 5, and 6. See also note 22 in chapter 2 above.

5. On the changes in the conventions of audience behavior and the transformation of Shakespeare and opera into "sacred" texts that were to be approached with reverence, see Levine, *Highbrow/Lowbrow*, 74, 89–90, 167–68, and chaps. 1 and 2 passim.

6. See my introduction, especially notes 15 and 19.

7. W. E. B. DuBois, *The Souls of Black Folk* (Greenwich, Conn.: Fawcett, 1961), v. Further references are cited in the text.

8. Jay Martin notes that "following the decline of instruction in Latin and Greek, Dickens, Cooper, Scott and other nineteenth-century novelists came to be known as 'classics'" (*Harvests of*

Change: American Literature, 1865–1914 [Englewood Cliffs, N.J.: Prentice Hall, 1967]), 19. See also Hart, *The Popular Book,* 183. Still, there were classics and Classics. On the shifting relation of books and "culture" at the end of the century, see Rubin, *The Making of Middlebrow Culture,* chap. 1, and Radway, *A Feeling for Books,* chap. 4.

9. As Kenneth W. Warren puts it, the passage "celebrates a possible high cultural transcendence of racial segregation" ("Troubled Black Humanity in *The Souls of Black Folk* and *The Autobiography of an Ex-Colored Man,*" in *The Cambridge Companion to American Realism and Naturalism,* ed. Donald Pizer [New York: Cambridge University Press, 1995]), 267. See also Levine, *Highbrow/Lowbrow,* chap. 3 ("The Sacralization of Culture"), and Brodhead, *Cultures of Letters,* 87–88. Whatever their own aspirations to high seriousness, however, novelists were not cultural icons at the turn of the century. Du Bois's group of authors is eclectic; it asserts his right to make discriminations of his own.

10. Individual chapters of *The Souls of Black Folk* were published in the *Atlantic Monthly, The World's Work, The Dial, New World,* and the *Annals of the American Academy of Political and Social Science,* all journals geared largely to a white, middle-class audience.

11. James Russell Lowell, "The Five Indispensable Authors," *Century Magazine* 47 (April–November 1893–94): 223–24.

12. Mary Antin, *The Promised Land* (1911, reprinted Boston: Houghton Mifflin, 1912), 340–41. Further references are cited in the text. Antin arrived in America at the age of fourteen in 1894.

13. Another point worth noting here is one that I have argued throughout this book: that sensitivity to the status and effect of particular rhetorical strategies does not prevent one from believing that one's "self" is deeply embedded in one's text and visible to others there. Writing to *Atlantic Monthly* editor Ellery Sedgwick about the idea of restricting the subject of *The Promised Land* to her years in America, Antin insisted that leaving out the Russian part would "leave *me* out of the book." Antin to Sedgwick, July 31, 1911, cited in Werner Sollors, Introduction to *The Promised Land* (New York: Penguin, 1997), xxvi. Sollors argues that Antin's "emigrant doubleness" may account for her having "view[ed] herself as separate from the subject of her autobiography" (xiv), insofar as she did so. Sollors raises cogent questions about Antin's relation to her imagined readers (xix–xxiv).

14. George Palmer Putnam, "Suggestions for Household Libraries," in *Hints for Home Reading: A Series of Chapters on Books and Their Use,* ed. Lyman Abbott (New York: G. P. Putnam's Sons, 1880), 13. The essay, and indeed the entire collection, represented just the kind of democratization that Lowell was attacking. Contributors included such distinguished men of letters as Charles Dudley Warner, F. B. Perkins, Hamilton W. Mabie, Edward Everett Hale, and Henry Ward Beecher. But the volume was part of a series of self-help books that also included titles such as *What to Eat, Till the Doctor Comes and How to Help Him, How to Educate Yourself, A Manual of Etiquette,* and *Hints on Dress by an American Woman.*

15. *The Book Lover: A Guide to the Best Reading* (1898) cites a passage from John Ruskin's *Sesame and Lilies* that was much quoted to promote the reading of "great authors" in this period. Relying on the familiar trope of books as people, these lines imply that to read certain authors would raise one's social standing: "Will you go and gossip with your housemaid or your stable boy when you may talk with kings and queens, while this eternal court is open to you, with its society wide as the world . . . the chosen, the mighty, of every place and time" (40–41). Putnam's "Suggestions for Household Libraries" used similar imagery and drew on similar sentiments (including class consciousness and social snobbery): "A man, says the old proverb, is known by his companions. How true is this of the companions of our better hours of ease and retirement, the volumes which we keep at hand" (112). Or again: "Reading is a very serious affair. . . . A man's library, assuming it be for use and not for display, is a better index to his character than the most detailed of external biographies. Show us the man at work in his library and we view him in his essence, not in his

seeming" ("Reading and Education" [1895], 101–2). Here as elsewhere, not only class but also gender is clearly marked. Such discussions regularly linked the idea of serious reading with the image of a man at work in his library or study. In most such discussions, the color line is not mentioned at all.

16. "I speak for thousands," Antin writes; "oh, for thousands!" (248). In Du Bois's formulation: "I have sought here to sketch, in vague, uncertain outline, the spiritual world in which ten thousand thousand Americans live and strive" ("The Forethought").

WORKS CITED

Abbott, Lyman, ed. *Hints for Home Reading: A Series of Chapters on Books and Their Use.* New York: G. P. Putnam's Sons, 1880.

Acocella, Joan. "Cather and the Academy." *New Yorker,* November 27, 1995.

Albee, John. "The Spectral Publisher." *The Dial* (May 1895).

Ammons, Elizabeth. *Edith Wharton's Argument with America.* Athens: University of Georgia Press, 1980.

Anderson, Benedict. *Imagined Communities: Reflections on the Origins and Spread of Nationalism* (London: Verso, 1991).

Anesko, Michael. *Friction with the Market.* Oxford: Oxford University Press, 1986.

Antin, Mary. *The Promised Land.* 1911. New York: Houghton Mifflin, 1912.

Auerbach, Jonathan. *Male Call: Becoming Jack London.* Durham: Duke University Press, 1996.

———. *The Romance of Failure: First-Person Fictions of Poe, Hawthorne, and James.* New York: Oxford University Press, 1989.

Augst, Thomas. "The Business of Reading in Nineteenth-Century America." *American Quarterly* 50.2 (June 1998).

———. "Composing the Moral Senses: Emerson and the Politics of Character in Nineteenth-Century America." *Political Theory* 27.1 (February 1999).

———. "The Fate of Eloquence and the Popular Science of Rhetoric in Nineteenth-Century America." Paper presented at the American Studies Association, Washington, D.C., 1997.

"Author, Agent, and Publisher." *The Critic,* December 23, 1895.

Baldwin, James. *The Booklover: A Guide to the Best Reading.* 1884. Chicago: McClurg & Co., 1898.

Banta, Martha. *Imaging American Women: Idea and Ideals in Cultural History.* New York: Columbia University Press, 1987.

Barish, Jonas A. *The Antitheatrical Prejudice.* Berkeley: University of California Press, 1981.

Barthes, Roland. "The Death of the Author." In *Image, Music, Text.* Trans. Stephen Heath. New York: Hill and Wang, 1977.

Baym, Nina. *Novels, Readers, and Reviewers: Responses to Fiction in Antebellum America.* Ithaca: Cornell University Press, 1984.

Becker, George, ed. *Documents of Modern Literary Realism.* Princeton: Princeton University Press, 1967.

Benjamin, Walter. "The Storyteller." In *Illuminations.* Trans. Harry Zohn. New York: Schocken, 1969.

Bennett, Tony. *Formalism and Marxism.* London: Methuen 1979.

Berger, John. *Ways of Seeing.* Harmondsworth: Penguin, 1972.

Blair, Juliet. "Private Parts in Public Places: The Case of Actresses." In *Women and Space: Ground Rules and Social Maps.* Ed. Shirley Ardener. New York: St. Martin's, 1981.

Bledstein, Burton. *The Culture of Professionalism: The Middle Class and the Development of Higher Education in America.* New York: Norton, 1976.

Bleich, David. *Subjective Criticism.* Baltimore: Johns Hopkins University Press, 1978.

Bleich, David, and Deborah Holstein, eds. *Personal Effects in Scholarly Writing.* New York: MLA, forthcoming.

Bloom, Harold, ed. *Edith Wharton.* New York: Chelsea House, 1986.

"Books That Stay By." *Atlantic* 98 (February 1906).

Booth, Wayne C. *The Rhetoric of Fiction.* 1961. Chicago: University of Chicago Press, 1967.

Borus, Daniel H. *Writing Realism: Howells, James, and Norris in the Mass Market.* Chapel Hill: University of North Carolina Press, 1989.

Bourdieu, Pierre. *The Field of Cultural Production: Essays on Art and Literature.* Ed. Randal Johnson. Cambridge: Polity Press, 1993.

Brantlinger, Patrick. *The Reading Lesson: The Threat of Mass Literacy in Nineteenth-Century British Fiction.* Bloomington: Indiana University Press, 1998.

Brodhead, Richard. *Cultures of Letters: Scenes of Reading and Writing in Nineteenth-Century America.* Chicago: University of Chicago Press, 1993.

Brooks, Peter. *Reading for the Plot: Design and Intention in Narrative.* New York: Knopf, 1985.

———. "The Tale vs. the Novel." *Novel* 21.1 (1988).

Burnett, Frances Hodgson. *Little Lord Fauntleroy.* London: Frederick Warne and Co., [n.d.].

✓ Butler, Judith. *Gender Trouble: Feminism and the Subversion of Identity.* New York: Routledge, 1990.

✓ Carlson, Julie. "Impositions of Form: Romantic Anti-Theatricalism and the Case against Particular Women." *English Literary History* 60 (1993).

Carroll, David. *The Matinee Idols.* New York: Galahad Books, 1972.

✓ Casper, Scott E. "Defining the National Pantheon: The Making of Houghton Mifflin's Biographical Series, 1880–1900." In *Reading Books: Essays on the Material Text and Literature in America.* Ed. Michele Moylan and Lane Stiles. Amherst: University of Massachusetts Press, 1996.

Cather, Willa. "Coming Aphrodite." In *Youth and the Bright Medusa.* New York: Alfred A. Knopf, 1920.

———. "Death in the Desert." In *"The Troll Garden" and Selected Stories by Willa Cather.* New York: Bantam, 1990.

———. "Du Maurier's *Trilby.*" *Nebraska Journal,* December 23, 1894. Reprinted in Slote, *Kingdom of Art.*

———. "Nanette: An Aside" in *Willa Cather: 24 Stories.* Ed. Sharon O'Brien. New York: Penguin, 1993.

———. "Peter." In *Willa Cather: 24 Stories.*

———. *The Song of the Lark.* New York: Penguin, 1991.

———. *Uncle Valentine and Other Stories: Willa Cather's Uncollected Short Fiction, 1915–29.* Ed. Bernice Slote. Lincoln: University of Nebraska Press, 1986.

Chartier, Roger. *The Order of Books.* Trans. Lydia G. Cochrane. Stanford: Stanford University Press, 1994.

———. "Texts, Printings, Readings." In *The New Cultural History.* Ed. Lynn Hunt. Berkeley: University of California Press, 1989.

Churchill, Winston. *The Celebrity: An Episode.* 1897. Reprinted New York: Grosset and Dunlap, 1906.

———. *Richard Carvel.* 1899. London: Macmillan, 1900.

Clarke, George. "The Novel-Reading Habit." *The Arena* 19 (May 1898).

Coates, Joseph H. "Sister Carrie." *North American Review* 186 (October 1907). Reprinted in Pizer, *Critical Essays.*

Cohn, Dorrit. *Transparent Minds: Narrative Modes for Presenting Consciousness in Fiction.* Princeton: Princeton University Press, 1978.

"Congress of Authors." *The Dial* 15 (July 1893).

"Contributors' Club." *Atlantic* 98 (February 1906).

Cooper, Anna Julia. *A Voice from the South.* 1892. New York: Oxford University Press, 1990.

Corson, Hiram. *The Aims of Literary Study.* New York: Macmillan & Co., 1894.

Crane, Stephen. *Maggie: A Girl of the Streets.* New York: W. W. Norton and Co., 1979.

Crawford, Francis Marion. *Marietta: A Maid of Venice.* New York: Macmillan, 1901.

———. *The Novel: What It Is.* 1893. Reprinted New York: Macmillan, 1908.

———. *A Roman Singer.* Leipzig: Bernhard Tauchnitz, 1884.

Crisler, Jesse S. "Norris's 'Library.'" *Frank Norris Studies* 5 (Spring 1988).

Crothers, Samuel McCord. "The Gentle Reader." *Atlantic* 86 (November 1900).

Crowley, J. Donald, ed. *Hawthorne: The Critical Heritage.* London: Routledge, 1970.

"Culture of the Old School." *Atlantic* 55 (January 1885).

Darnton, Robert. "First Steps toward a History of Reading." In *The Kiss of Lamourette: Reflections in Cultural History.* New York: W. W. Norton and Co., 1989.

———. "Readers Respond to Rousseau: The Fabrication of Romantic Sensitivity." In *The Great Cat Massacre and Other Episodes of French Cultural History.* New York: Basic Books, 1984.

Dauber, Kenneth. *The Idea of Authorship in America: Democratic Poetics from Franklin to Melville.* Madison: University of Wisconsin Press, 1990.

Davidson, Cathy N., ed. *Reading in America: Literature and Social History.* Baltimore: Johns Hopkins University Press, 1989.

———. *Revolution and the Word: The Rise of the Novel in America.* New York: Oxford University Press, 1986.

Davison, Richard Allan. "The Remaining Seven of Frank Norris's 'Weekly Letters.'" *American Literary Realism* 3 (Summer 1968).

Dickinson, Emily. Letter to Thomas Wentworth Higginson. In *The Norton Anthology of American Literature.* Shorter 4th edition. Ed. Nina Baym et al. New York: Norton, 1995.

Dimock, Wai Chee. "Debasing Exchange: Edith Wharton's *The House of Mirth.*" In Bloom, *Edith Wharton.*

✓ ———. "Feminism, New Historicism, and the Reader." In Machor, *Readers in History.*

Dreiser, Theodore. *A Book about Myself.* New York: Boni and Liveright, 1922.

———. *The Financier.* New York: A. L. Burt, 1912.

———. *The Financier.* New York: New American Library, 1981.

———. "A Lesson from the Aquarium." *Tom Watson's Magazine* 3 (1906). Reprinted in Pizer, *Dreiser: Uncollected Prose.*

———. *The Letters of Theodore Dreiser: A Selection.* Vol. 1. Ed. Robert H. Elias. Philadelphia: University of Pennsylvania Press, 1959.

———. *Sister Carrie.* New York: Norton, 1970.

———. "Talks with Four Novelists: Mr. Dreiser." *New York Times Saturday Review of Books,* June, 15, 1907, reprinted in Pizer, *Dreiser: Uncollected Prose.*

———. "Theodore Dreiser." In Pizer, *Dreiser: Uncollected Prose.*

Drinker, Elizabeth Sandwith. *The Diary of Elizabeth Sandwith Drinker.* Ed. Elaine Forman Crane. Boston: Northeastern University Press, 1991.

Du Bois, W. E. B. *The Souls of Black Folk.* Greenwich, Conn.: Fawcett, 1961.

Du Maurier, George. *Trilby.* London: Osgood, McIlvaine & Co., 1895.

Dunn, Martha. "A Plea for the Shiftless Reader." *Atlantic* 85 (January 1900).

Edel, Leon, ed. *Henry James and H. G. Wells: A Record of Their Friendship, Their Debate on the Art of Fiction, and Their Quarrel.* London: Rupert Hart-Davis, 1959.

———. *The Life of Henry James.* 2 vols. New York: Penguin, 1977.

Eliot, T. S. "Tradition and the Individual Talent." In *Selected Prose of T. S. Eliot.* Ed. Frank Kermode. New York: Harcourt Brace and Jovanovich, 1975.

Fay, Susan Barrera. "A Modest Celebrity: Literary Reputation and the Marketplace in Antebellum America." Ph.D. diss., George Washington University, 1992.

✓ Feldstein, Richard. "Reader, Text, Referentiality." In *Feminism and Psychoanalysis.* Ed. Richard Feldstein and Judith Roof. Ithaca: Cornell University Press, 1989.

Fetterley, Judith. "Impersonating 'Little Women': The Radicalism of Alcott's *Behind a Mask.*" *Women's Studies* 10 (1983).

———. "Reading about Reading: 'A Jury of Her Peers,' 'The Murders in the Rue Morgue,' and 'The Yellow Wallpaper.'" In Flynn and Schweickart, *Gender and Reading.*

———. *The Resisting Reader: A Feminist Approach to American Fiction.* Bloomington: Indiana University Press, 1978.

———. "'The Temptation to Be a Beautiful Object': Double Standard and Double Bind in *The House of Mirth.*" *Studies in American Fiction* 5.2 (1977).

Fish, Stanley. *Is There a Text in This Class? The Authority of Interpretive Communities.* Cambridge, Mass.: Harvard University Press, 1980.

Fisher, Philip. *Hard Facts: Setting and Form in the American Novel.* New York: Oxford University Press, 1985.

Fitzgerald, F. Scott. *The Letters of F. Scott Fitzgerald.* Ed. Andrew Turnbull. New York: Charles Scribner's Sons, 1963.

Fliegelman, Jay. *Declaring Independence: Jefferson, Natural Language, and the Culture of Performance.* Stanford: Stanford University Press, 1993.

Flynn, Elizabeth A., and Patrocinio P. Schweickart, eds. *Gender and Reading: Essays on Readers, Texts, and Contexts.* Baltimore: Johns Hopkins University Press, 1986.

Forster, E. M. *Aspects of the Novel.* New York: Harcourt, Brace and Co., 1927.

Foucault, Michel. "What Is an Author?" In *Language, Counter-Memory, Practice: Selected Essays and Interviews.* Ed. Donald F. Bouchard. Trans. Donald F. Bouchard and Sherry Simon. Ithaca: Cornell University Press, 1977.

"Four Views on the Place of the Personal in Scholarship." *PMLA* 111.5 (October 1996).

Freund, Elizabeth. *The Return of the Reader: Reader-Response Criticism.* London: Methuen, 1987.

Fried, Michael. *Realism, Writing, Disfiguration: On Thomas Eakins and Stephen Crane.* Chicago: University of Chicago Press, 1987.

Fryer, Judith. *Felicitous Space: The Imaginative Structures of Edith Wharton and Willa Cather.* Chapel Hill: University of North Carolina Press, 1986.

Garvey, Ellen Gruber. *The Adman in the Parlor: Magazines and the Gendering of Consumer Culture, 1880s to 1910s.* New York: Oxford University Press, 1996.

Gates, Henry Louis. "Introduction" to Wilson, *Our Nig.*

Gennette, Gérard. *Narrative Discourse.* Trans. Jane E. Lewin. Ithaca: Cornell University Press, 1980; first published 1972 as a portion of *Figures Three.*

Gibson, Walker. "Authors, Speakers, Readers, and Mock Readers." In Tompkins, *Reader-Response Criticism.*

Gilder, Jeannette. *Authors at Home: Personal and Biographical Sketches of Well-Known American Writers.* New York: Cassell Publishing Co., 1888.

Gilman, Charlotte Perkins. "The Yellow Wallpaper." New York: The Feminist Press, 1973.

Gilmore, Michael T. *American Romanticism and the Marketplace.* Chicago: University of Chicago Press, 1985.

Ginzburg, Carlo. *The Cheese and the Worms: The Cosmos of a Sixteenth-Century Miller.* Trans. John and Anne Tedeschi. Baltimore: Johns Hopkins University Press, 1980.

Glazener, Nancy. *Reading for Realism: The History of a U.S. Literary Institution.* Durham: Duke University Press, 1997.

Goffman, Erving. "The Theatrical Frame." In *Frame Analysis: An Essay On the Organization of Experience.* New York: Harper and Row, 1974.

Golden, Catherine. "The Writing of 'The Yellow Wallpaper': A Double Palimpsest." *Studies in American Fiction* 17.2 (1989).

Graff, Gerald. *Professing Literature.* Chicago: University of Chicago Press, 1987.

Graham, Don. *Frank Norris: The Aesthetic Context.* Columbia: University of Missouri Press, 1978.

Grossman, Julie. "Hardy's *Tess* and 'The Photograph': Images to Die For." *Criticism* 35.4 (1993).

"The Hap-Hazard of Our Friendships." *Atlantic* 57 (June 1886).

✓ Hart, James. *The Popular Book: A History of America's Literary Taste.* New York: Oxford University Press, 1950.

"Henry James." *Atlantic* 55 (May 1885).

Henry, Katherine. "Angelina Grimké's Rhetoric of Exposure." *American Quarterly* 49.2 (June 1997).

Higham, John. *Strangers in the Land: Patterns of American Nativism, 1860–1925.* New York: Atheneum, 1975.

Hochman, Barbara. *The Art of Frank Norris, Storyteller.* Columbia: University of Missouri Press, 1988.

———. "*The Awakening* and *The House of Mirth:* Plotting Experience and Experiencing Plot." In *Cambridge Companion to American Realism and Naturalism.* Ed. Donald Pizer. New York: Cambridge University Press, 1995.

———. "A Portrait of the Artist as a Young Actress: The Rewards of Representation in *Sister Carrie.*" In *New Essays on "Sister Carrie."* Ed. Donald Pizer. New York: Cambridge University Press, 1991.

———. "The Rewards of Representation: Edith Wharton, Lily Bart, and the Writer/Reader Interchange." *Novel: A Forum on Fiction* 24.2 (Winter 1991).

✓ Holland, Norman N. *The Dynamics of Literary Response.* New York: W. W. Norton & Co., 1975.

Homestead, Melissa J. "'Links of Similitude': The Narrator of *The Country of the Pointed Firs* and Author-Reader Relations at the End of the Nineteenth Century." In *Jewett and Her Contemporaries: Reshaping the Canon.* Ed. Karen L. Kilcup and Thomas S. Edwards. Gainesville: University Press of Florida, 1999.

Horwitz, Howard. "To Find the Value of X: *The Pit* as a Renunciation of Romance." In *American Realism.* Ed. Eric J. Sundquist. Baltimore: Johns Hopkins University Press, 1982.

Horwitz, Morton. *The Transformation of American Law: 1780–1860.* Cambridge, Mass.: Harvard University Press, 1977.

Howard, June. *Form and History in American Literary Naturalism.* Chapel Hill: University of North Carolina Press, 1985.

Howells, William Dean. "My Favorite Novelist and His Best Book." *Munsey's Magazine* (April 1897), reprinted in *European and American Masters.* Ed. Clara Marburg Kirk and Rudolf Kirk. New York: Collier Books, 1963.

———. "Novel-Writing and Novel-Reading: An Impersonal Explanation." 1899. *Bulletin of the New York Public Library* 62 (January–February 1958).

———. *The Rise of Silas Lapham.* New York: W. W. Norton and Co., 1982.

Hunter, Paul J. "The Loneliness of the Long-Distance Reader." *Genre* 10 (Winter 1977).

Iser, Wolfgang. *The Act of Reading: A Theory of Aesthetic Response.* London: Routledge and Kegan Paul, 1978.

———. "Indeterminacy and the Reader's Response in Prose Fiction." In *Aspects of Narrative: Selected Papers from the English Institute.* Ed. J. Hillis Miller. New York: Columbia University Press, 1971.

James, Henry. "Anthony Trollope." In *The Art of Fiction and Other Essays by Henry James.* New York: Oxford University Press, 1948.

———. "The Art of Fiction." In Miller, *Theory of Fiction.*

———. The Aspern Papers. In *The Aspern Papers and The Turn of the Screw.* London: Penguin, 1986.

———. *The Bostonians.* New York: Random House, 1956.

———. "The Figure in the Carpet." In *"The Figure in the Carpet" and Other Stories.* London: Penguin, 1986.

———. "The Future of the Novel." 1899. In Miller, *Theory of Fiction.*

———. "Gustave Flaubert." In Miller, *Theory of Fiction.*

———. "Guy de Maupassant." In Miller, *Theory of Fiction.*

———. "Ivan Turgenieff." In Miller, *Theory of Fiction.*

———. "The Lesson of Balzac." In Miller, *Theory of Fiction.*

———. "The New Novel." In Miller, *Theory of Fiction.*

———. "The Novels of George Eliot." *Atlantic* 18 (October 1866).

———. *The Portable James.* Ed. Morton Dauwen Zabel. New York: Viking, 1958.

———. *The Portrait of a Lady.* New York: Norton, 1975.

———. "Preface" to *The Golden Bowl.* In *The Art of the Novel.* New York: Charles Scribner's Sons, 1950.

———. "The Private Life." In *"The Figure in the Carpet" and Other Stories.* London: Penguin, 1986.

———. "Some Notes on the Theatre." *The Nation,* March 11, 1875. Cited in *The American Theatre as Seen by Its Critics, 1752–1934.* Ed. Montrose J. Moses and John Mason Brown. New York, 1934.

———. *The Tragic Muse.* New York: Penguin, 1984.

James, William. *Psychology: Briefer Course.* New York: Collier, 1962.

Jauss, Hans Robert. *Toward an Aesthetic of Reception.* Trans. Timothy Bahti. Minneapolis: University of Minnesota Press, 1982.

Jenkins, Emily. "*Trilby:* Fads, Photographers, and 'Over-Perfect' Feet." *Book History* 1 (1998).

Joyce, James. *A Portrait of the Artist as a Young Man.* In *The Essential James Joyce.* Ed. Harry Levin. Harmondsworth: Penguin, 1967.

Kacandes, Irene. "Are You in the Text?: The 'Literary Performative' in Post-modernist Fiction." *Text and Performance Quarterly* 13 (1993).

Kaplan, Amy. "Manifest Domesticity." *American Literature* 70.3 (September 1998).

———. *The Social Construction of American Realism.* Chicago: University of Chicago Press, 1988.

Kazin, Alfred. "Two Educations." In *On Native Grounds.* New York: Harcourt Brace and Co., 1942.

Kelley, Mary. *Private Woman, Public Stage: Literary Domesticity in Nineteenth-Century America*. New York: Oxford University Press, 1985.

———. "Reading Women/Women Reading: The Making of Learned Women in Antebellum America." *Journal of American History* 83 (September 1996).

Kendrick Walter. *The Novel Machine*. Baltimore: Johns Hopkins University Press, 1980.

Kijinsky, John, L. "John Morley's 'English Men of Letters' Series and the Politics of Reading." *Victorian Studies* 34.1 (1990).

Klein, Marcus. *Easterns, Westerns, and Private Eyes: American Matters, 1870–1900*. Madison: University of Wisconsin Press, 1994.

Kolodny, Annette. "A Map for ReReading: Or, Gender and the Interpretation of Literary Texts." In *The Captive Imagination: A Casebook on "The Yellow Wallpaper."* Ed. Catherine Golden. New York: The Feminist Press, 1992.

Lears, T. J. Jackson. *No Place of Grace: Antimodernism and the Transformation of American Culture (1880–1920)*. New York: Pantheon Books, 1981.

Lee, Gerald Stanley. *The Lost Art of Reading*. New York: G. P. Putnam's Sons, 1902.

Leverenz, David. *Manhood and the American Renaissance*. Ithaca: Cornell University Press, 1989.

Levine, Lawrence W. *Highbrow/Lowbrow: The Emergence of Cultural Hierarchy in America*. Cambridge, Mass.: Harvard University Press, 1988.

Lewis, R. W. B. *Edith Wharton: A Biography*. London: Constable, 1975.

"The Life and Poetry of Wordsworth." *North American Review* 73 (1851).

London, Jack, "Getting into Print." *The Editor*, March 1903.

———. *Letters from Jack London*. Ed. King Hendricks and Irving Shepard. New York: Odyssey Press, 1965.

———. *Martin Eden*. New York: Penguin, 1993.

———. *"The Sea-Wolf" and Other Stories*. London: Penguin, 1989.

Long, Elizabeth. "Textual Interpretation as Collective Action." In *The Ethnography of Reading*. Ed. Jonathan Boyarin. Berkeley: University of California Press, 1993.

Lowell, James Russell. "The Five Indispensable Authors." *Century Magazine* 47 (April–November 1893–94).

Lubbock, Percy. *The Craft of Fiction*. 1921. New York: Peter Smith, 1947.

Mabie, Hamilton. "The Feeling for Literature." *The Bookman* 1 (June 1895).

Machor, James L. "Fiction and Informed Reading in Early Nineteenth-Century America." *Nineteenth-Century Literature* 47.3 (1992).

———. Respondent's Comments, "Historical Readers: Reconstructive Strategies." Modern Language Association Convention, Toronto, December 1997.

Machor, James L., ed. *Readers in History: Nineteenth-Century American Literature and the Contexts of Response*. Baltimore: Johns Hopkins University Press, 1993.

Mailloux, Steven. "The Rhetorical Use and Abuse of Fiction: Eating Books in Late Nineteenth-Century America." *Boundary 2* 17.1 (1990).

Marshall, David. *The Figure of Theater*. New York: Columbia University Press, 1986.

Martin, Jay. *Harvests of Change: American Literature, 1865–1914*. Englewood Cliffs, N.J.: Prentice Hall, 1967.

Matthews, Brander. "On Pleasing the Taste of the Public." In *Aspects of Fiction and Other Ventures in Criticism*. New York: Charles Scribner's Sons, 1902.

Matthiessen, F. O., *American Renaissance: Art and Expression in the Age of Emerson and Whitman*. New York: Oxford University Press, 1968.

McElrath, Joseph R., Jr. "Frank Norris: Early Posthumous Responses." *American Literary Realism* 12 (1974).

———. *Frank Norris Revisited*. New York: Macmillan, 1992.

McGill, Meredith. "The Matter of the Text: Commerce, Print Culture, and the Authority of the State in American Copyright Law." *American Literary History* 9.1 (Spring 1997).

Melville, Herman. "Hawthorne and His Mosses." In *Norton Anthology of American Literature*. Shorter 4th ed. New York: Norton, 1995.

"Men, Women, and Books." *The Critic*, February 15, 1896.

Mencken, H. L. "Dreiser's Novel." *New York Times Review of Books*, November 10, 1912. Reprinted in Pizer, *Critical Essays*.

———. Review of *The Financier*. In Pizer, *Critical Essays*.

Merish, Lori. "Engendering Naturalism: Narrative Form and Commodity Spectacle in U.S. Naturalist Fiction." *Novel* 29.3 (1996).

Meynell, Alice. "*The House of Mirth*." *Bookman* 29 (1905). Reprinted in Tuttleton, Lauer, and Murray, *Edith Wharton: The Contemporary Reviews*.

Michaels, Walter Benn. *The Gold Standard and the Logic of Naturalism: American Literature at the Turn of the Century*. Berkeley: University of California Press, 1987.

———. *Our America: Nativism, Modernism, and Pluralism*. Durham: Duke University Press, 1995.

Michelson, Bruce. "Edith Wharton's 'House Divided.'" *Studies in American Fiction* 12.2 (1984).

Miller, D. A. *Narrative and Its Discontents*. Princeton: Princeton University Press, 1981.

Miller, Edwin Haviland. "Frank Norris's *The Pit* as Autobiography." *Hartford Studies in Literature* 17.3 (1985).

Miller, E. James, ed. *Theory of Fiction: Henry James*. Lincoln: University of Nebraska Press, 1972.

Mitchell, Lee Clark. *Determined Fictions: American Literary Naturalism*. New York: Columbia University Press, 1989.

———. "'When You Call Me That . . .': Tall Talk and Male Hegemony in *The Virginian*." *PMLA* 102.1 (1987).

Mitchell, S. Weir. "Books and the Man." New York: The New York Public Library. Astor, Lenox, and Tilden Foundations, 1905.

———. *Doctor and Patient*. Philadelphia: J. B. Lippincott, 1887.

———. *Hugh Wynne: Free Quaker*. 1896. Reprinted New York: The Century Co., 1905.

Moddelmog, William E. "Disowning 'Personality': Privacy and Subjectivity in *The House of Mirth*." *American Literature* 70.2 (1998).

Mott, Frank Luther. *Golden Multitudes: The Story of Best Sellers in the United States*. New York: Macmillan, 1947.

Mulvey, Laura. "Visual Pleasure and Narrative Cinema." *Feminism and Film Theory.* Ed. Constance Penley. New York: Routledge, 1988.

Newbury, Michael. "Eaten Alive: Slavery and Celebrity in Antebellum America." *English Literary History* 61 (Spring 1994).

Nicholson, Bruce. "Frank Norris's 'Dedication' in *The Pit.*" *Frank Norris Studies* 25 (Spring 1998).

Norris, Charles. *Frank Norris.* New York: Doubleday, 1914.

Norris, Frank. "The American Public and 'Popular' Fiction." February 2, 1903. Reprinted in Pizer, *Literary Criticism of Frank Norris.*

———. "Dying Fires." In *The Complete Edition of Frank Norris.* Vol. 4. New York: Doubleday Doran and Co., 1928.

———. "The Jongleur of Taillebois." In *The Complete Edition of Frank Norris.* Vol. 10. New York: Doubleday, Doran & Co., 1928.

———. *Letters of Frank Norris.* Ed. Franklin Walker. San Francisco: Book Club of California, 1956.

———. "A Neglected Epic." *World's Work* (December 1902). Reprinted in Pizer, *Literary Criticism.*

———. *The Octopus.* New York: New American Library, 1964.

———. *The Pit.* New York: Grove Press, 1956.

———. "A Problem in Fiction: Truth vs. Accuracy." *Boston Evening Transcript,* November 6, 1901. Reprinted in Pizer, *Literary Criticism.*

———. "The Responsibilities of the Novelist." *Critic* 41 (December 1902). Reprinted in Pizer, *Literary Criticism.*

———. "Simplicity in Art." January 15, 1902. Reprinted in Pizer, *Literary Criticism.*

———. "Storytellers vs. Novelists." *World's Work* (March 1902). Reprinted in Pizer, *Literary Criticism.*

———. "Weekly Letter." *Chicago American.* July 13, 1901. Reprinted in Pizer, *Literary Criticism.*

———. "Weekly Letter." *Chicago American.* (August 3, 1901). Reprinted in Pizer, *Literary Criticism.*

O'Brien, Sharon. "Becoming Noncanonical: The Case against Willa Cather." *American Quarterly* 40 (March 1988).

Ong, Walter J. "The Writer's Audience Is Always a Fiction." *PMLA* 90.1 (January 1975).

Page, Philip. "The Curious Narration of *The Bostonians.*" *American Literature* 46 (November 1974).

Perloff, Marjorie. "Forum." *PMLA* 112.5 (October 1997).

Philes, George. *How to Read a Book.* New York, 1873.

Pizer, Donald. *The Novels of Theodore Dreiser: A Critical Study.* Minneapolis: University of Minnesota Press, 1976.

———, ed. *Critical Essays on Theodore Dreiser.* Boston: G. K. Hall & Co., 1981.

———. *The Literary Criticism of Frank Norris.* New York: Russell & Russell, 1976.

———. *Theodore Dreiser: A Selection of Uncollected Prose.* Detroit: Wayne State University Press, 1977.

Porter, Noah. *Books and Reading: What Books Shall I Read and How Shall I Read Them?* New York: Charles Scribners, 1871, reprinted 1882.

Potter, A. *A Handbook for Readers.* New York: Harper and Bros., 1843.

Poulet, Georges. "Criticism and the Experience of Interiority." In Tompkins, *Reader-Response Criticism.*

———. "The Self and Other in Critical Consciousness." *Diacritics* 2 (1972).

Purcell, L. Edward. "*Trilby* and *Trilby*-Mania: The Beginning of the Bestseller System." *Journal of Popular Culture* 11 (Summer 1977).

Putnam, George Palmer. "Suggestions for Household Libraries." In Abbott, *Hints for Home Reading.*

Rabinowitz, Peter. *Before Reading: Narrative Conventions and the Politics of Interpretation.* Ithaca: Cornell University Press, 1987.

Radway, Janice. *A Feeling for Books: The Book-of-the-Month Club, Literary Taste, and Middle-Class Desire.* Chapel Hill: University of North Carolina Press, 1997.

———. "Reading Is Not Eating: Mass-Produced Literature and the Theoretical, Methodological, and Political Consequences of a Metaphor." *Book Research Quarterly* 2 (Fall 1986).

———. *Reading the Romance: Women, Patriarchy, and Popular Culture.* Chapel Hill: University of North Carolina Press, 1984.

Railton, Stephen. "The Address of the Scarlet Letter." In Machor, *Readers in History.*

"Reading and Education." *The Dial* 18 (February 16, 1895).

"The Reading Habit." *The Critic,* July 30, 1892.

"Recent Novels." Review of Wister, *The Virginian. The Nation* 23 (October 1902).

Reed, Henry Hope. *The New York Public Library: Its Architecture and Decoration.* New York: W. W. Norton and Co., 1986.

Reedy, William Marion. "A Strangely Strong Novel in a Queer Milieu." *St. Louis Mirror,* January 10, 1901, reprinted in Pizer, *Critical Essays.*

Rees, J. Rogers. *The Diversions of a Book Worm.* New York: George J. Coombes, 1887.

Review of Corson, *The Aims of Literary Study. The Bookman* 1 (February 1895).

Review of "The Life and Correspondence of Robert Southey." *North American Review* 73 (July 1851).

Review of *Representative Men. North American Review* 70 (1850).

Review of *The Scarlet Letter. North American Review* 71 (1850).

Richardson, Charles. *The Choice of Books.* New York: American Book Exchange, 1881.

Richardson, Joanna. *Sarah Bernhardt and Her World.* New York: Putnam's, 1977.

Rimmon-Kenan, Shlomith. *Narrative Fiction: Contemporary Poetics.* London: Methuen, 1983.

Rose, Jonathan. "ReReading the English Common Reader: A Preface to a History of Audiences." *Journal of the History of Ideas* 53 (1992).

Rose, Mark. *Authors and Owners: The Invention of Copyright.* Cambridge, Mass.: Harvard University Press, 1993.

Rosenblatt, Louise. "On the Aesthetic as the Basic Model of the Reading Process." *Bucknell Review* 26.1 (1981).

Rowe, John Carlos. *The Theoretical Dimensions of Henry James.* Madison: University of Wisconsin Press, 1984.

Rubin, Joan Shelley. *The Making of Middlebrow Culture.* Chapel Hill: University of North Carolina Press, 1992.

Samuels, Shirley. *Romances of the Republic: Women, the Family, and Violence in the Liter-ature of the Early American Nation.* New York: Oxford University Press, 1996.

Scarry, Elaine. *The Body in Pain: The Making and Unmaking of the World.* New York: Oxford University Press, 1985.

Schudson, Michael. *The Origins of the Ideal of Objectivity in the Professions: American Journalism and American Law, 1830–1940.* New York: Garland Publishing, 1990.

Scudder, Horace. "Literature in Schools: An Address and Two Essays." In *Methods of Teaching.* New York: Houghton Mifflin & Co., 1888.

Sedgwick, Catherine. "Cacoethes Scribendi." In *Tales and Sketches.* Philadelphia: Carey, Lea, and Blanchard, 1835.

Sedgwick, Henry Dwight. "The Novels of Mrs. Wharton." *Atlantic* 98 (August 1906).

Seltzer, Mark. *Bodies and Machines.* London: Routledge, 1992.

Sherman, Stuart P. "The Naturalism of Mr. Dreiser." In Becker, *Documents.*

Shoemaker, J. W. *Best Things from Best Authors: Humor, Pathos, and Eloquence Designed for Public and Social Entertainment and for Use in Schools and Colleges.* Philadelphia, 1882.

Showalter, Elaine. "The Death of the Lady (Novelist): Wharton's *House of Mirth.*" In Bloom, *Edith Wharton.*

———. "Introduction." In *Alternative Alcott.* Ed. Elaine Showalter. New Brunswick, N.J.: Rutgers University Press, 1988.

———. "Tradition and the Female Talent: *The Awakening* as a Solitary Book." In *New Essays on "The Awakening."* Ed. Wendy Martin. New York: Cambridge University Press, 1988.

Shreyer, Alice D. "Copyright and Books in Nineteenth-Century America." In *Getting the Books Out: Papers of the Chicago Conference on the Book in Nineteenth-Century America.* Washington, D.C.: Center for the Book, Library of Congress, 1987.

Sicherman, Barbara. "Reading and Ambition: M. Carey Thomas and Female Hero-ism." *American Quarterly* 45.1 (March 1993).

———. "Reading *Little Women:* The Many Lives of a Text." In *U.S. History as Women's History: New Feminist Essays.* Ed. Linda K. Kerber, Alice Kessler-Harris, and Kathryn Kish Sklar. Chapel Hill: University of North Carolina Press, 1995.

———. "Sense and Sensibility: A Case Study of Women's Reading in Late Victorian America." In Davidson, *Reading in America.*

Simmel, Georg. "Female Culture." In *On Women, Sexuality, and Love.* 1911. Trans. Guy Oakes. New Haven: Yale University Press, 1984.

Slote, Bernice, ed. *The Kingdom of Art: Willa Cather's First Principles and Critical State-ments, 1893–96.* Lincoln: University of Nebraska Press, 1966.

Smith-Rosenberg, Carroll. *Disorderly Conduct: Visions of Gender in Victorian America.* New York: Oxford University Press, 1985.

Sollors, Werner. Introduction to Mary Antin, *The Promised Land.* New York: Penguin, 1997.

Sorrentino, Paul. "A Biographical Connection between Jack London and Kate Douglas Wiggin." *American Literary Realism* 32.1 (Fall, 1999).

Spiller, Robert E., Willard Thorp, Thomas A. Johnson, and Henry Seidel Canby, eds. *The Literary History of the United States.* New York: Macmillan, 1955.

"The Star System in Literature." *The Dial,* May 16, 1900.

Steig, Michael. *Stories of Reading: Subjectivity and Literary Understanding.* Baltimore: Johns Hopkins University Press, 1989.

Stewart, Garrett. *Dear Reader: The Conscripted Audience in Nineteenth-Century British Fiction.* Baltimore: Johns Hopkins University Press, 1996.

Sundquist, Eric, ed. *American Realism: New Essays.* Baltimore: Johns Hopkins University Press, 1982.

Susman, Warren I. "'Personality' and the Making of Twentieth-Century Culture." In *Culture as History: The Transformation of American Society in the Twentieth Century.* New York: Pantheon Books, 1984.

Taine, Hippolyte A. *History of English Literature.* Vol. 4. Trans. H. Van Laun. New York: Frederick Ungar, 1965.

Thayer, W. R. "The New Story-Tellers and the Doom of Realism." *Forum* 18 (1894).

Thomas, Brook. *American Literary Realism and the Failed Promise of Contract.* Berkeley: University of California Press, 1997.

Thoreau, Henry David. *Walden, or Life in the Woods.* In *"Walden" and Other Writings of Henry David Thoreau.* New York: Random House, 1950.

Tompkins, Jane P., ed. *Reader-Response Criticism: From Formalism to Post-Structuralism.* Baltimore: Johns Hopkins University Press, 1980.

———. *Sensational Designs: The Cultural Work of American Fiction, 1790–1860.* New York: Oxford University Press, 1985.

Trachtenberg, Alan. *The Incorporation of America.* New York: Hill and Wang, 1982.

Trilling, Lionel. *The Liberal Imagination.* New York: Viking Press, 1950.

Tuttleton, James, Kristin O. Lauer, and Margaret P. Murray. *Edith Wharton: The Contemporary Reviews.* New York: Cambridge University Press, 1992.

"Uncut." *Atlantic* 98 (April 1906).

Veblen, Thorstein. *The Rise of the Leisure Class: An Economic Study in the Evolution of Institutions.* New York: Penguin, 1981.

Vrettos, Athena. *Somatic Fictions: Imagining Illness in Victorian Culture.* Stanford: Stanford University Press, 1995.

Walsh, William. *Authors and Authorship.* New York: G. P. Putnam's Sons, 1882.

Warhol, Robyn R. *Gendered Interventions: Narrative Discourse in the Victorian Novel.* New Brunswick, N.J.: Rutgers University Press, 1989.

Warner, Charles Dudley. *Fashions in Literature and Other Literary and Social Essays and Addresses.* New York: Dodd, Mead, and Co., 1902.

Warner, Michael. *Letters of the Republic: Publication and the Public Sphere in Eighteenth-Century America.* Cambridge, Mass.: Harvard University Press, 1990.

Warren, Kenneth W. *Black and White Strangers: Race and American Literary Realism.* Chicago: University of Chicago Press, 1993.

———. "Troubled Black Humanity in *The Souls of Black Folk* and *The Autobiography of an Ex-Colored Man.*" In *Cambridge Companion to American Realism and*

Naturalism. Ed. Donald Pizer. New York: Cambridge University Press, 1995.

Warren, Samuel D., and Louis D. Brandeis. "The Right to Privacy." *Harvard Law Review* 4.5 (1890). Reprinted in *The Philosophical Dimensions of Privacy: An Anthology.* Ed. Ferdinand D. Schoeman. New York: Cambridge University Press, 1984.

Wharton, Edith. *The Age of Innocence.* New York: Penguin, 1984.

———. *A Backward Glance.* New York: Scribner's Sons, 1985.

———. "Copy: A Dialogue." 1901. In *Crucial Instances.* New York: AMS, 1969.

———. *The House of Mirth.* In *Novels.* New York: Library of America, 1985.

———. *The Letters of Edith Wharton.* Ed. R. W. B. Lewis and Nancy Lewis. New York: Scribner's Sons, 1988.

———. "The Vice of Reading." *North American Review* 177 (1903).

———. "Visibility in Fiction." *Yale Review* 18 (March 1929).

———. *The Writing of Fiction.* New York: Charles Scribner's Sons, 1925.

———. "Xingu." In *"The Muse's Tragedy" and Other Stories.* New York: New American Library, 1990.

Wharton, Edith, and Ogden Codman, Jr. *The Decoration of Houses.* 1902. New York: W. W. Norton and Co., 1978.

Whipple, Edwin. *Lectures on Subjects Connected with Literature and Life.* 2nd ed. Boston: Ticknor and Fields, 1850.

Wiebe, Robert H. *The Search for Order: 1877–1920.* New York: Hill and Wang, 1967.

Wiggin, Kate Douglas. *Rebecca of Sunnybrook Farm.* Boston: Houghton Mifflin and Co., 1904.

Williams, Susan. "Widening the World: Susan Warner, Her Readers, and the Assumption of Authorship." *American Quarterly* 42.4 (December 1990).

Wilson, Christopher. *The Labor of Words.* Athens: University of Georgia Press, 1985.

———. "The Rhetoric of Consumption: Mass-Market Magazines and the Demise of the Gentle Reader." In *The Culture of Consumption.* Ed. Richard W. Fox and T. J. Jackson Lears. New York: Pantheon, 1983.

Wilson, Harriet E. *Our Nig.* 1859. New York: Vintage Books, 1983.

Wister, Owen. *The Virginian: A Horseman of the Plains.* 1902. New York: Macmillan, 1967.

Wolff, Cynthia Griffin. *A Feast of Words: The Triumph of Edith Wharton.* Oxford: Oxford University Press, 1977.

Wolff, Erwin. "Der Intendirte Leser." *Poetica* 4 (1971).

"A Word for Pepys." *Atlantic* 55 (February 1885).

"A Word for Silent Partners." *Atlantic* 61 (January 1888).

Zboray, Ronald. *A Fictive People: Antebellum Economic Development and the American Reading Public.* New York: Oxford University Press, 1993.

Zboray, Ronald J., and Mary Saracino Zboray. "Books, Reading, and the World of Goods in Antebellum New England." *American Quarterly* 48.4 (December 1996).

———. "'Have You Read . . . ?': Real Readers and Their Responses in Antebellum

Boston and Its Region." *Nineteenth-Century Literature* 52 (September 1997).

————. "Reading and Everyday Life in Antebellum Boston: The Diary of Daniel F. and Mary D. Child." *Libraries and Culture* 32.3 (Summer 1997).

Zimmerman, David A. "The Mesmeric Sources of Frank Norris's *The Pit.*" *Frank Norris Studies* 26 (Autumn 1998).

INDEX

BARBARA HOCHMAN is senior lecturer in the Department of Foreign Literatures and Linguistics at Ben-Gurion University of the Negev in Israel. She has written *The Art of Frank Norris, Storyteller* (1988) and essays on Theodore Dreiser, Edith Wharton, Henry James, F. Scott Fitzgerald, and others. She is the recent recipient of a Gilder Lehrman Fellowship in American History for a new project on nineteenth-century practices and the "reading revolution."